AF598738

BEACHES

CELEBRATING STONES, SAND, AND SURF

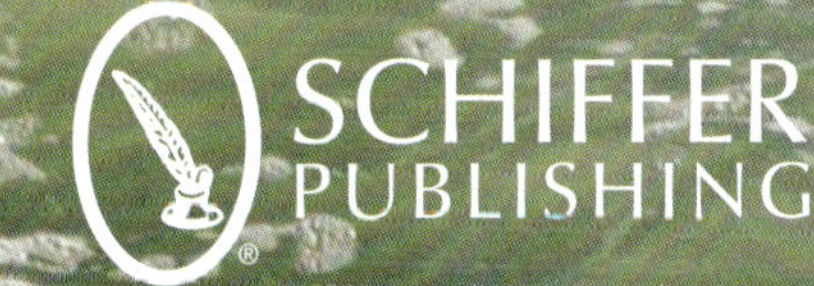

1080 Lower Valley Road • Atglen, PA 19310

"Every beautiful page evokes feelings of whimsy, wonder, play, joy, and awe—the very things that make life feel alive. Every photo makes me want to slow down and stay here."

—Lisa Genova, neuroscientist and author of *New York Times* bestsellers *Still Alice, Left Neglected, Love Anthony, Inside the O'Briens, Every Note Played,* and *Remember.*

Other Schiffer Books by Amy Dykens:
My Heart Rocks, ISBN 978-0-7643-5063-4

Other Schiffer Books on Related Subjects:
The Ever-Changing Coastline: Tidal Forces at Work,
Joseph R. Votano, ISBN 978-0-7643-5487-8

East Coast Atlantic Beaches, Michael Kahn, ISBN 978-0-7643-5931-6

Library of Congress Control Number: 2022944431

Design by Brenda McCallum
Cover design by Molly Shields
Type set in Cinzel Decorative/Agenda-Light

ISBN: 978-0-7643-6585-0
Printed in China
10 9 8 7 6 5 4 3 2

Published by Schiffer Publishing, Ltd.
4880 Lower Valley Road
Atglen, PA 19310
Phone: (610) 593-1777; Fax: (610) 593-2002
Email: Info@schifferbooks.com
Web: www.schifferbooks.com

For our complete selection of fine books on this and related subjects, please visit our website at www.schifferbooks.com. You may also write for a free catalog.

Schiffer Publishing's titles are available at special discounts for bulk purchases for sales promotions or premiums. Special editions, including personalized covers, corporate imprints, and excerpts, can be created in large quantities for special needs. For more information, contact the publisher.

We are always looking for people to write books on new and related subjects. If you have an idea for a book, please contact us at proposals@schifferbooks.com.

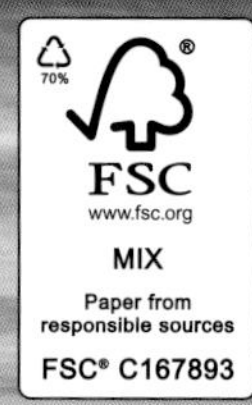

FOR MY PARENTS, WITH LOVE

The sea, once it casts its spell, holds one in its net of wonder forever.

—Jacques Yves Cousteau

INTRODUCTION

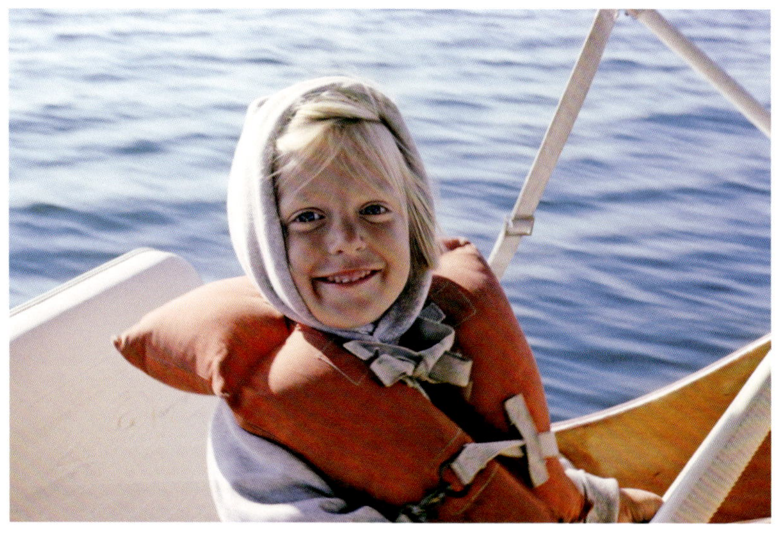

Amy on the boat at age five, photo by her dad

Spending time at the beach is my idea of pure joy. My enduring fondness for beaches blossomed early, fostered by summer boat rides to the outer beaches of Cape Cod. Although those trips were fun, I couldn't wait to get my feet off the boat and into the sand. After a day spent wading in the cooling salt water and collecting shells, a healthy fatigue set in at sunset, my salty skin a reminder of my adventures.

Many people consider a day at the beach the cure for all things. Beach days offer solace when deserted, and communal happiness when crowded and noisy. Rockhounds are among this kindred group and are easily recognized, as they pause on their beach walk to bend over and examine something that caught their eye. My good friends know exactly which kinds and colors of rocks light me up. Of course, I still favor heart rocks, but, as you'll see here, I also love shooting rocks underwater and on dry sand—making rock portraits. I also declare my fondness for beach rocks by leaving behind ephemeral cairns, tiny rock towers that express not only my affection for rocks, but also the tranquility I cherish: a "gift from the sea." I build a cairn on every beach walk, knowing full well that after I photograph it, high tide and waves will carry the rocks away.

The sea is blue and green, a function of ever-changing light combined with the whims of the weather. I have attempted to show this variation in my photos. I've noticed sea colors all my life—the intense turquoise of the clear Caribbean waters are the icing on my cake. The translucent colors in a backlit wave, the bottle green of a wave barrel, the deep blue of the sea on a sunny day—I observe all with delight.

One of the first things I notice at a beach is the sand: How warm sand gets on sunny summer days, but also how cold it gets in winter. How different sand can look at different spots on the same beach. How sand can vary in size and types of minerals and shells. How waves and currents create sinuous sand sculptures. Sometimes these sand sculptures mimic the sky above—a wonderful discovery.

Beach photography gives me peace. The quiet observation of nature, and the time spent waiting for the just-right shot, can be meditative. I am often of two minds: Do I freeze the motion of the water with a fast shutter speed, or use a slower camera speed to catch its inexorable march toward the beach? I delight in this shoreline dilemma, capturing "fast" or "slow" movement of the spray, foam, and crest versus the reflections and peace of a calm ocean.

My dear friends and family, who have patiently walked beaches with me, understand that I wander off and take my time. These are some of my happiest, most cherished hours.

I hope that you, too, enjoy these beaches.

The cure for anything is salt water: sweat, tears, or the sea.

—Isak Dinesen

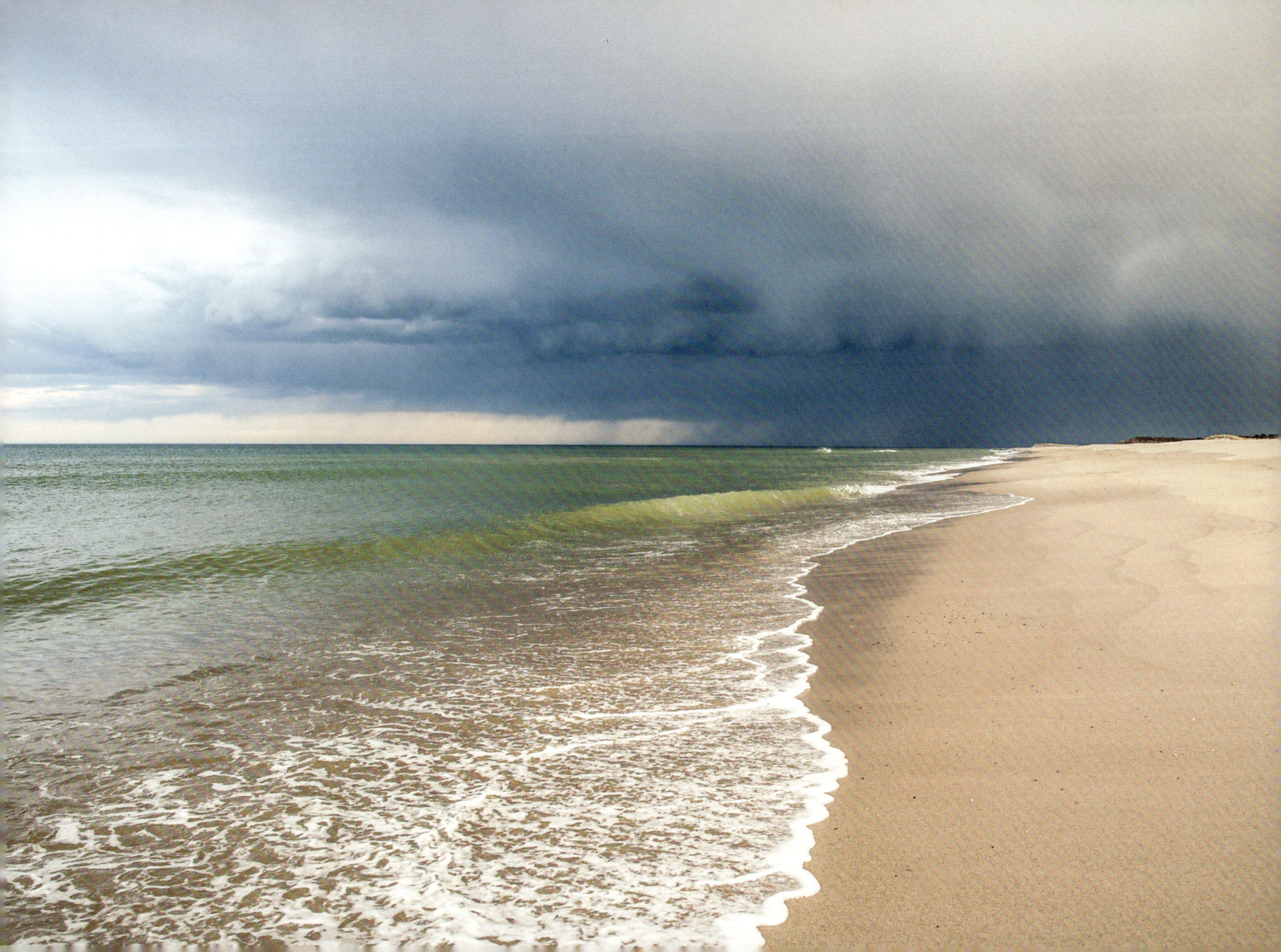

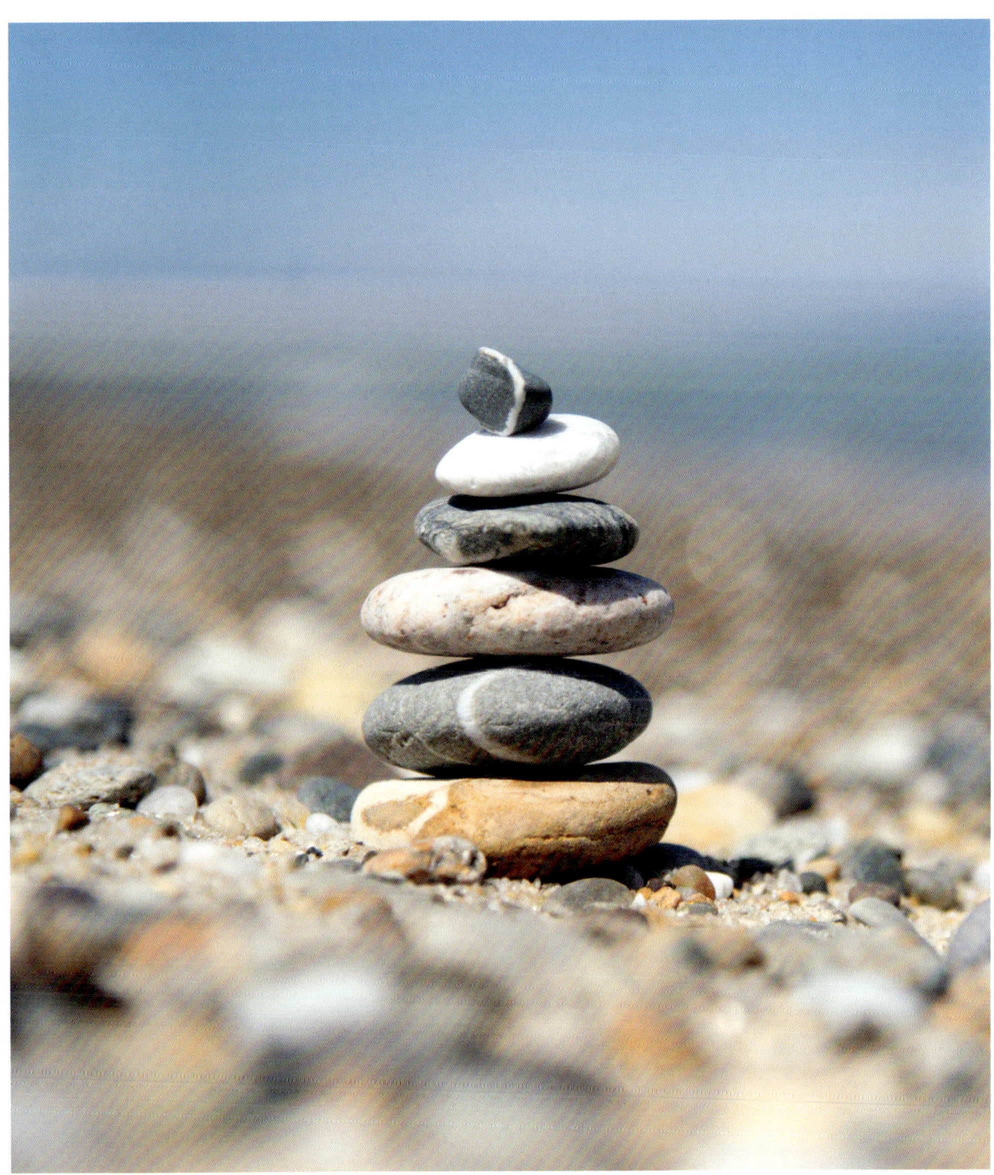

Stormy Evening

The light before this storm was stunning. The sky reminded me of time spent painting with watercolors and dragging a wet brush over the sky, only hoping for these results.

Colorful Cairn

Cairn is a Gaelic word meaning "heap of stones." They were originally used as trail markers, and in many other cultures as navigational tools, monuments, and ceremonial symbols. Building a cairn is peaceful and meditative, and this one highlights the beach's bountiful variety.

Plover View

One of my favorite things to do is lie in the sand and watch the birds, imagining what they see from their point of view. They are so small, yet completely in charge of their shoreline home.

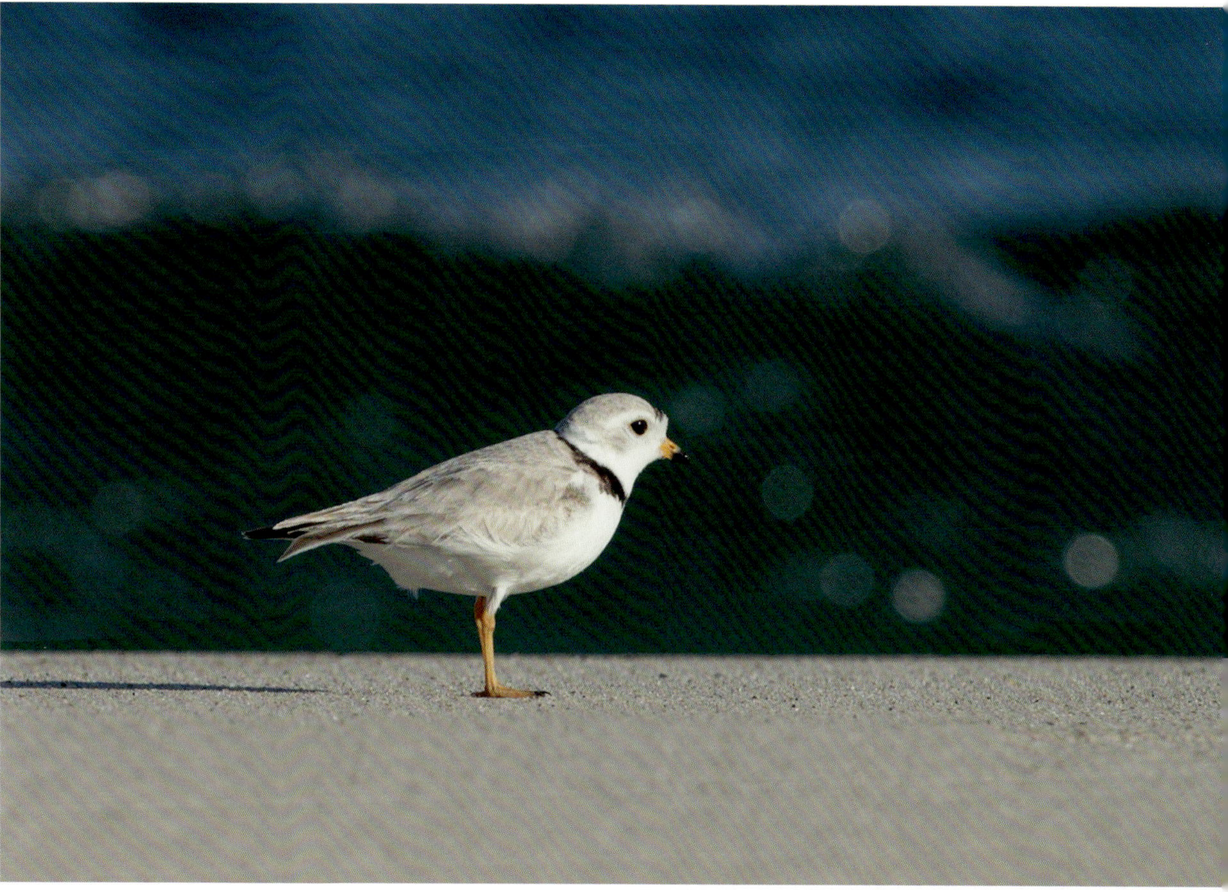

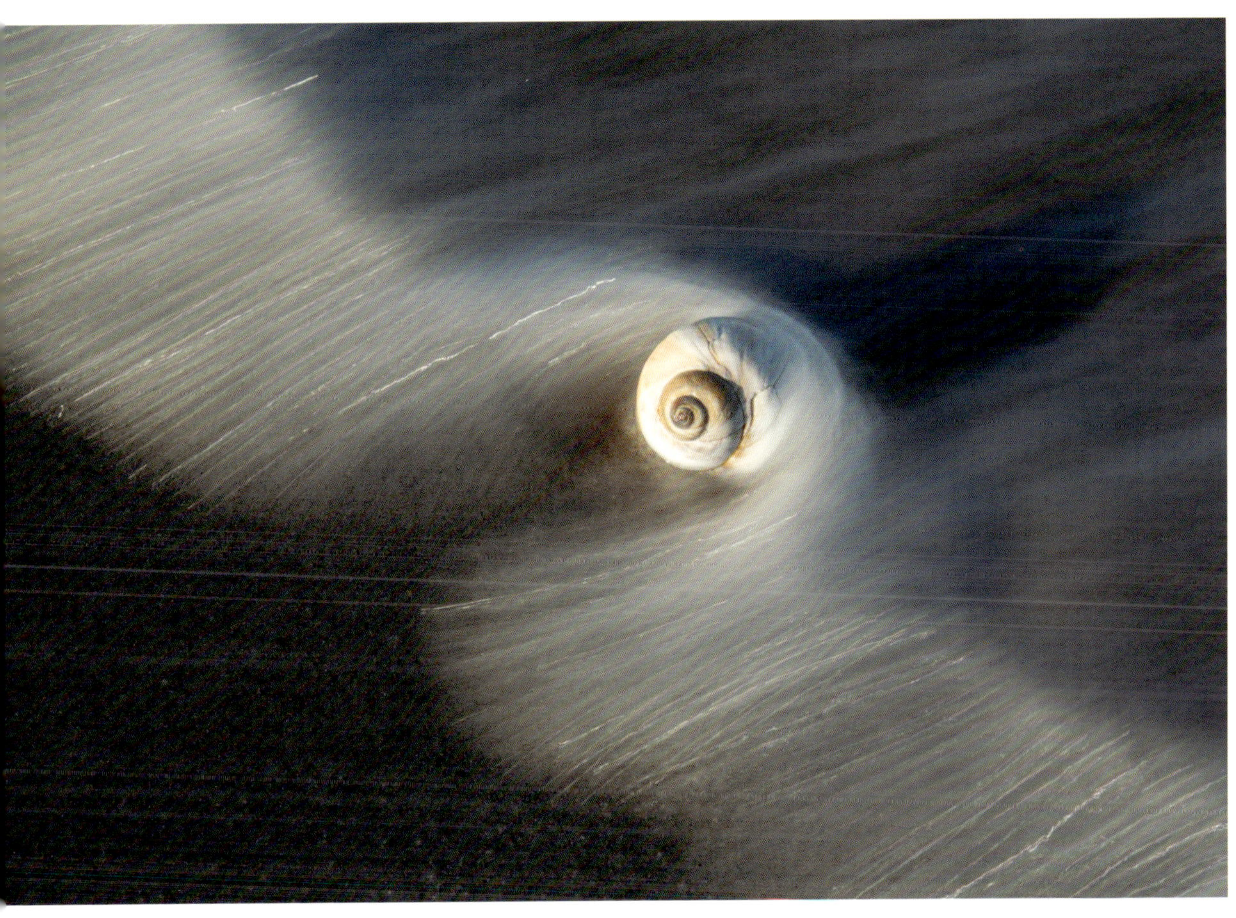

Angel Wings

Mother Nature has many types of wings.

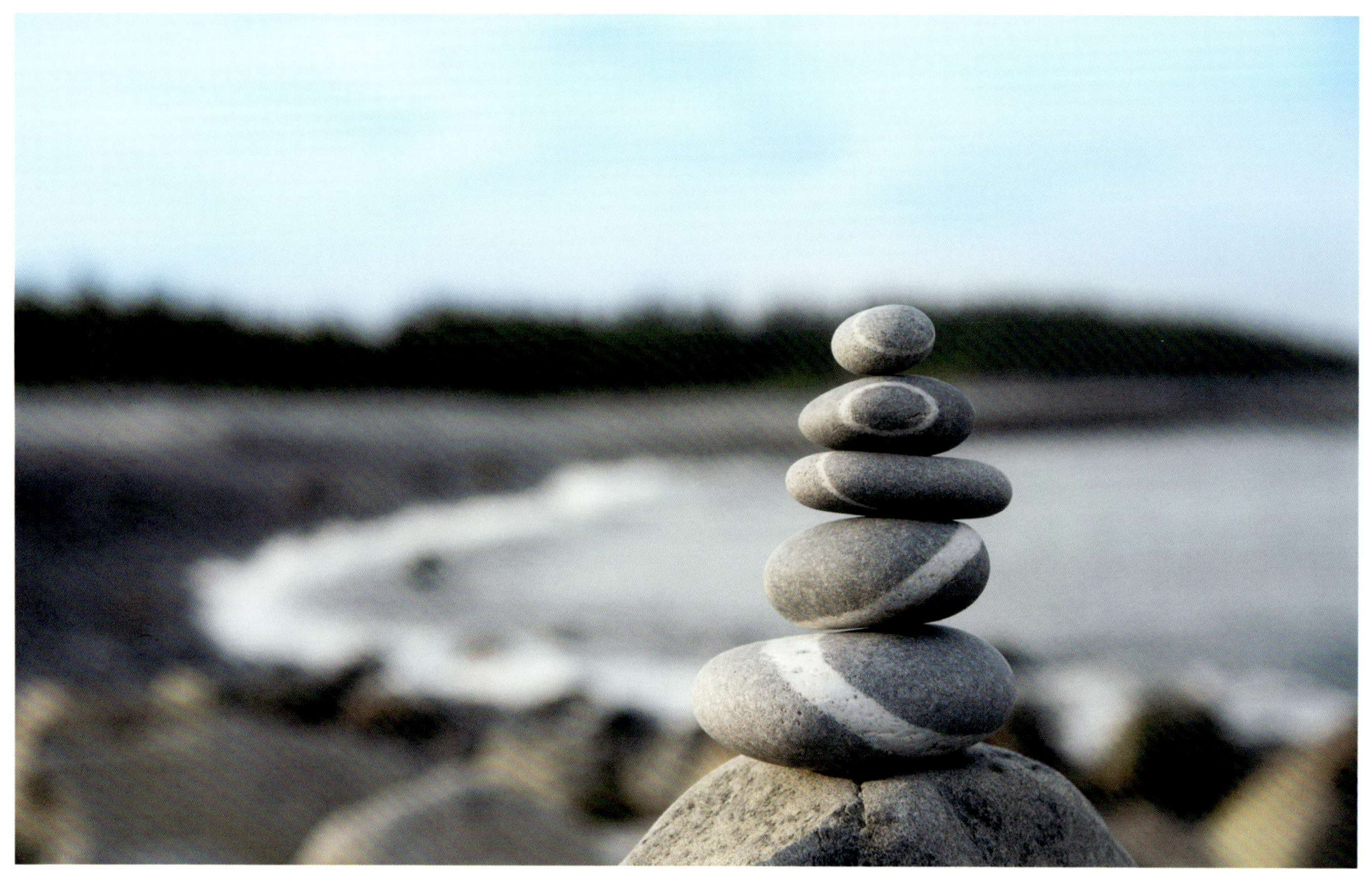

Wishing Rocks

I have been collecting lucky stones since I was a child. This is one of my favorite places in Nova Scotia to collect rocks and build cairns.

Spray Display

The sea was mesmerizing on this day. The spray was as beautiful as the waves.

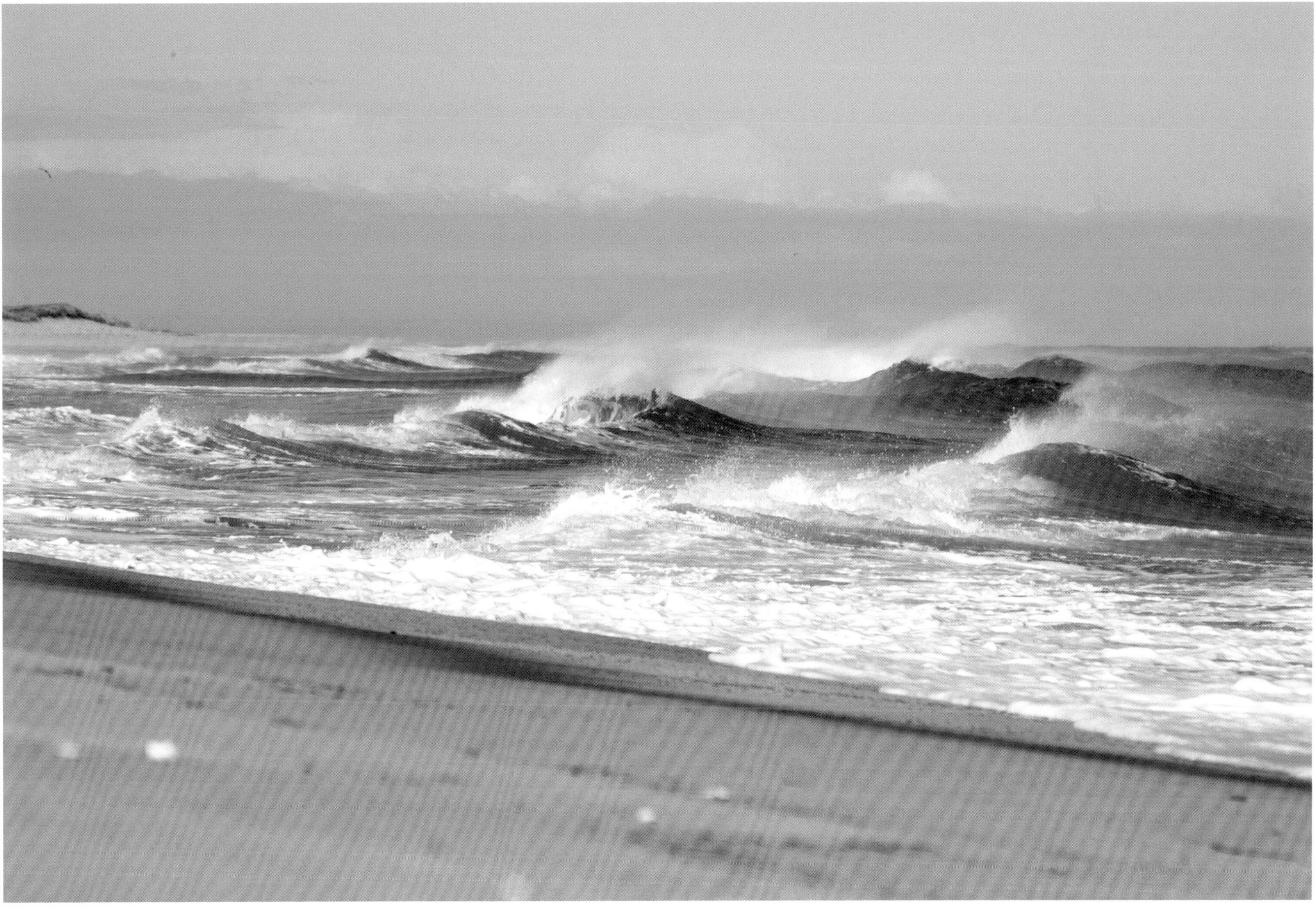

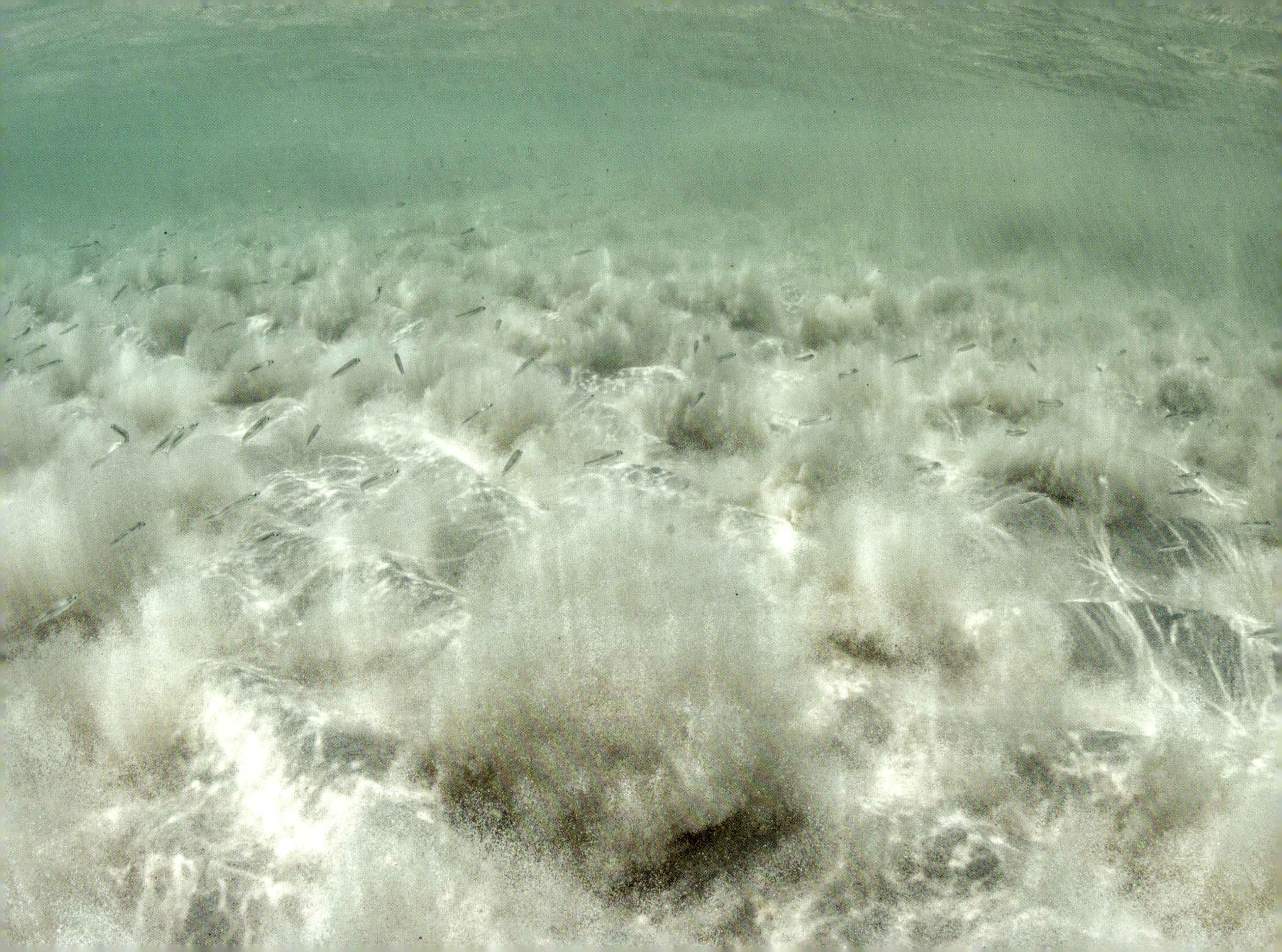

Powder Puffs

The soft sand in the Caribbean floats up in perfect powder puffs when waves pass over.

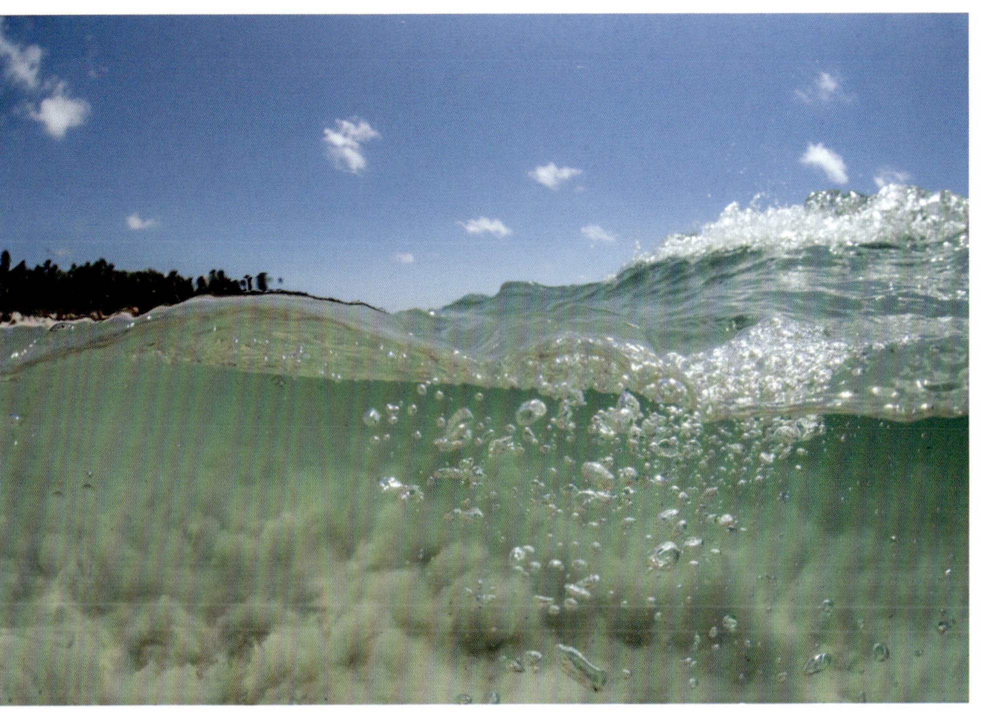

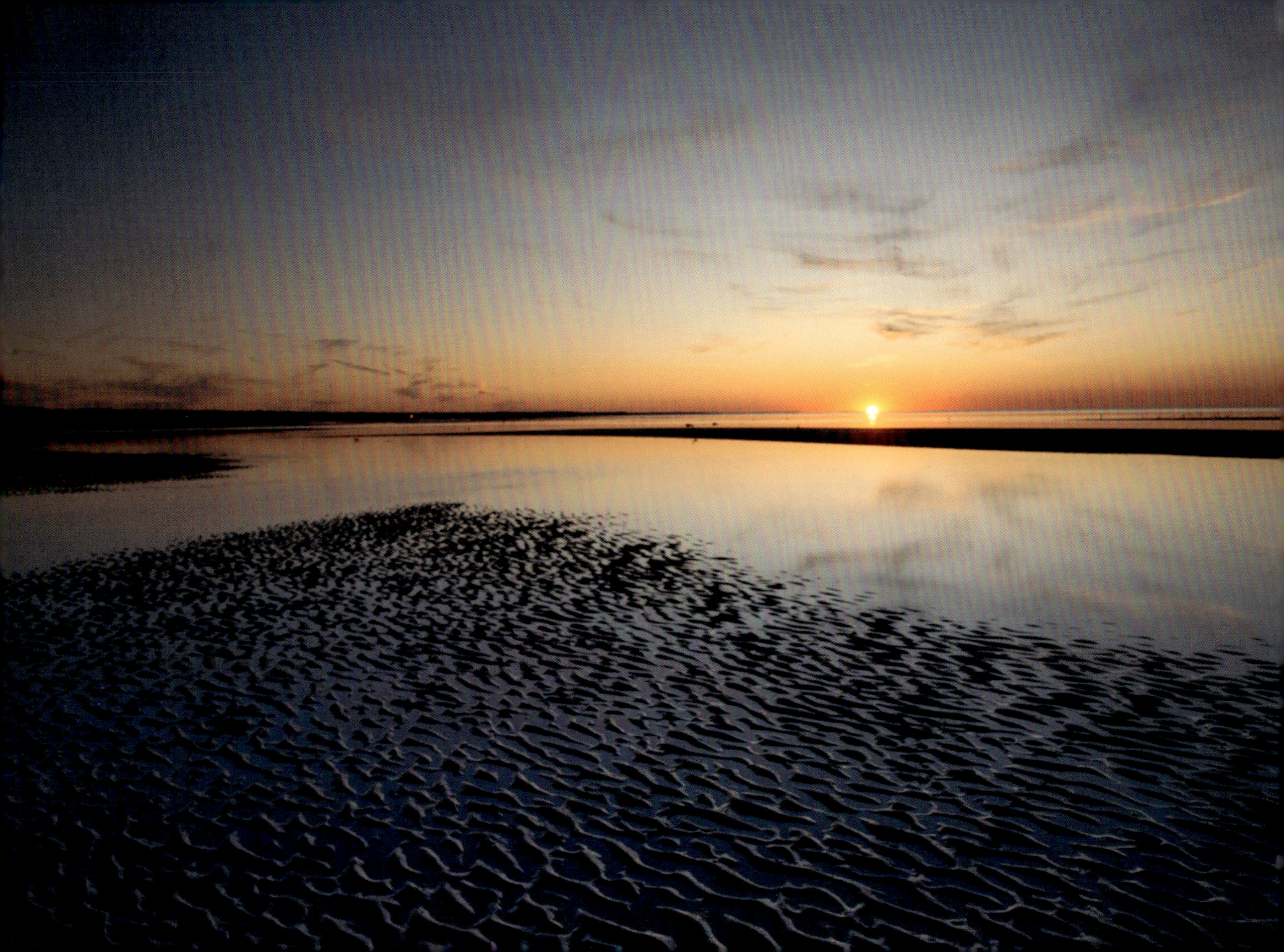

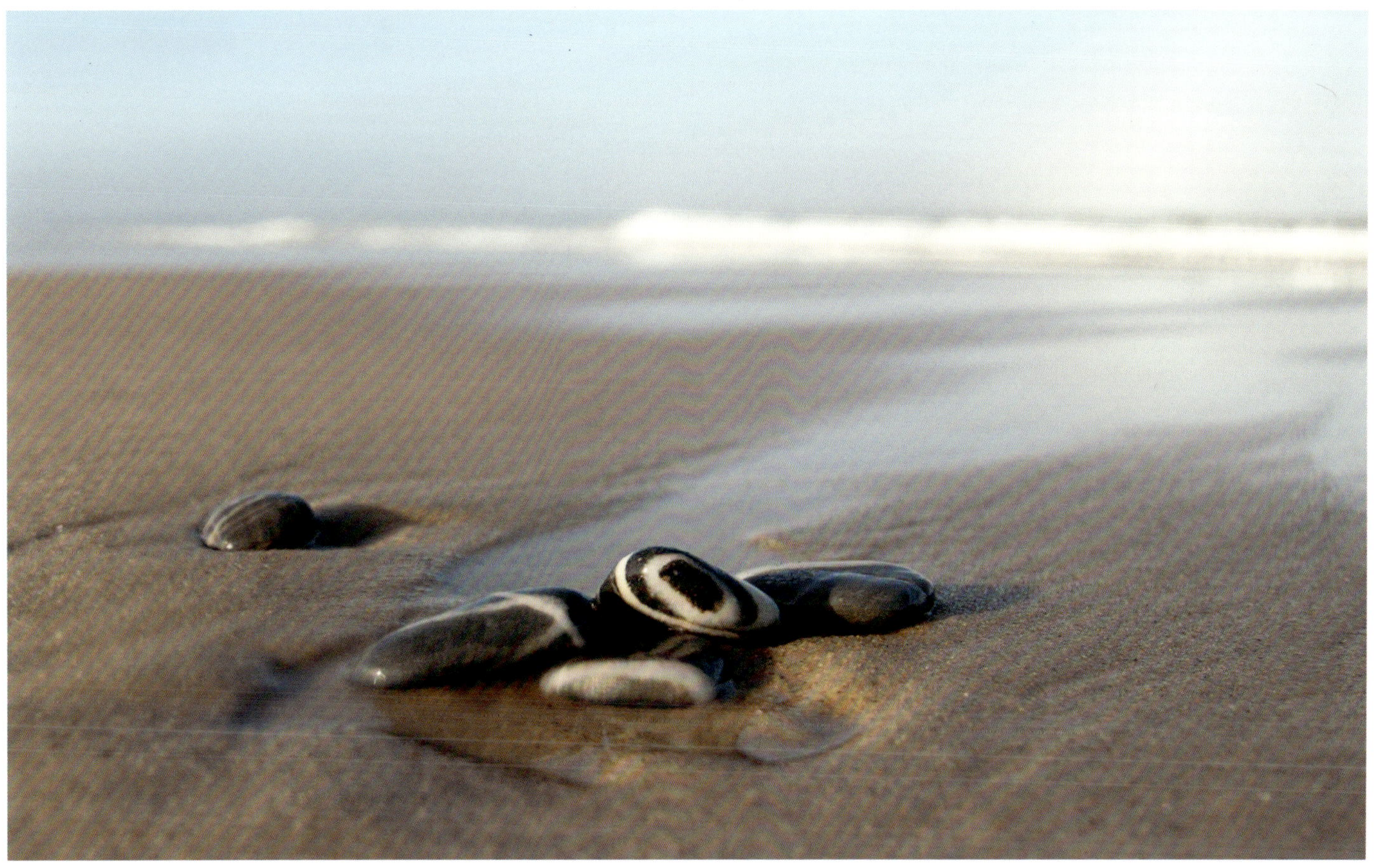

Last Light

The last light of the day skims across the flats.

Lucky Stripes

As children, we would make wishes on striped rocks and throw them into the sea, pass them on, or keep them close by for good luck.

Glass Menagerie

These sea glass pieces are from my sister-in-law's extensive collection. As I look at their varied shapes, ages, and sizes, I ponder their origins. What trips did they take to end up here on Cape Cod?

Up for Air

Swimming with the sea turtles in Mexico—the water was crystal clear, the light perfect.

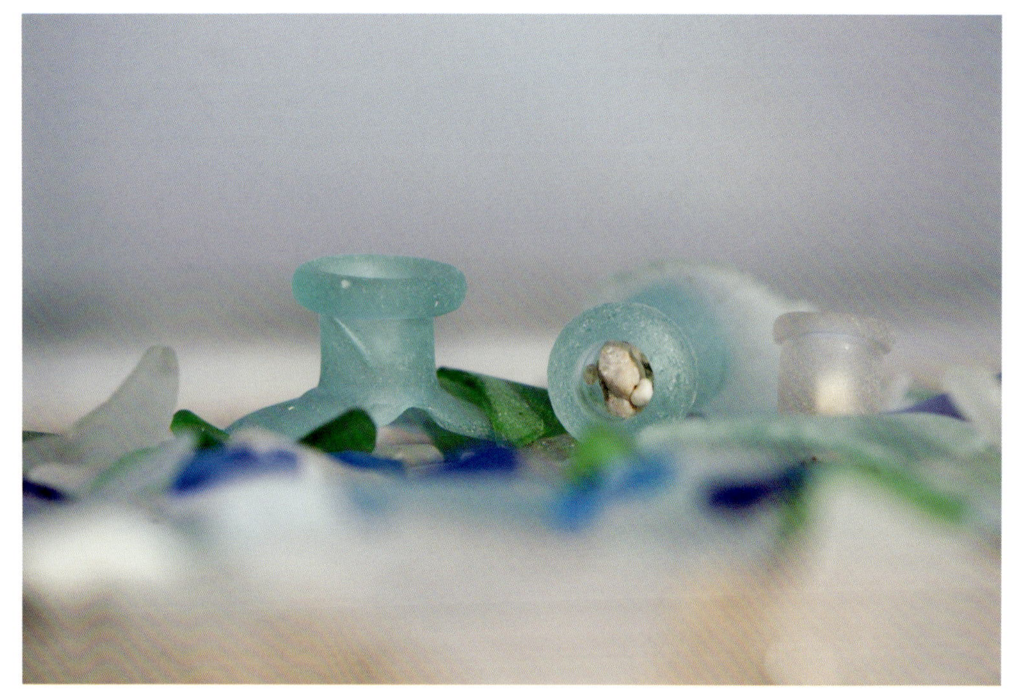

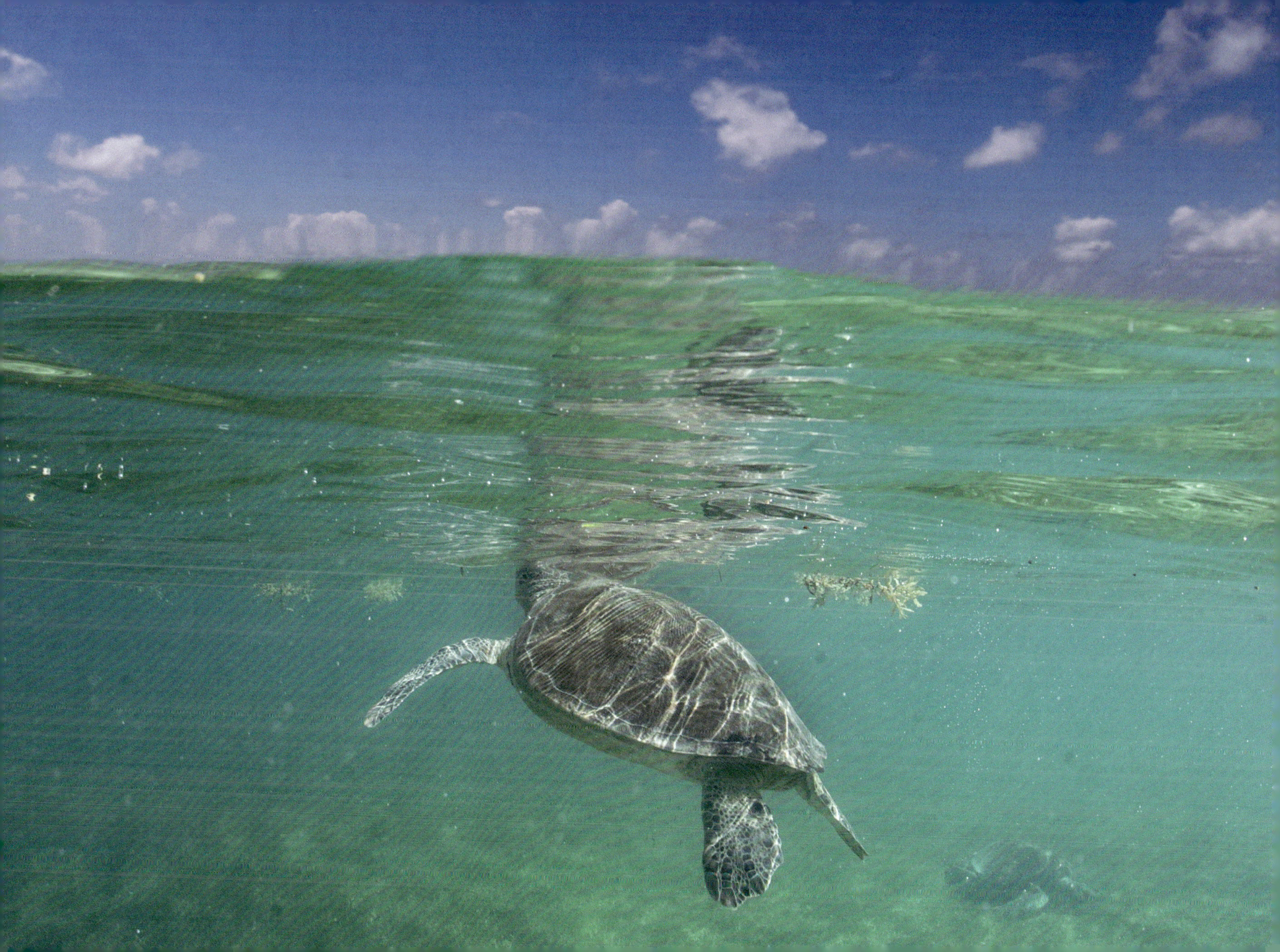

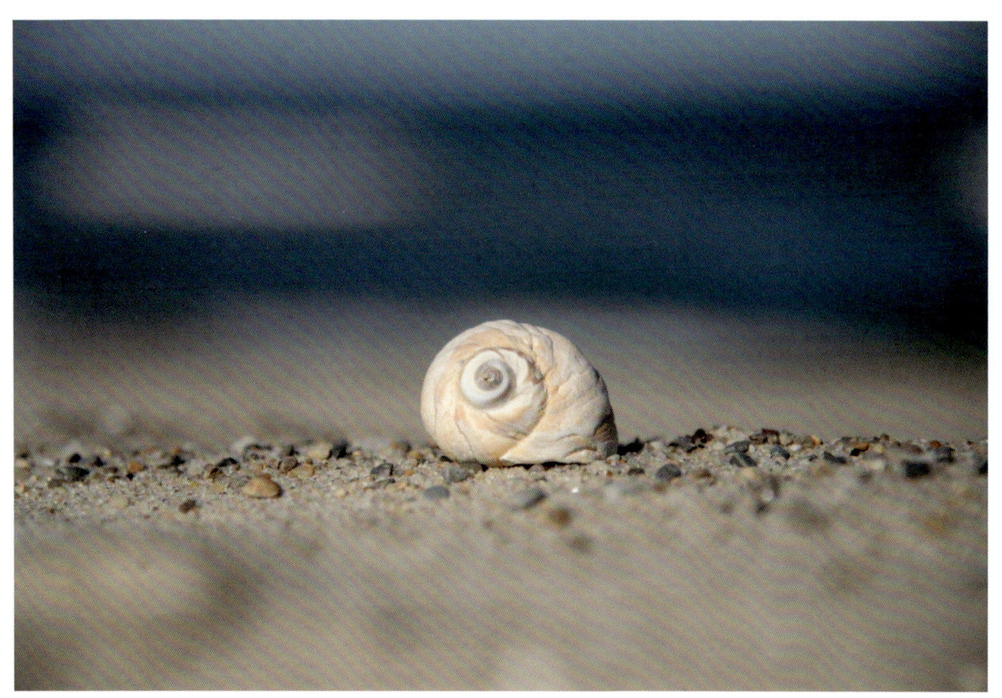

A Closer Look

If you look closely, you can discover the beach's many types of sand.

Winter Walks

One of the best things about living on Cape Cod is the solitude it offers during the off-season.

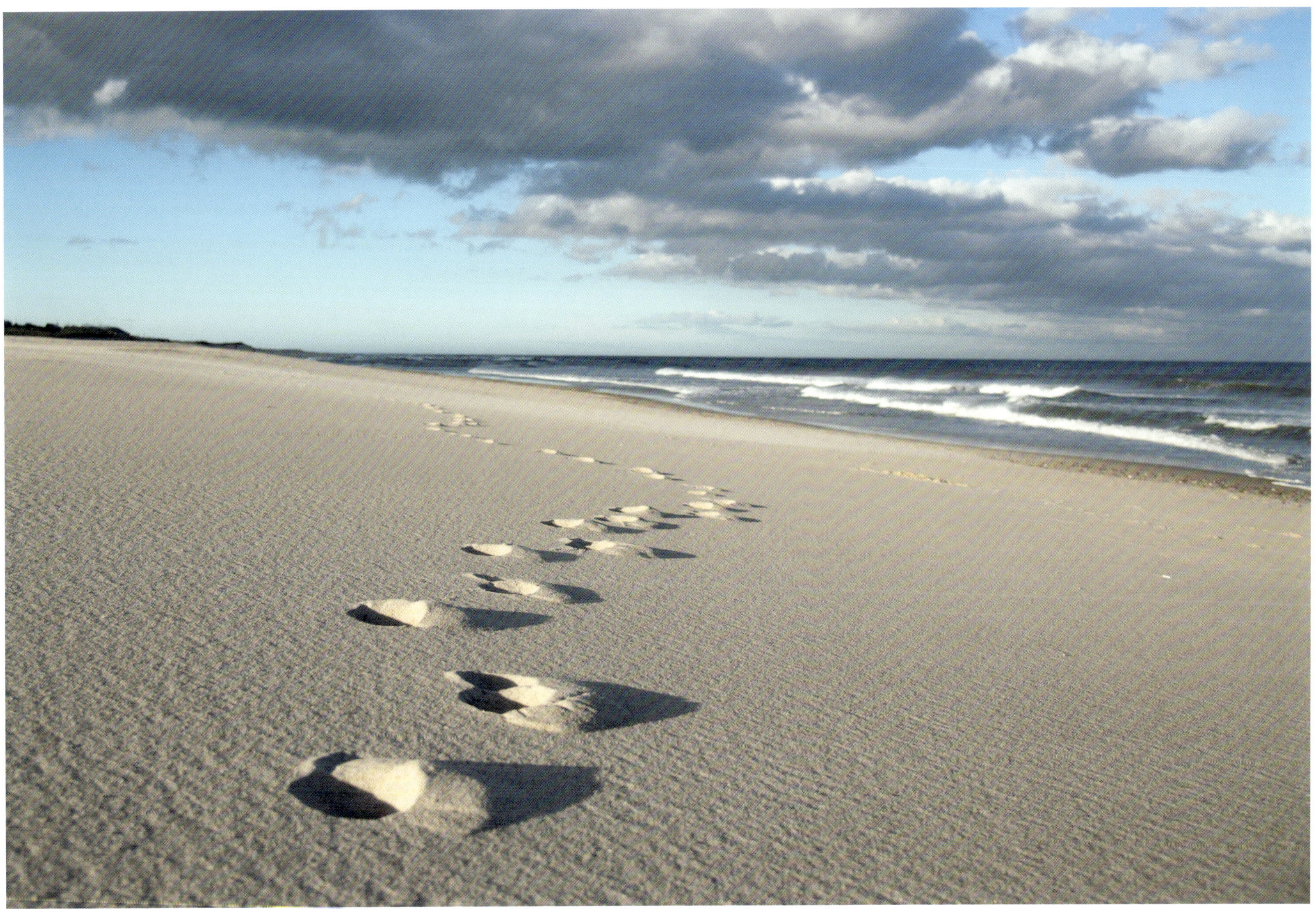

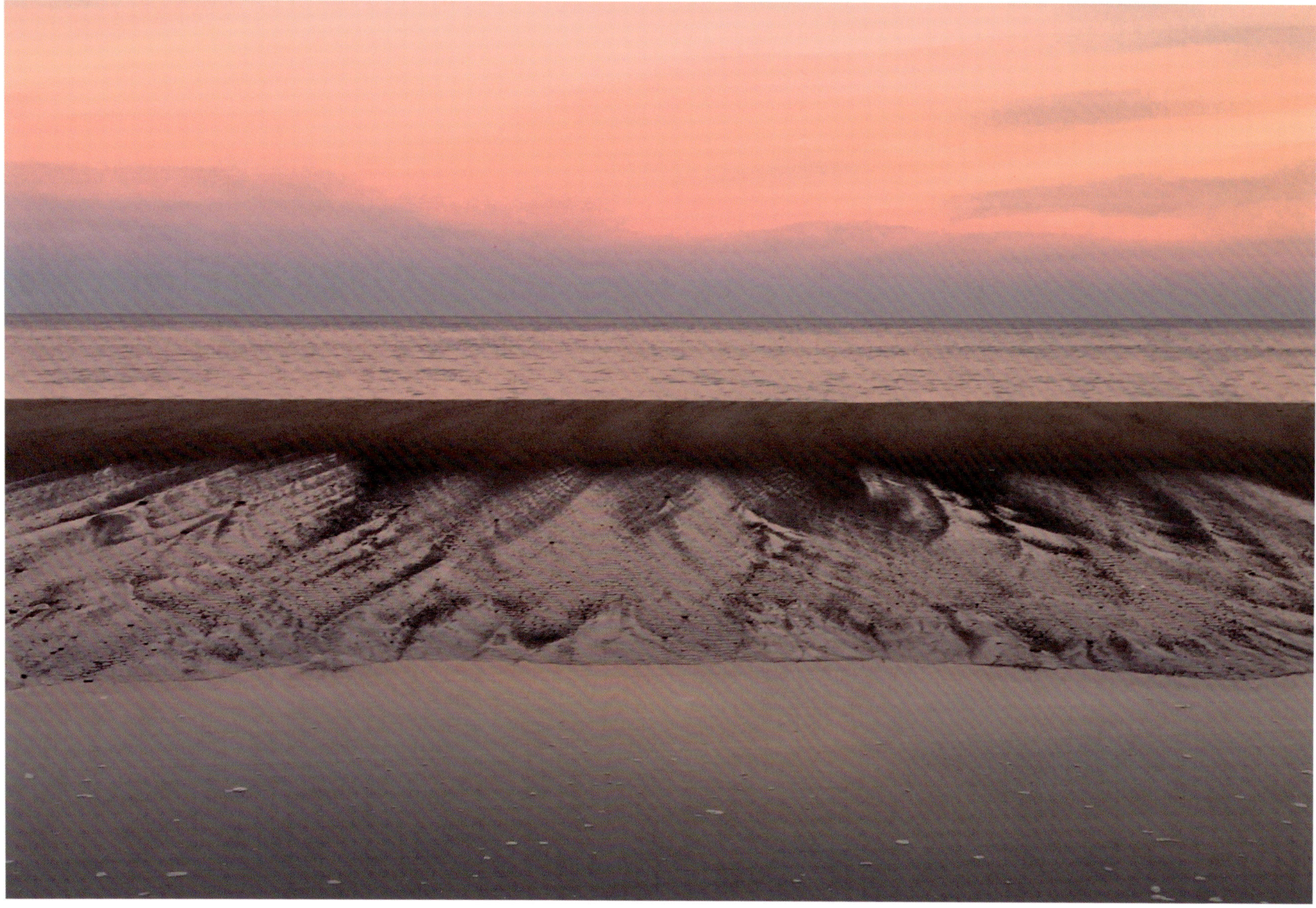

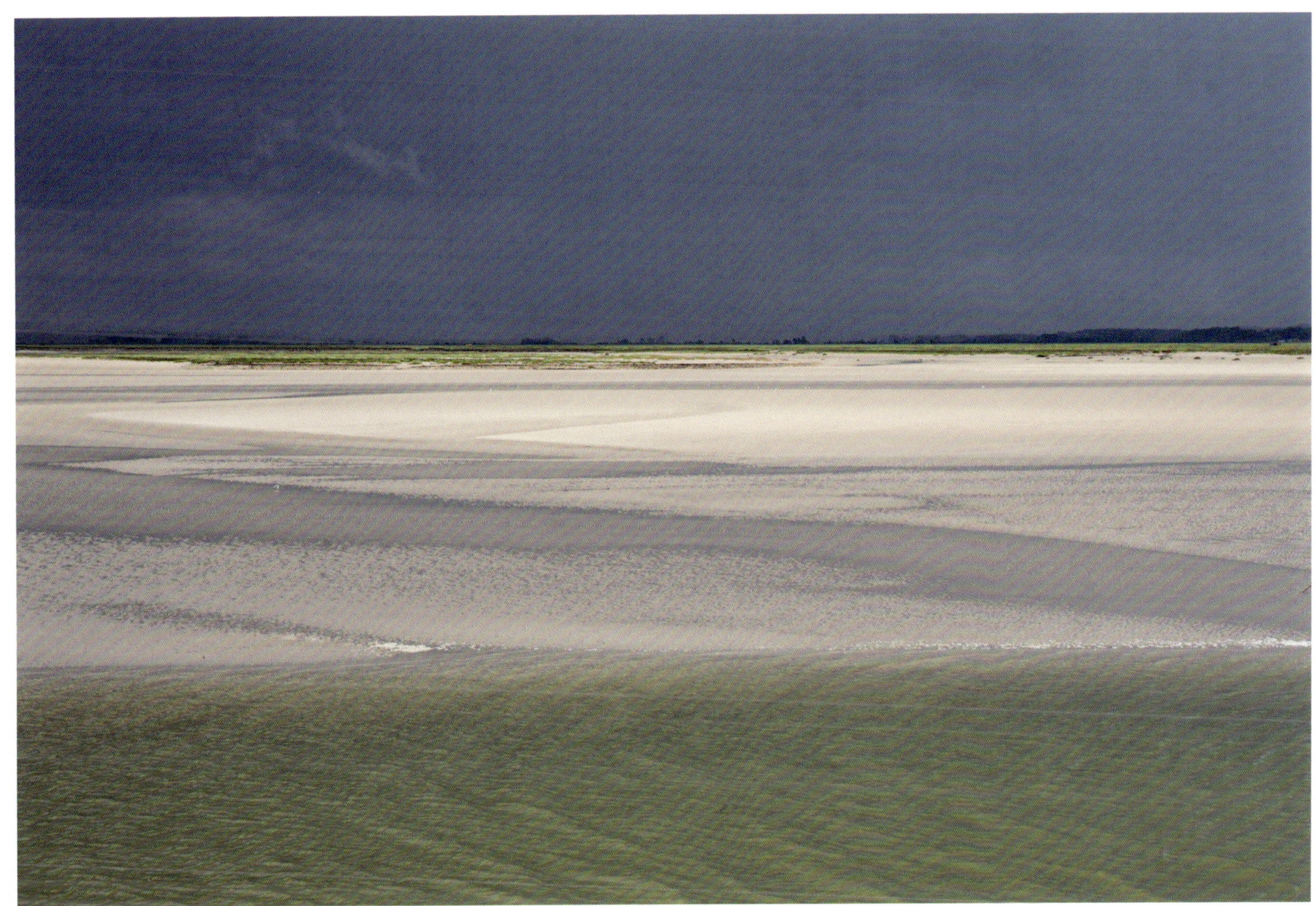

Coastal Colors

These colors take my breath away!

Beach Day

I tend to seek out remote beaches, but I also love the collective vibe at a crowded beach—everybody's happy place.

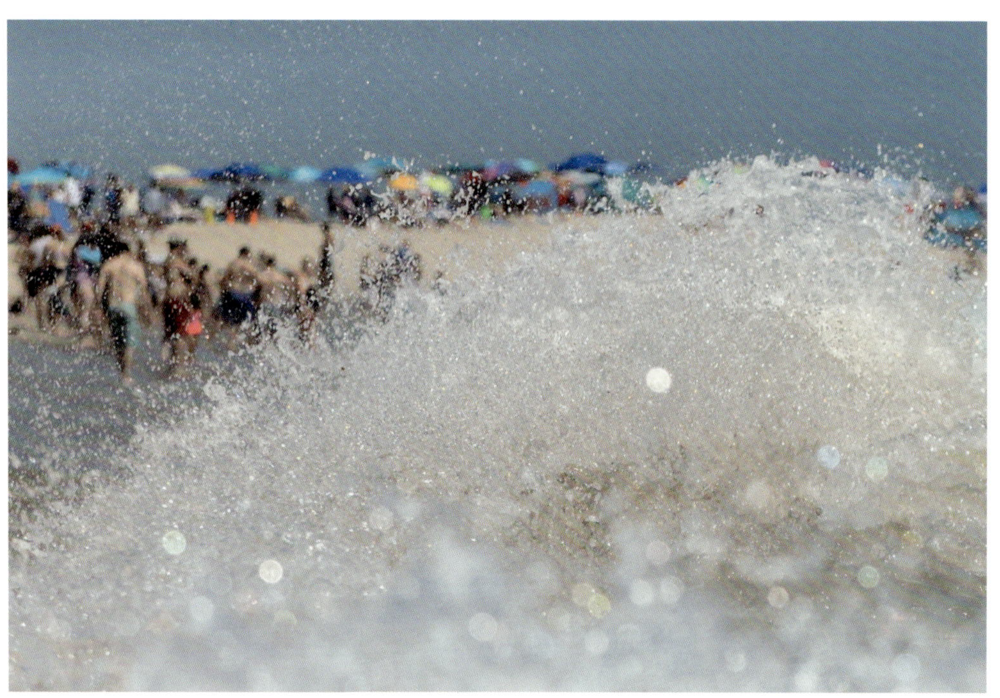

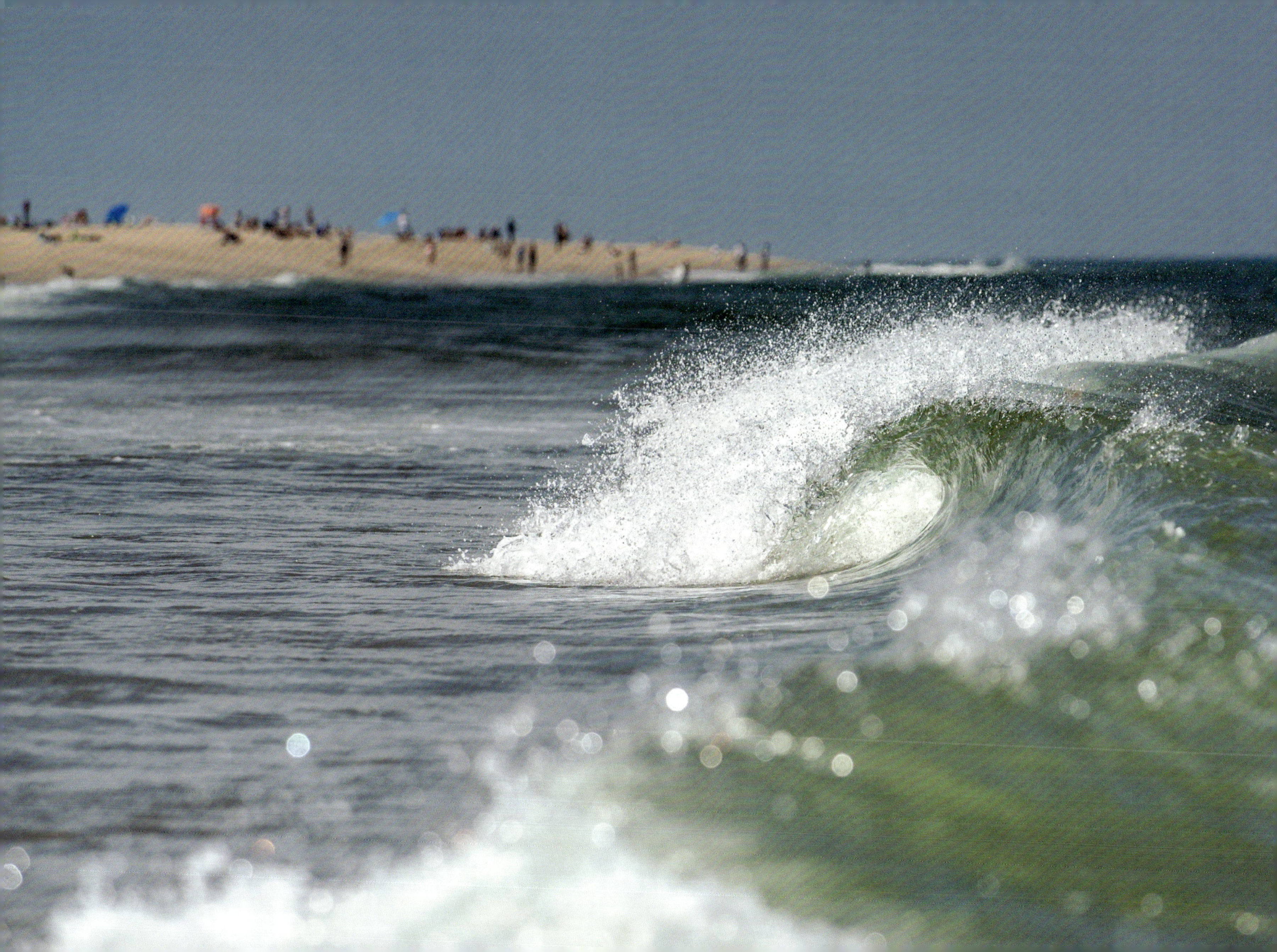

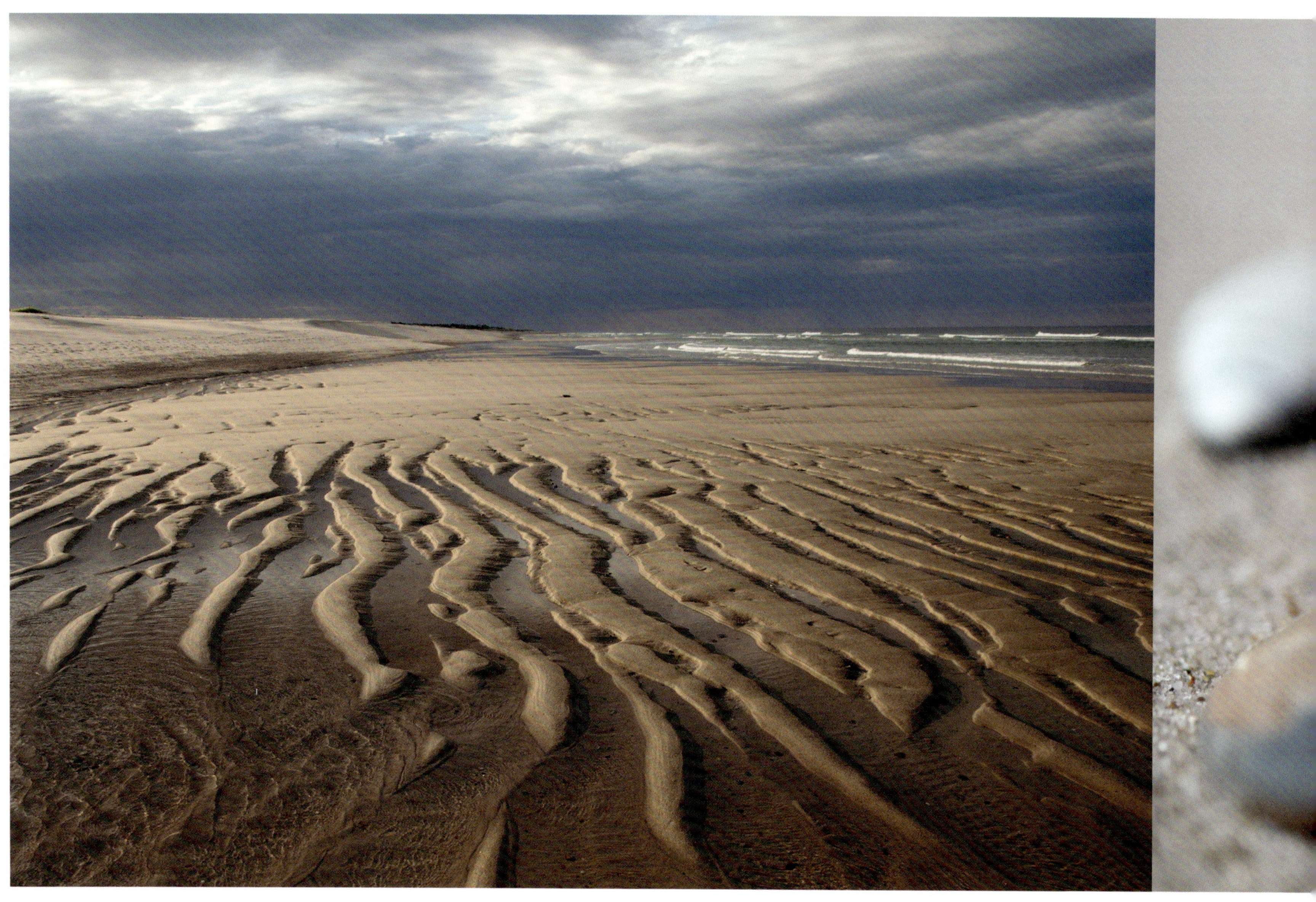

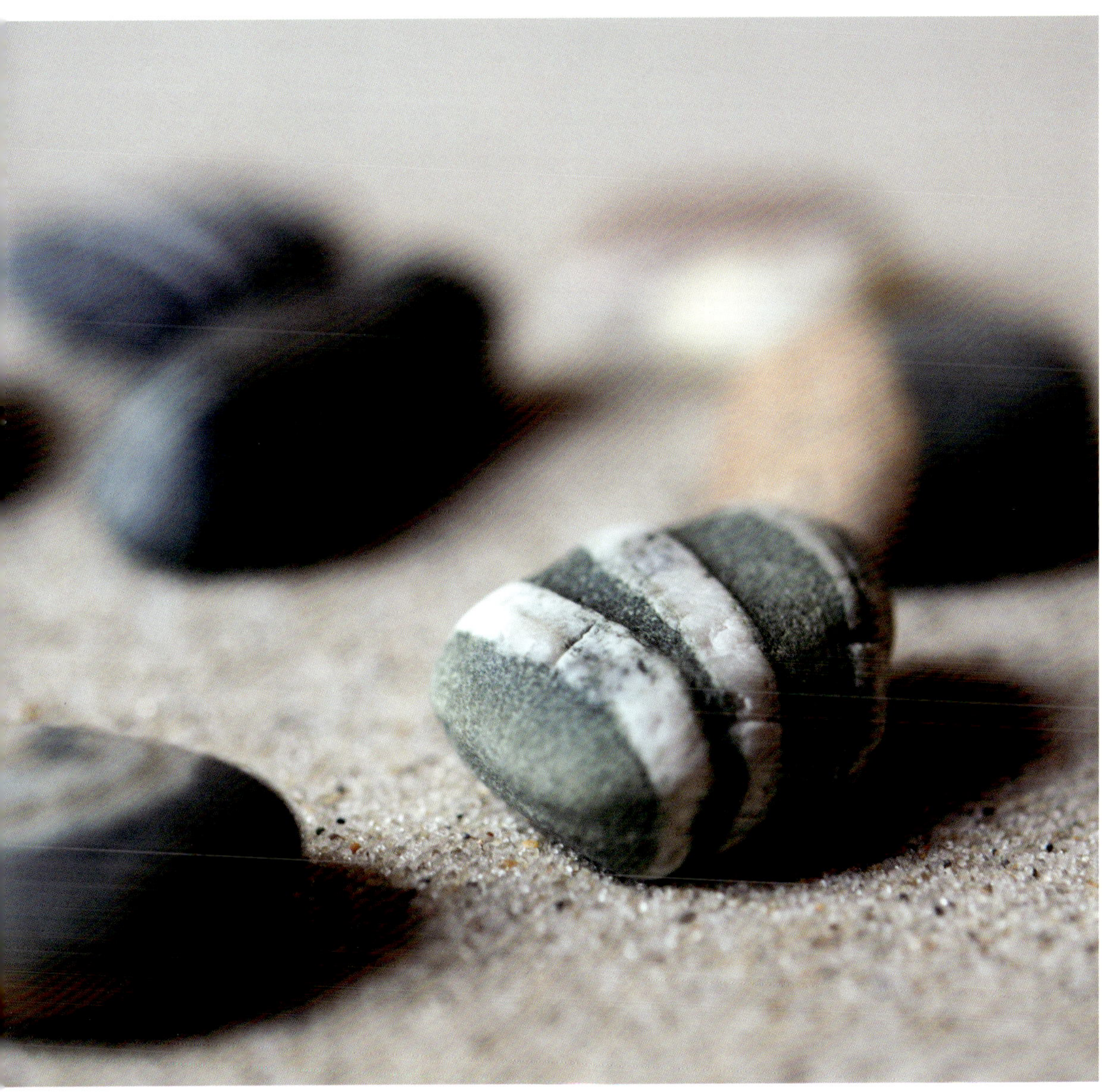

Special Stones

When my sister-in-law found this beautiful striped stone as we walked along the beach, I knew immediately how I wanted to photograph it—among other beach beauties in a simple pre-cairn composition.

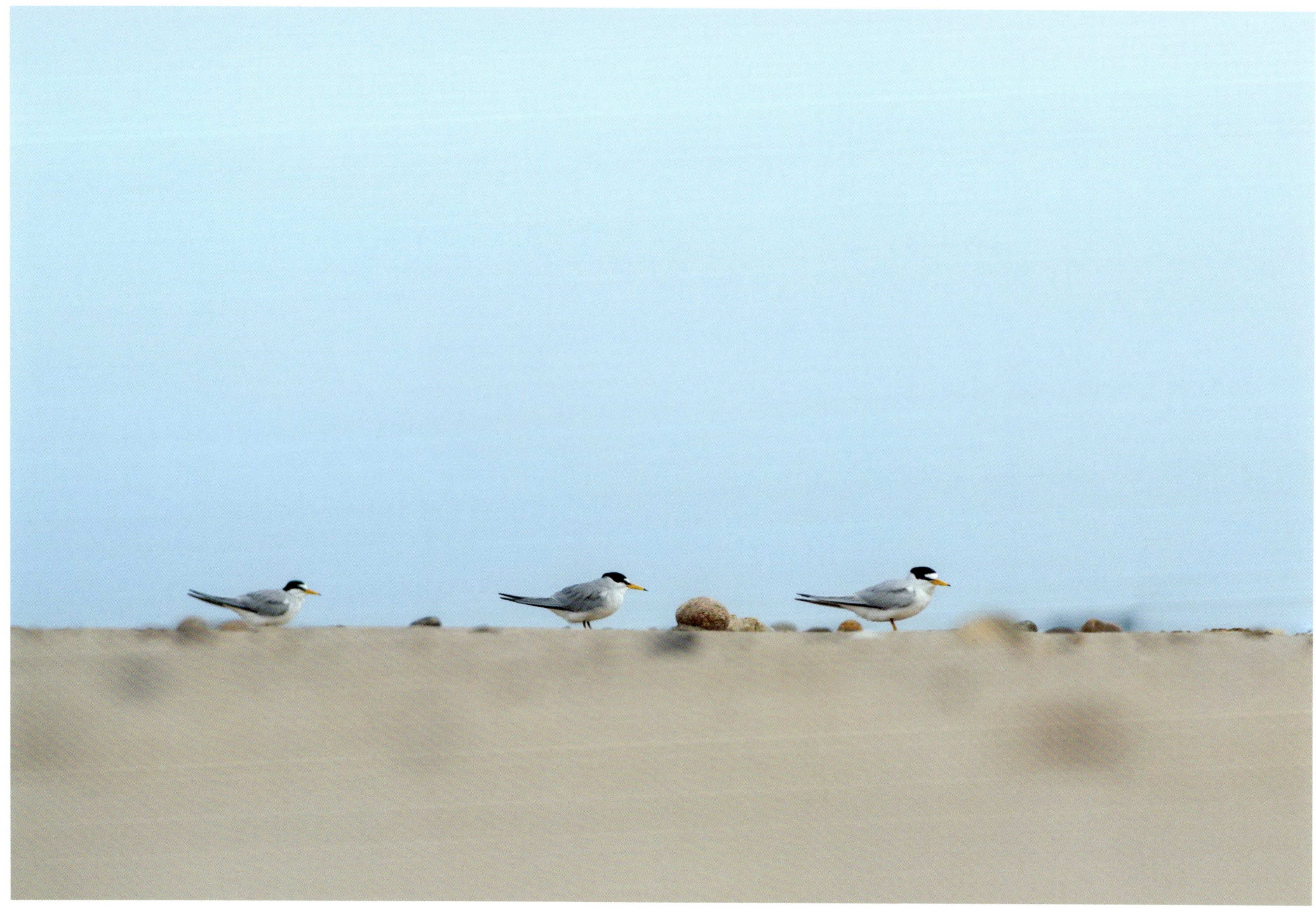

Taking Terns

These terns seem happy just watching the surf.

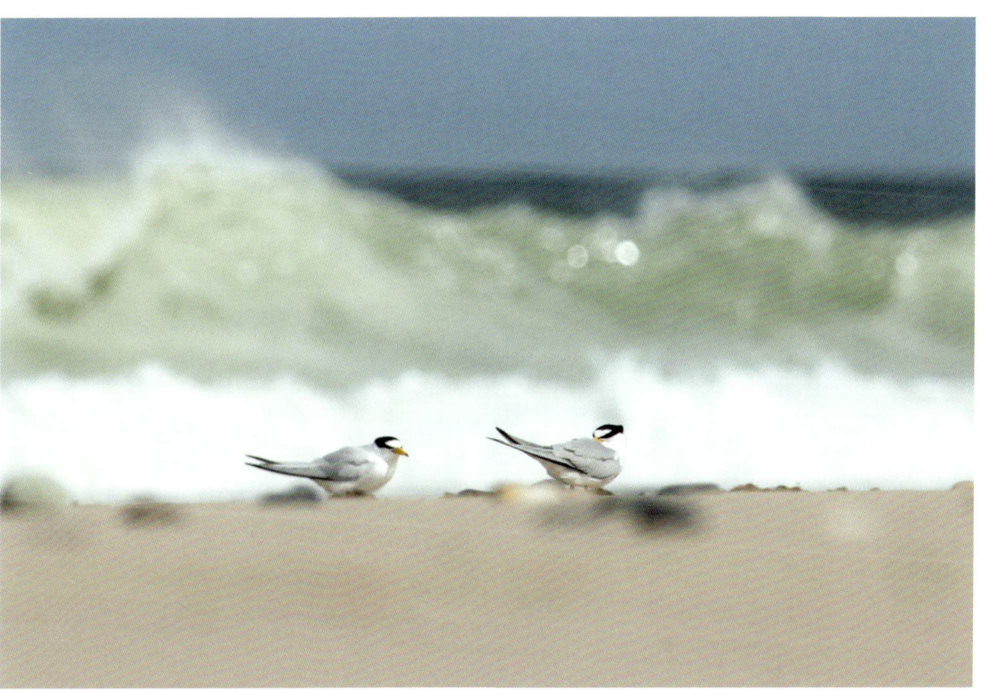

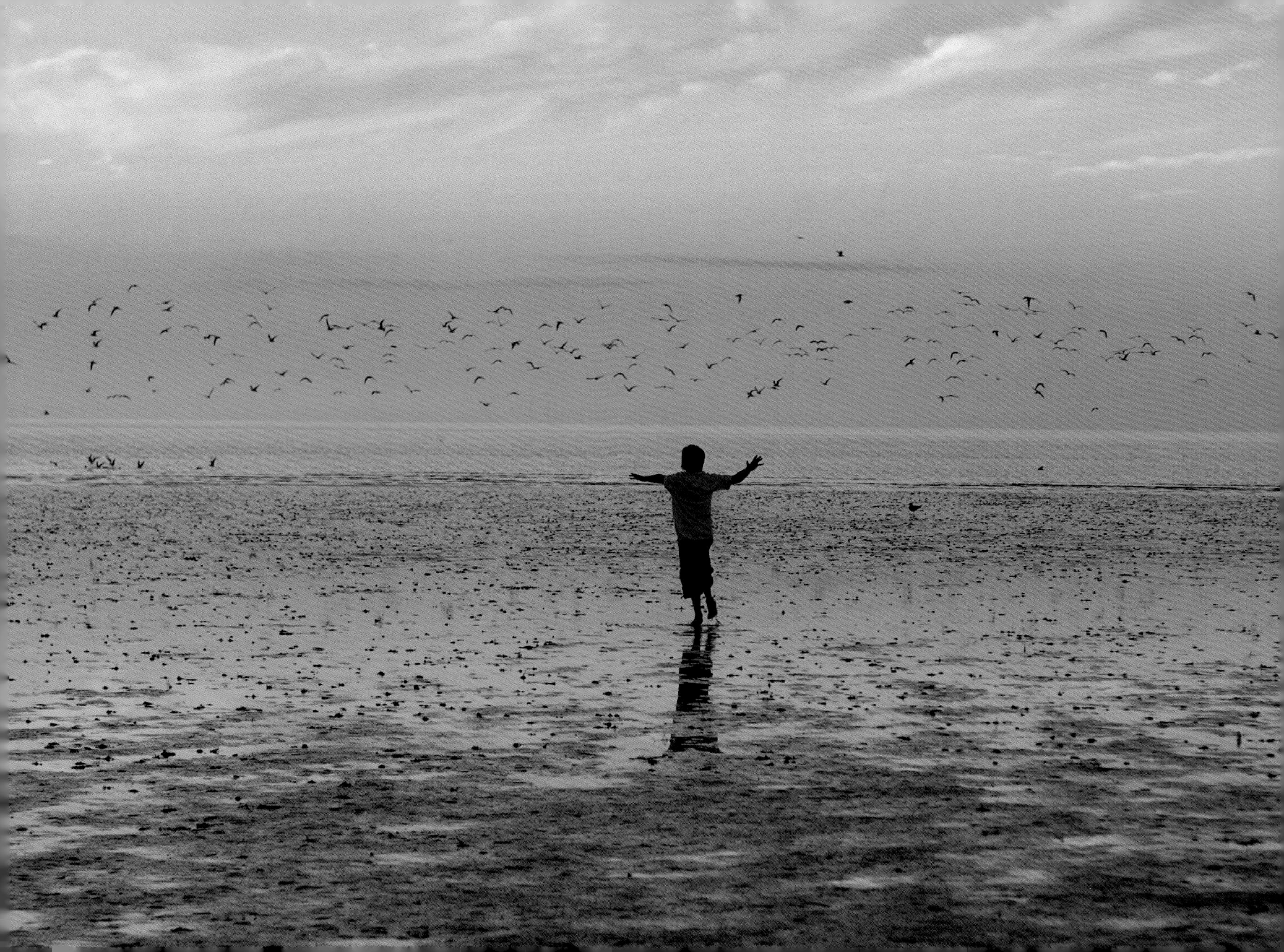

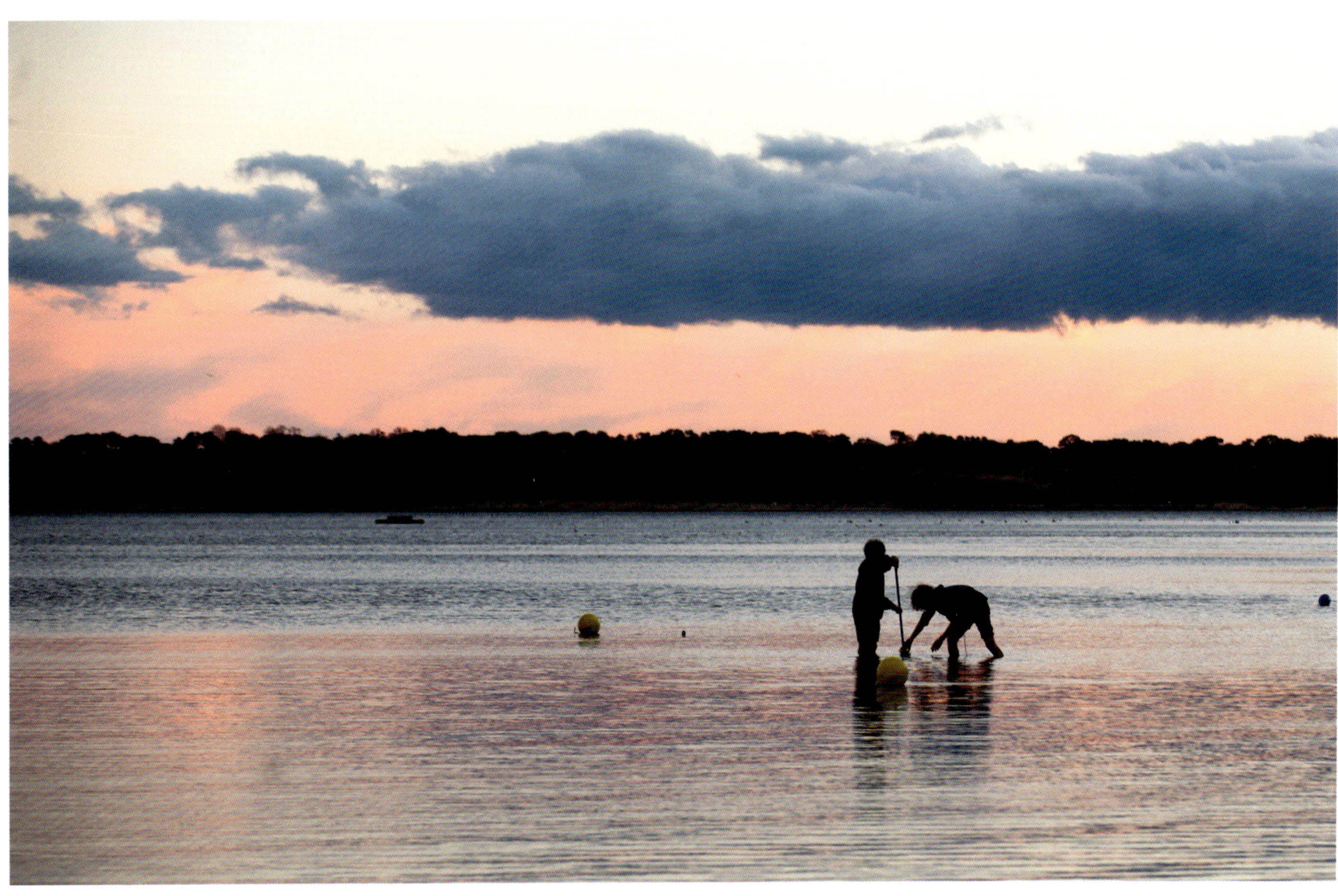

Taking Flight

This boy wanted to fly

Cape Kids

Scenes like this take me back to my childhood on Cape Cod and the many delightful summers exploring with my siblings.

Beach Portrait

These three enjoyed their portrait session. They displayed their personalities perfectly.

Shoreline Dilemma

A delightful shoreline dilemma is whether to freeze the wave with a fast shutter speed, or amplify the wave's motion with a slow exposure.

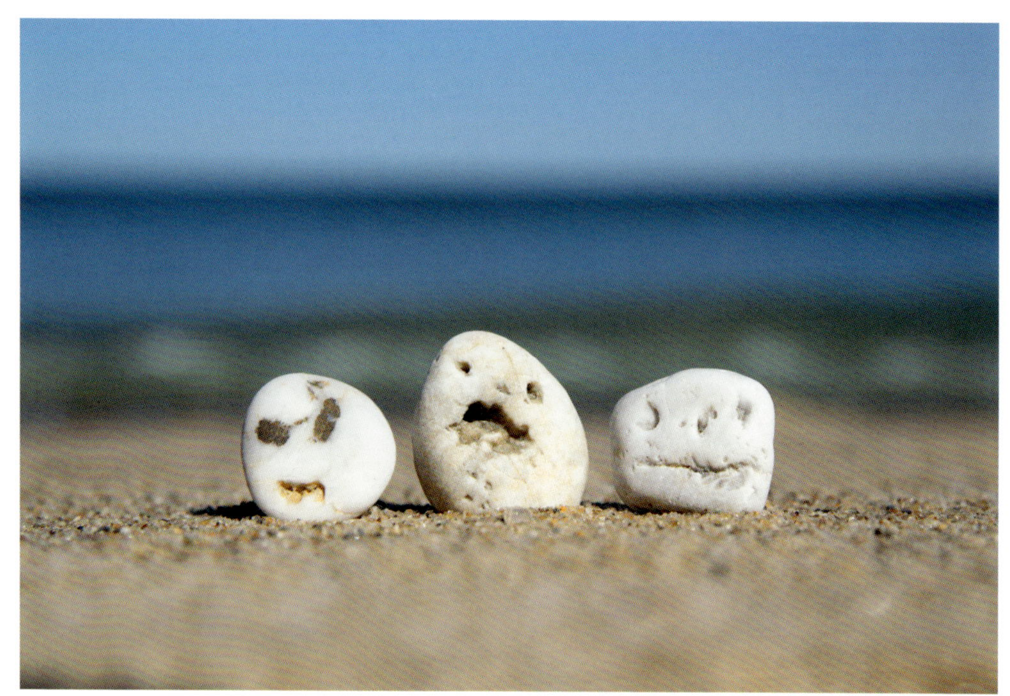

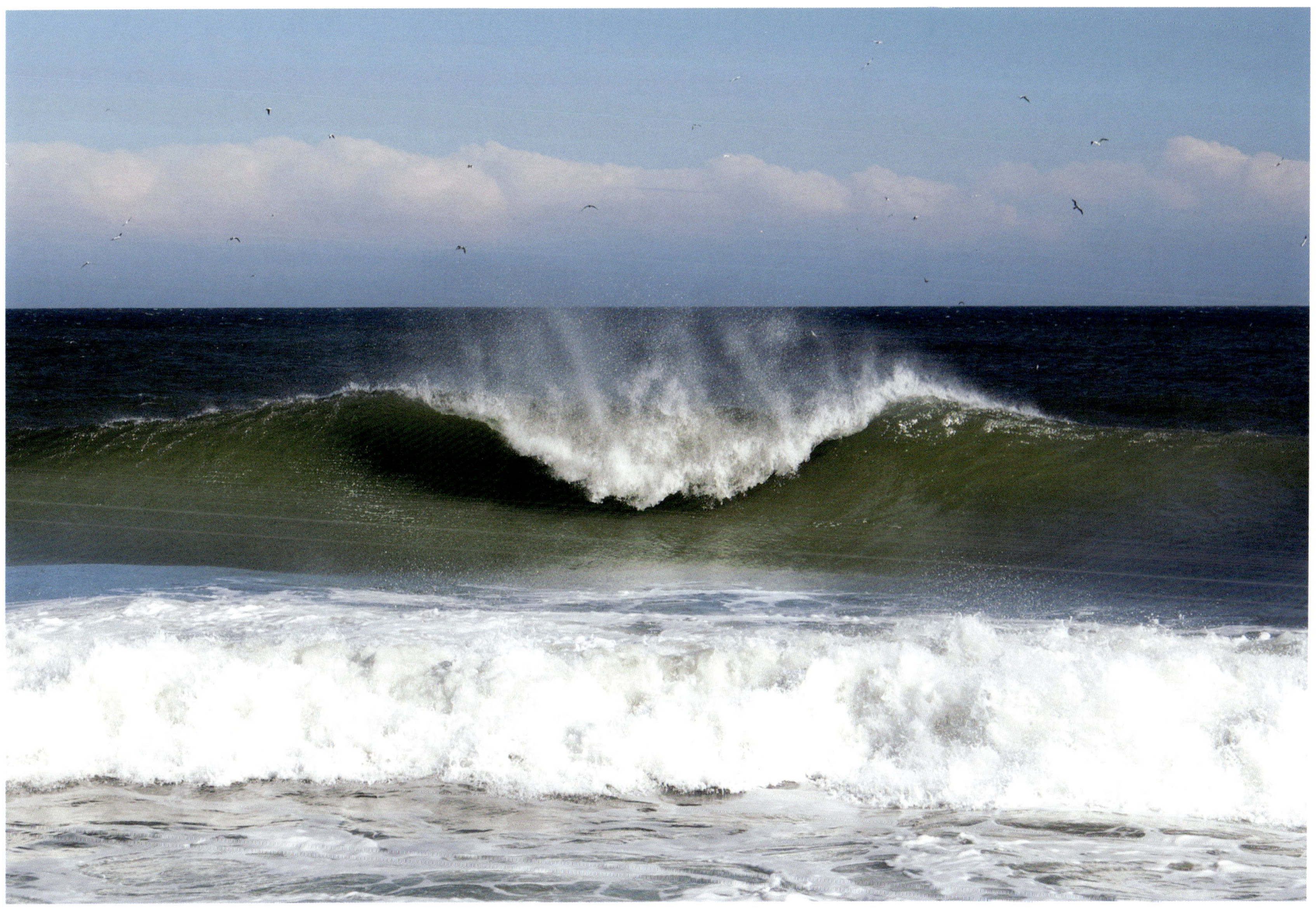

Glass Cairn

Like gems, light falling on sea glass creates a subtle kind of beauty.

Cloud and Shadow

After spending years photographing waves from the shore, I wanted to capture what was happening below. In this wave cross section, the shadow beneath the wave front mimics the cloud above.

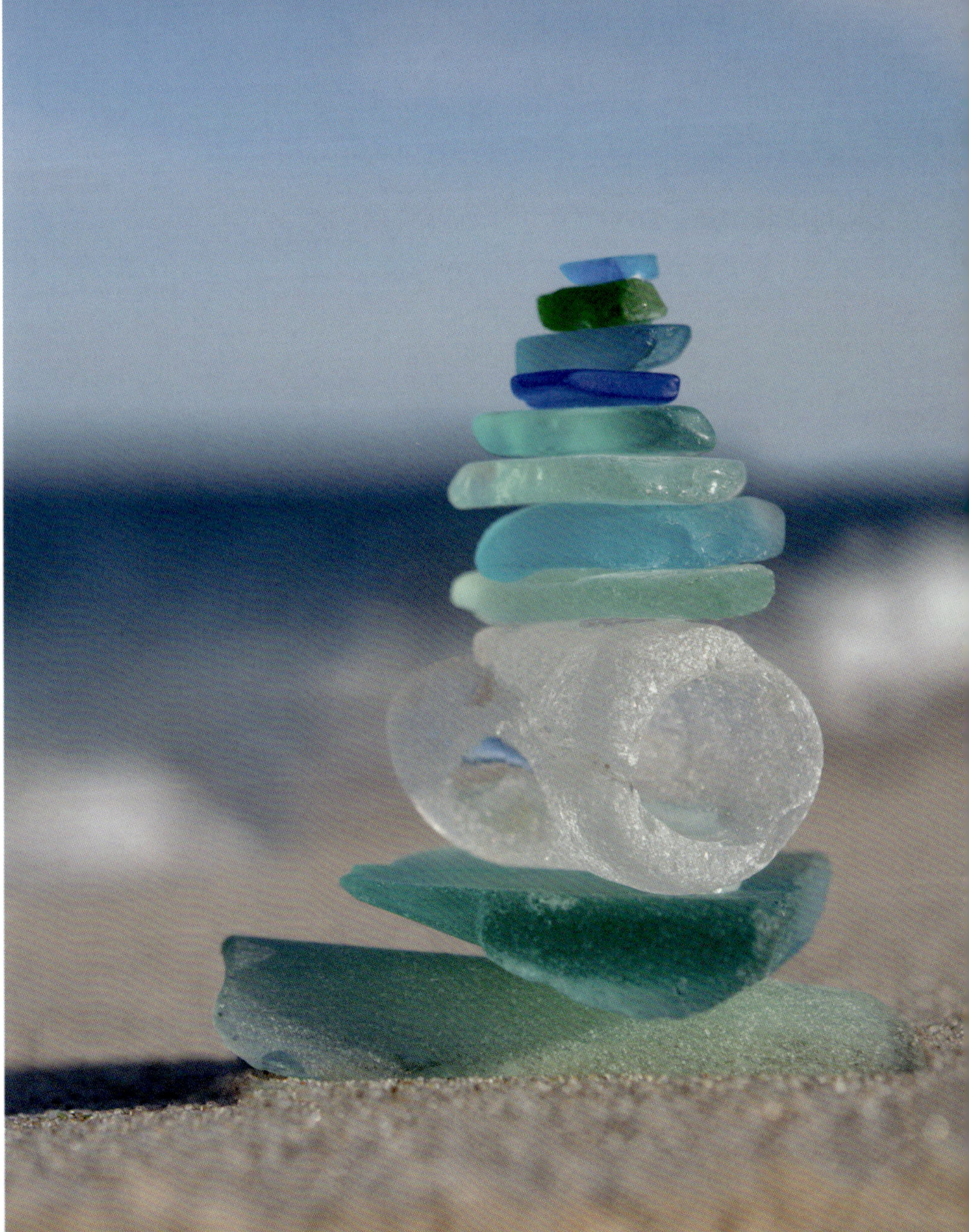

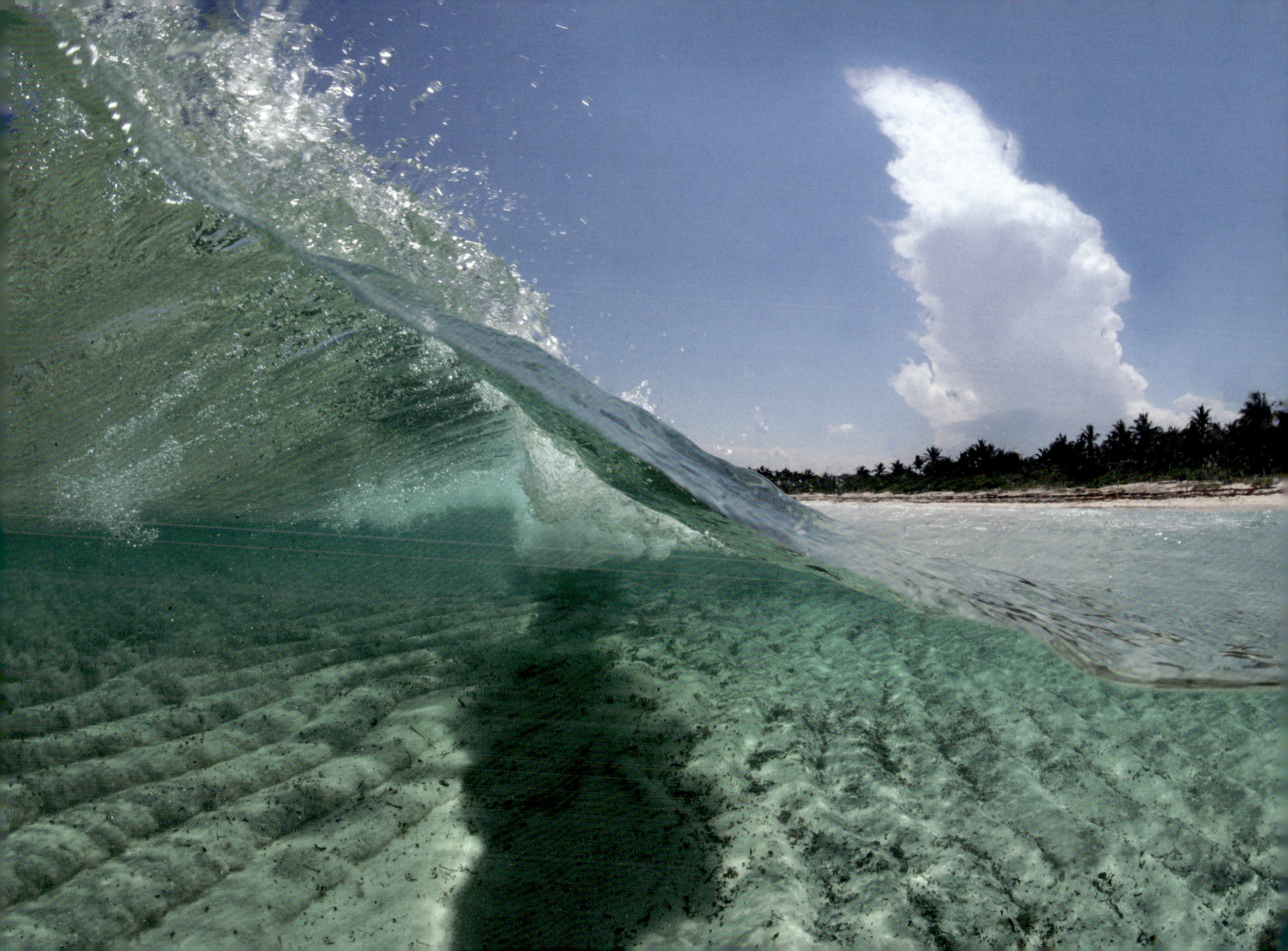

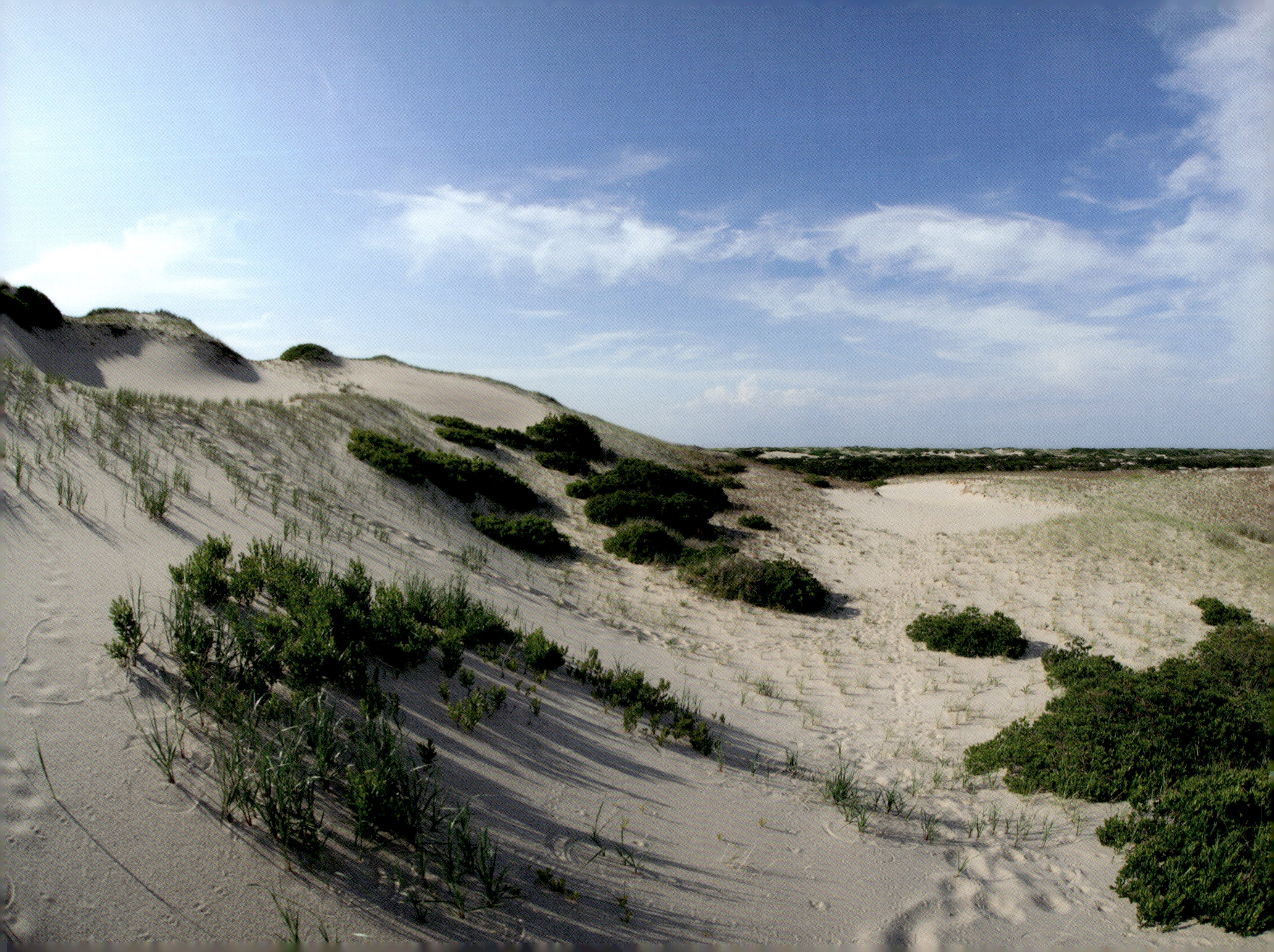

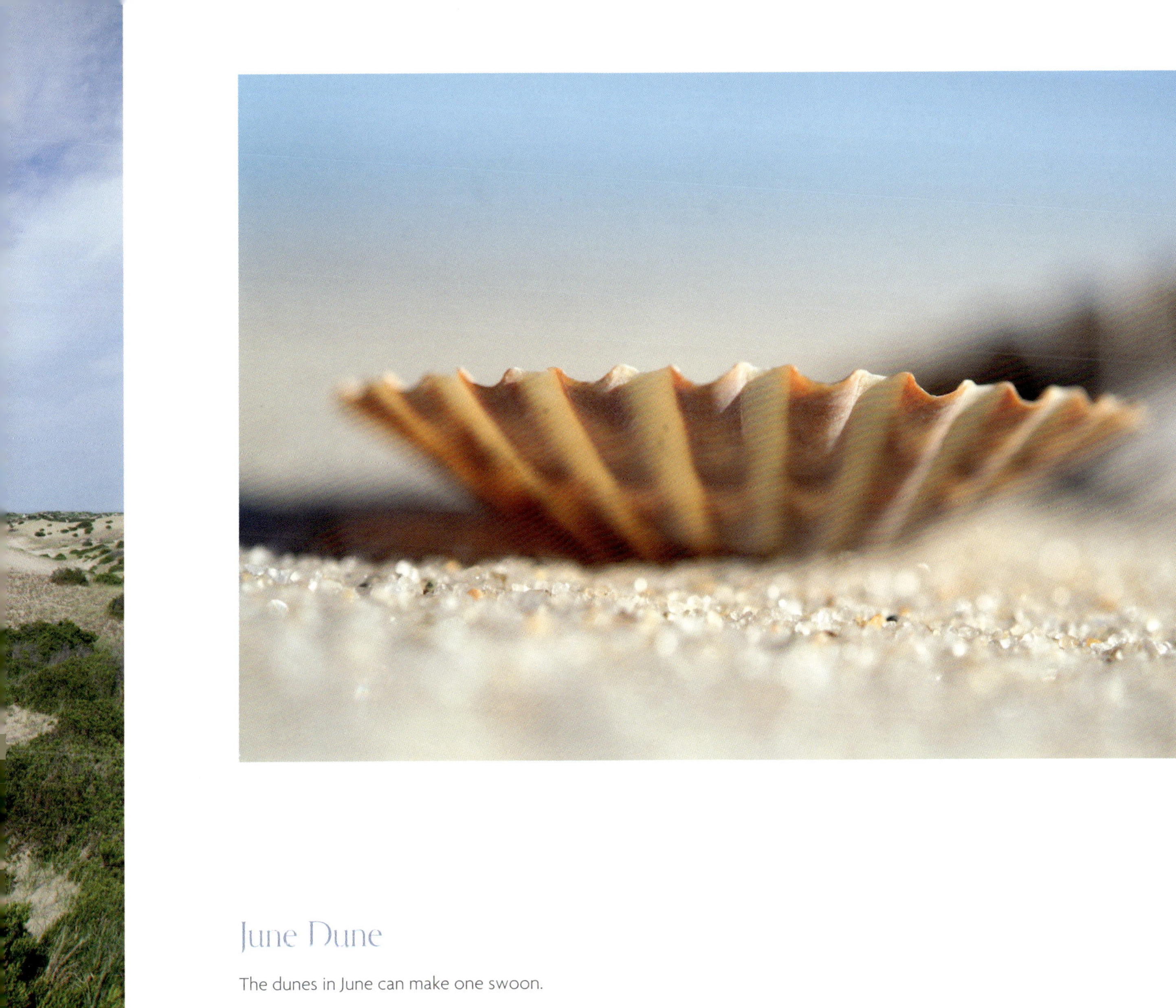

June Dune

The dunes in June can make one swoon.

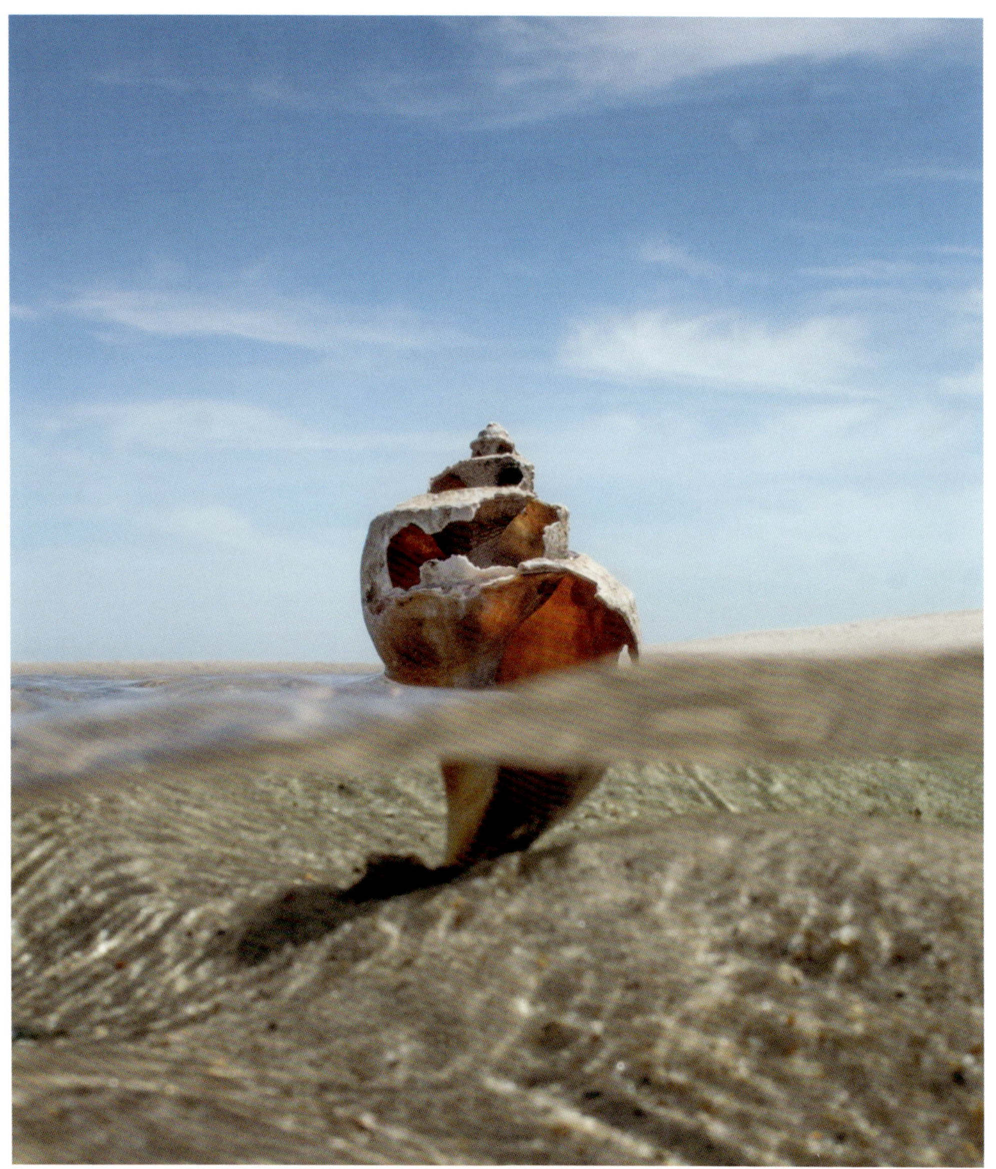

Translucence

I love shells because of how the light moves through them. My favorites are perfectly imperfect.

Selfie

Self-portrait: my favorite spot on my favorite beach

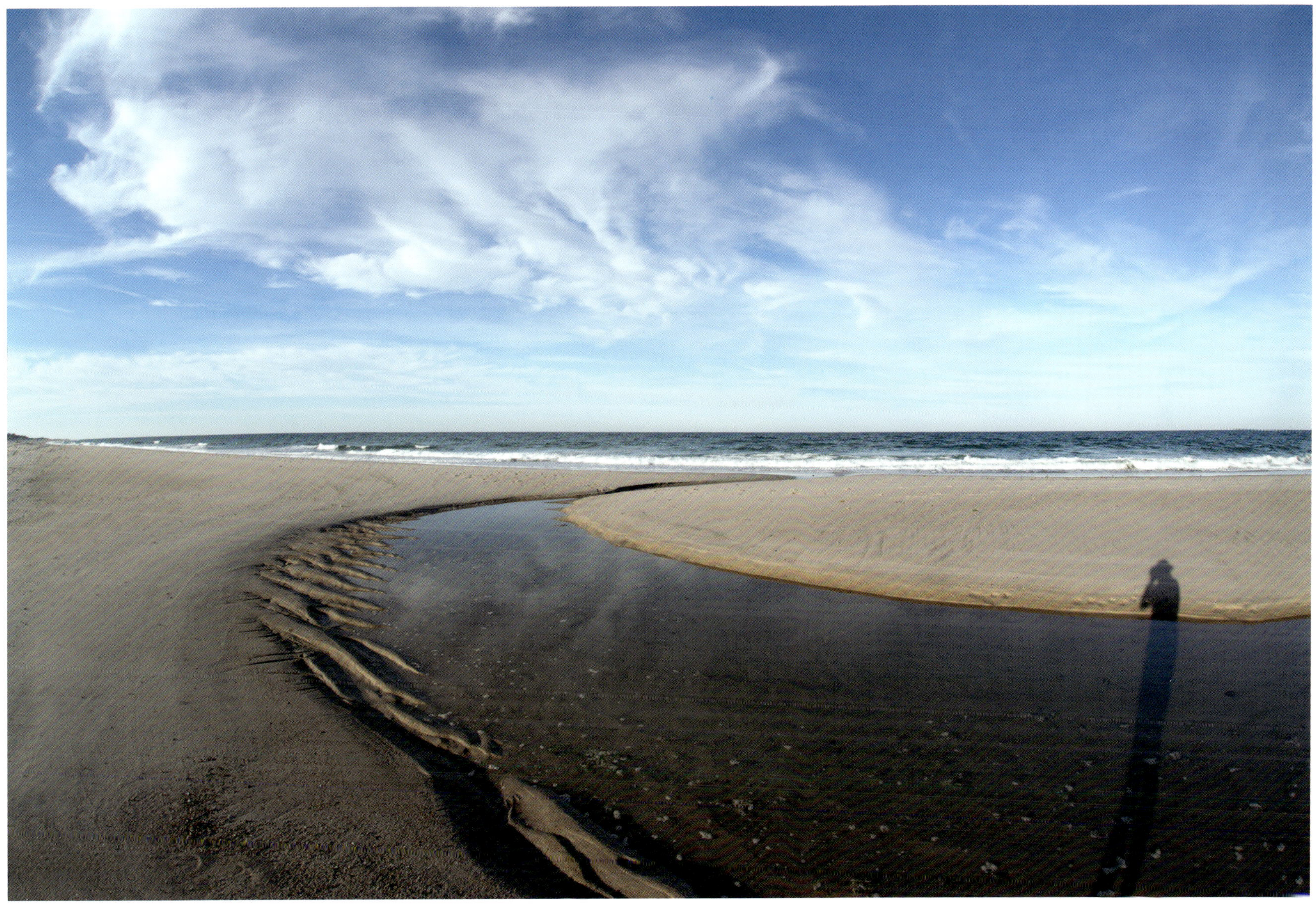

I spy

I spy with my little eye . . . eight hearts.

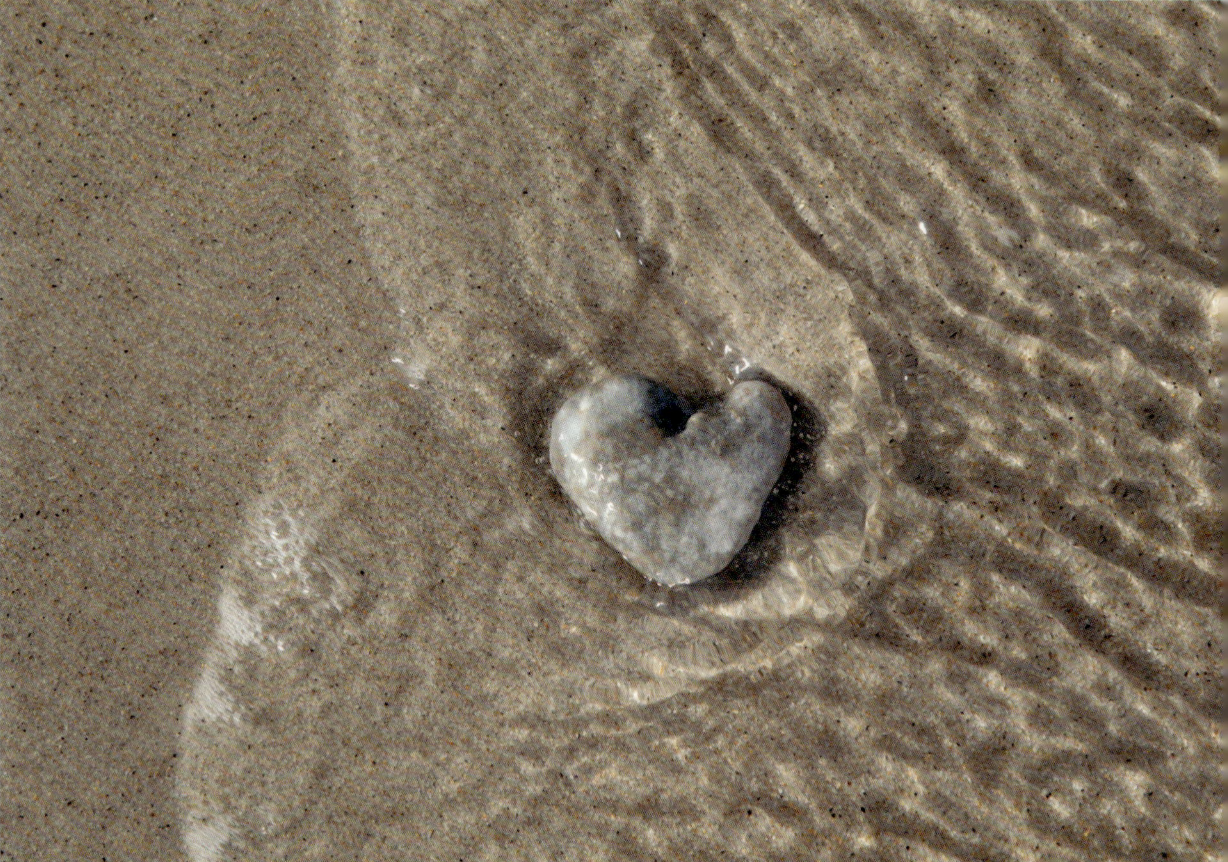

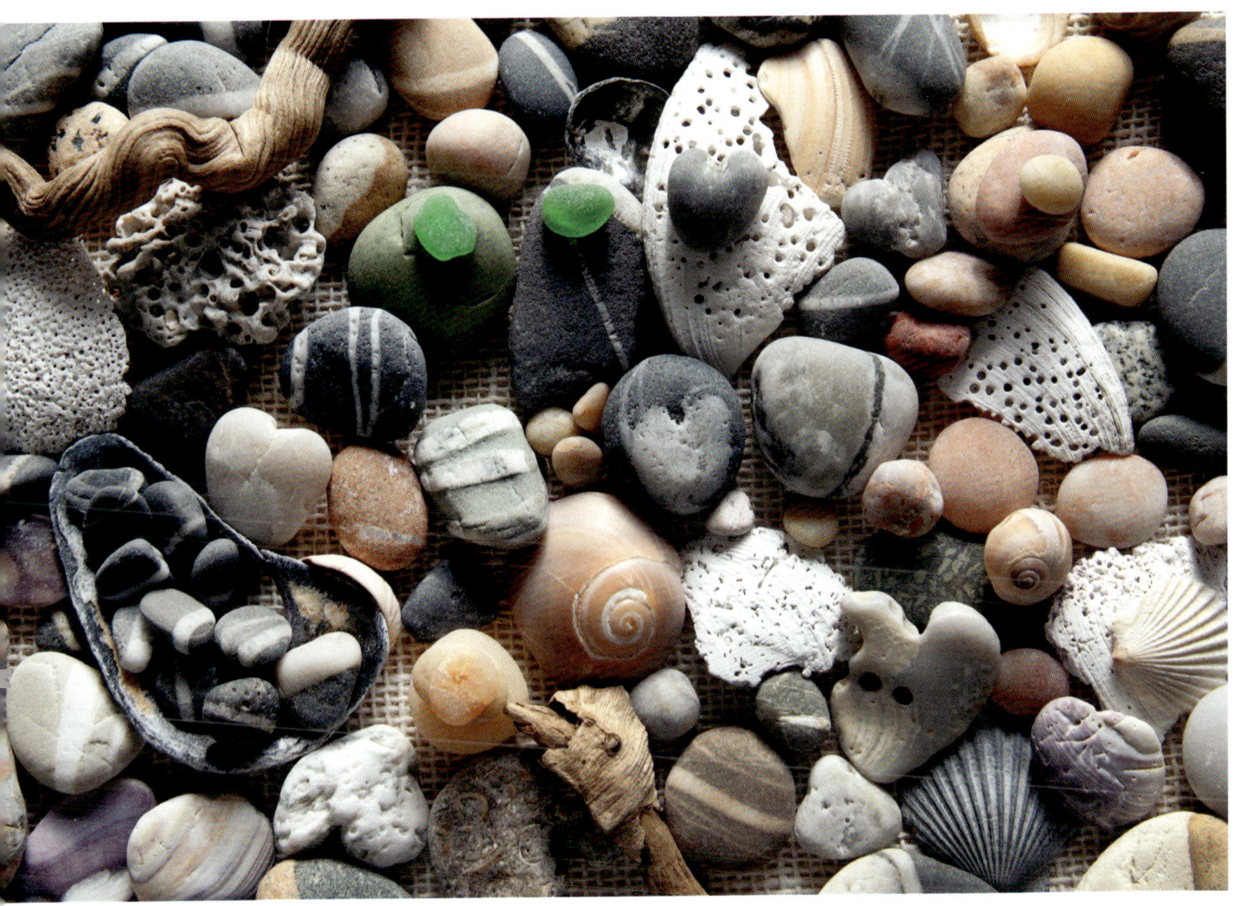

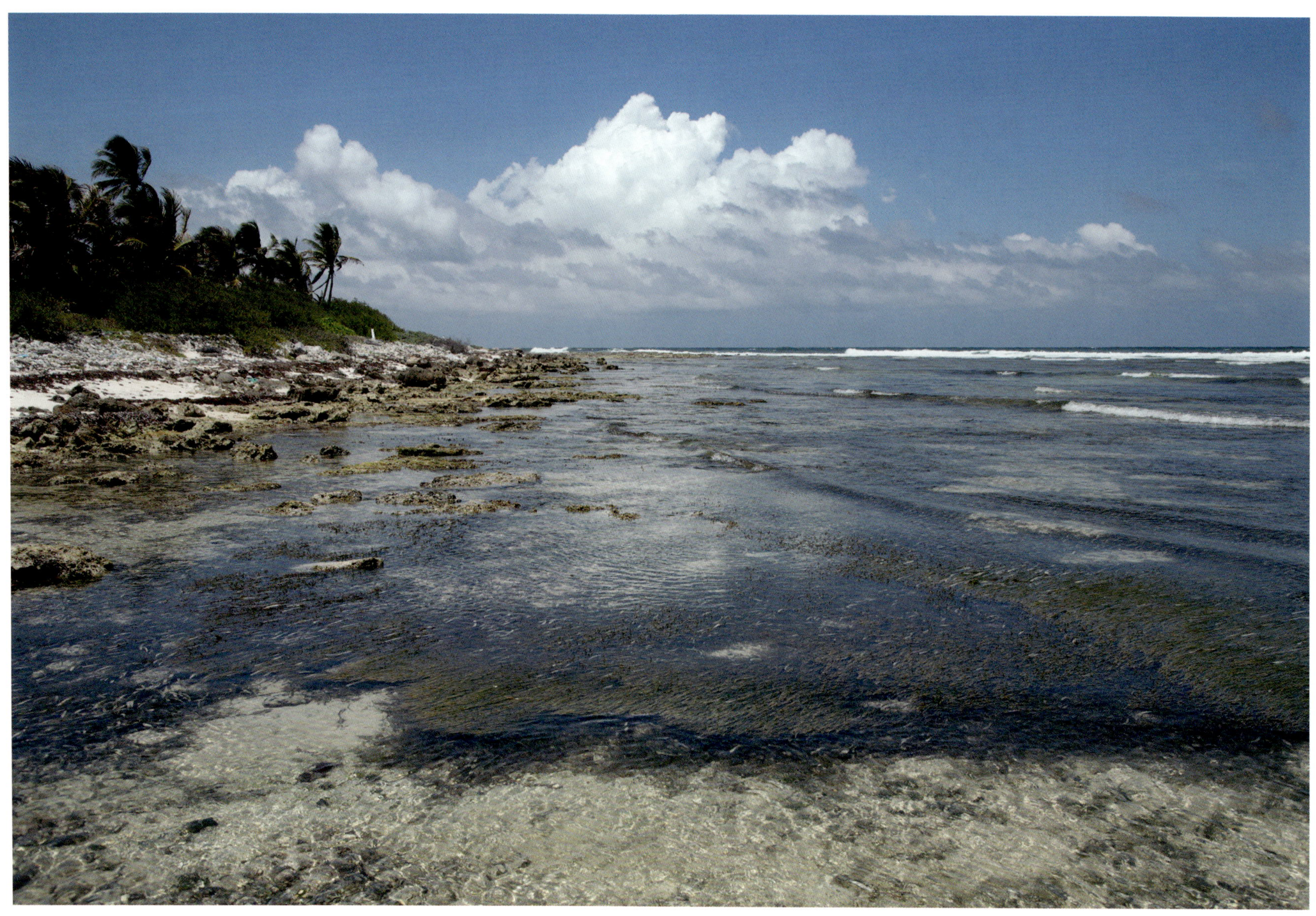

High Low

These two images were created in the exact same spot—one above the water, and one partly below it. I was mesmerized by how quickly the waves slowed when they reached the long eelgrass beds.

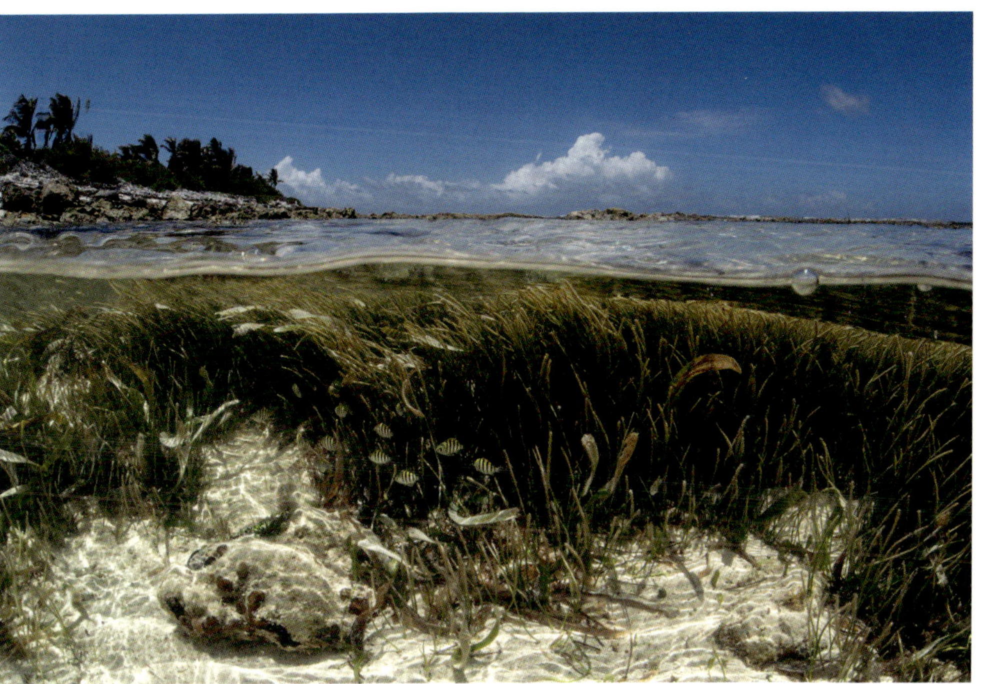

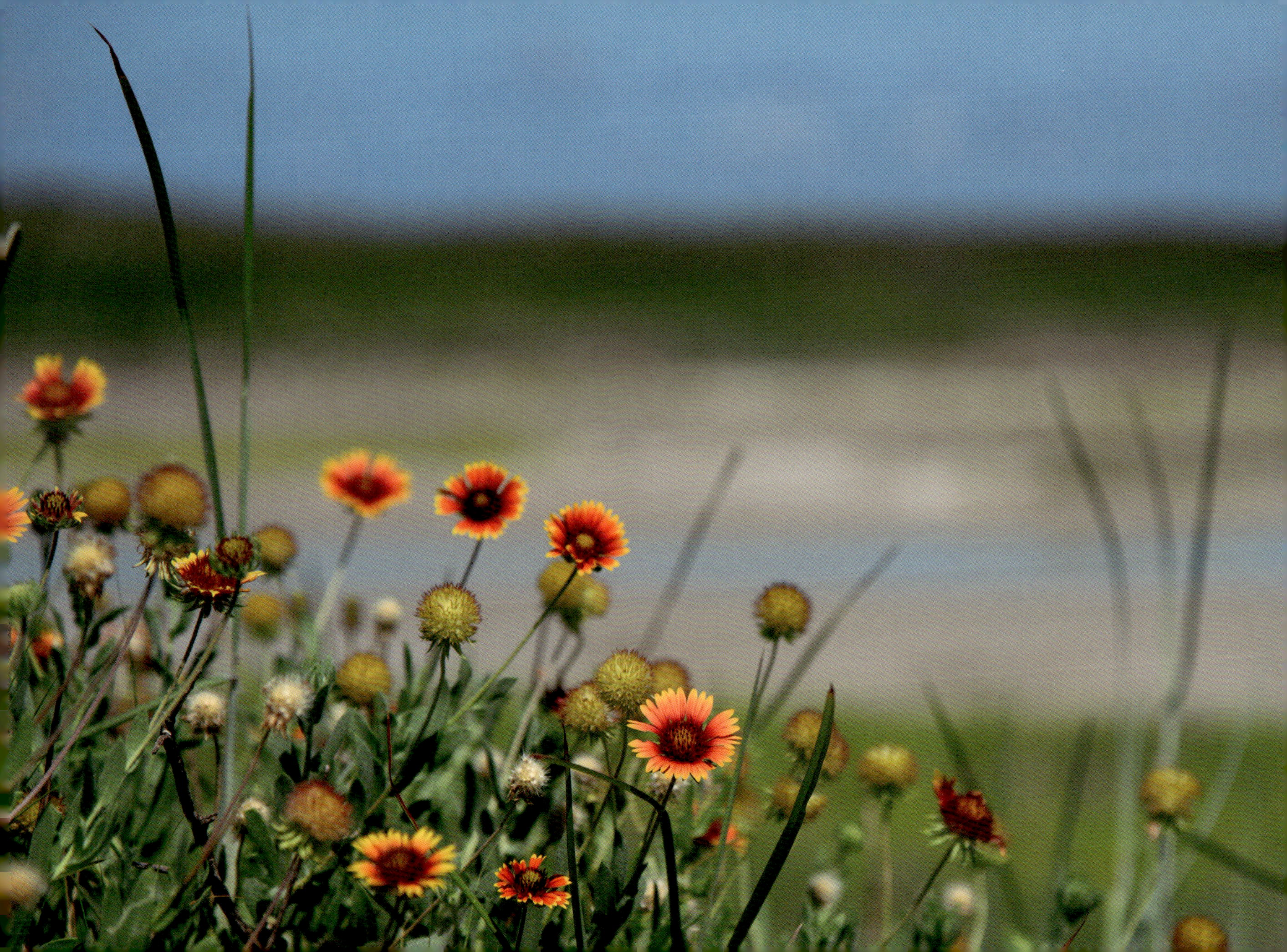

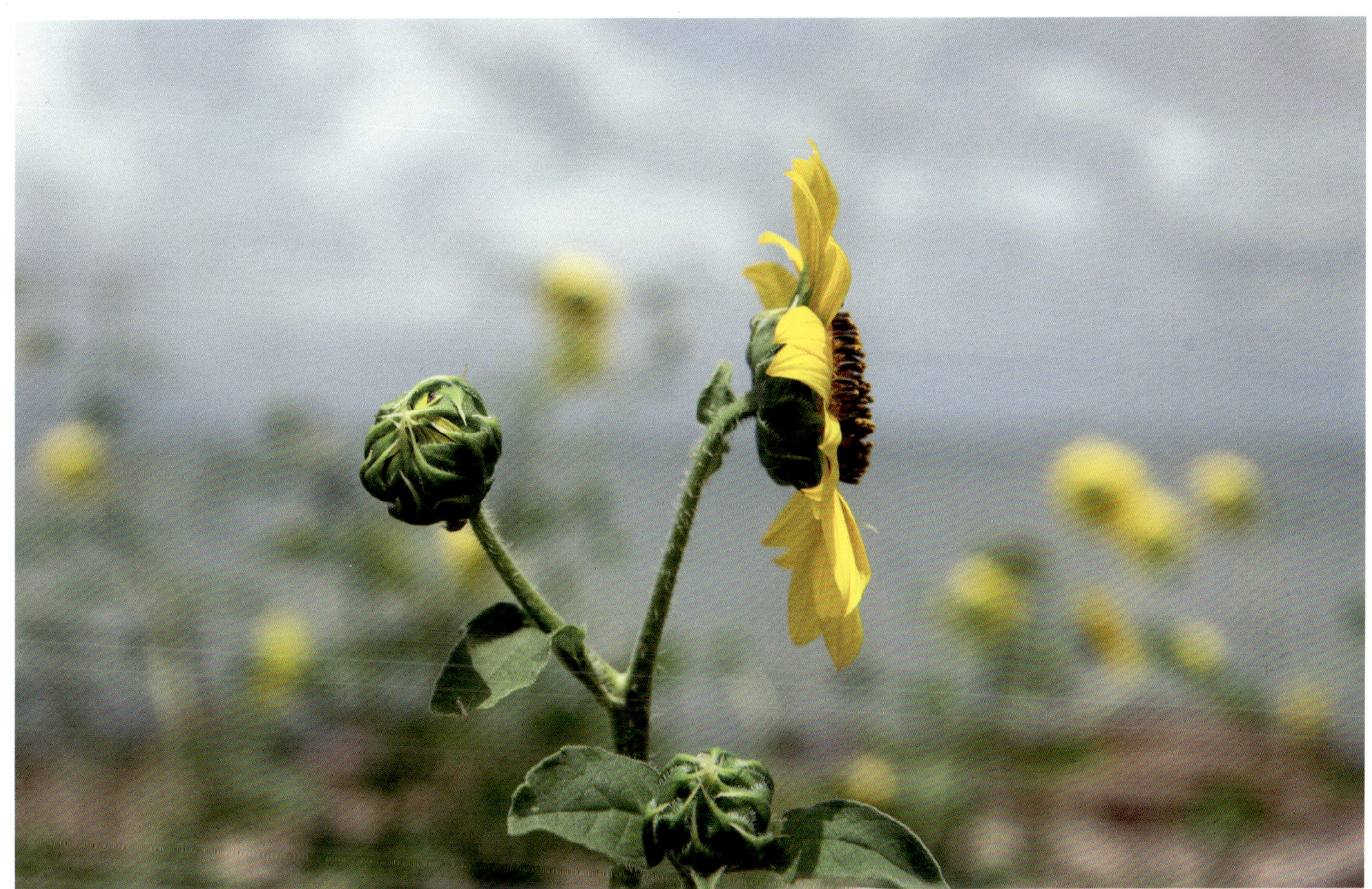

Texas Seaside

I love to visit new beaches and explore the nearby plants. These Texas wildflowers caught my attention.

My Heart Rocks

My heart is still rocking.

Two of Hearts

Nauset Beach shared its love with two sea spray hearts in the surf.

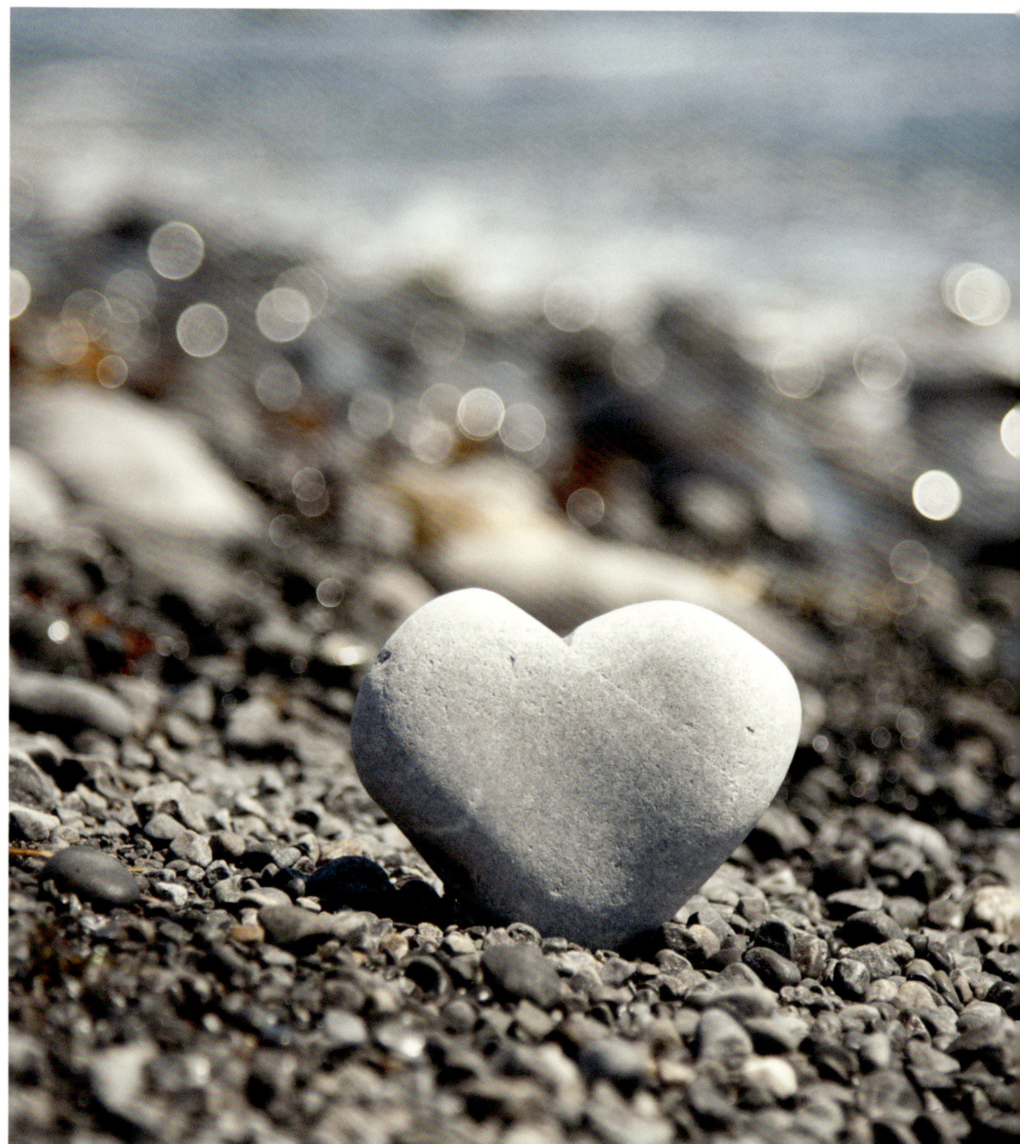

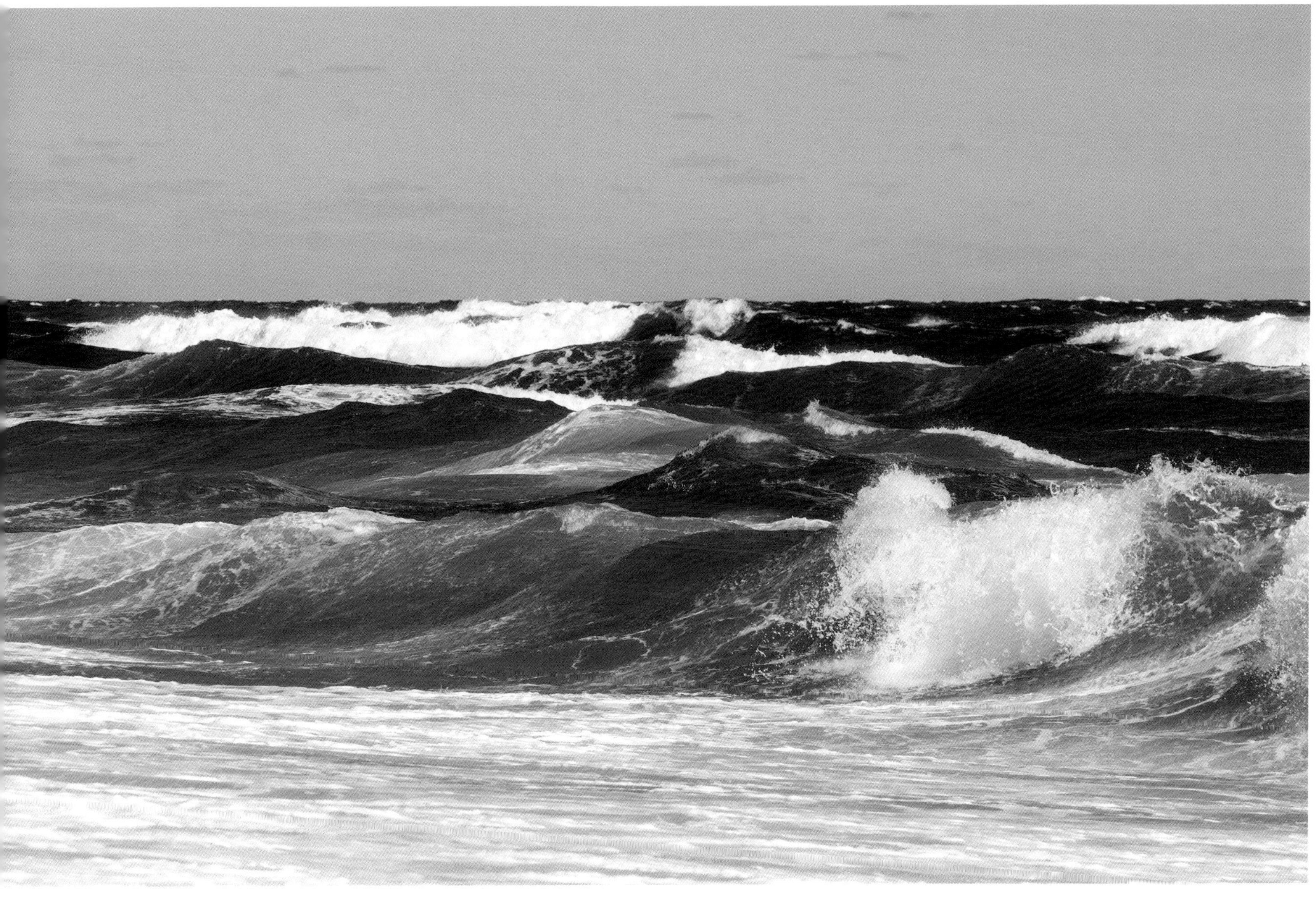

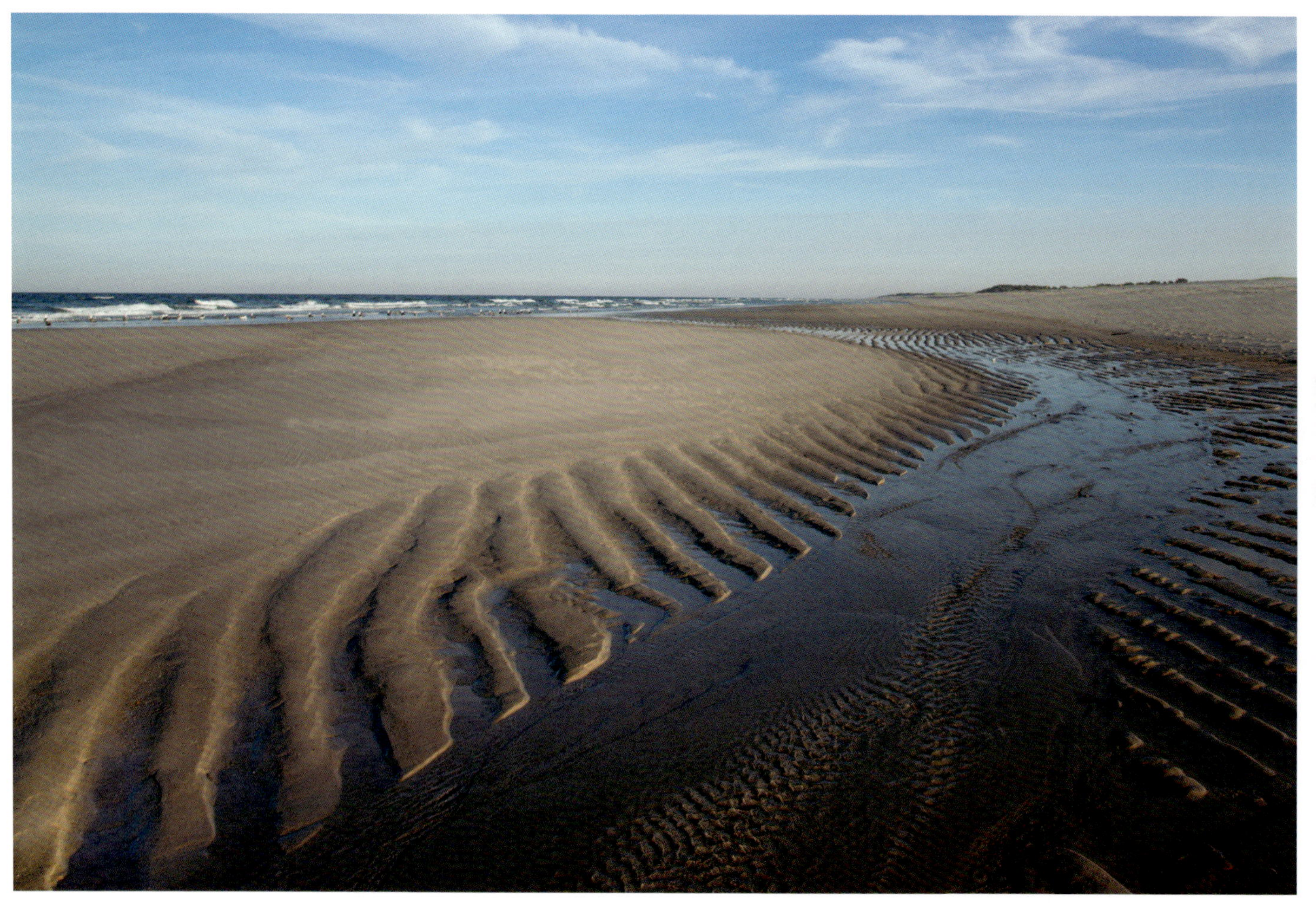

Natural Cogs

Whenever I see this pattern in the sand, I think of gear cogs.

Beach Bliss

Everybody goes to the beach for their own kind of fun.

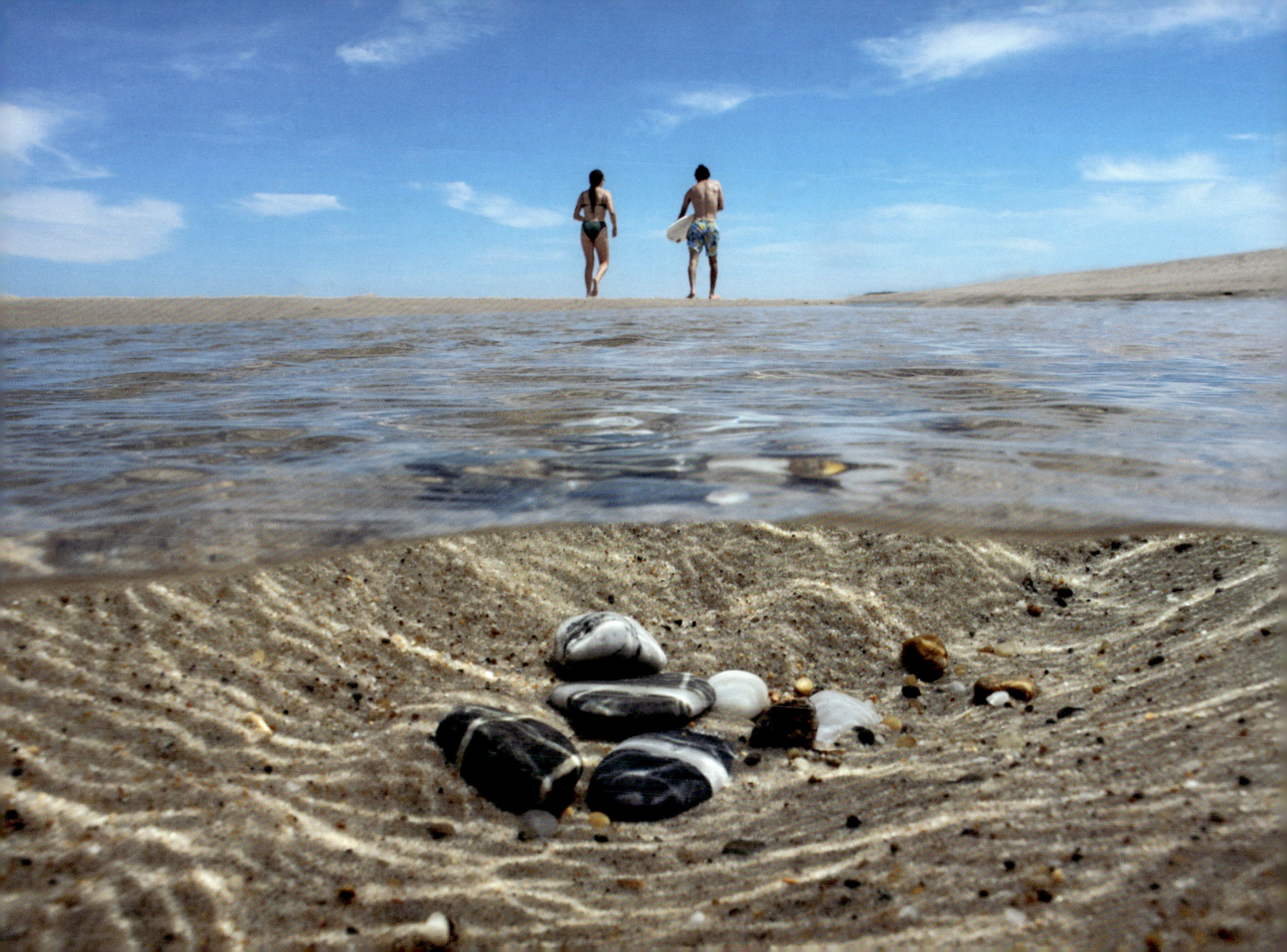

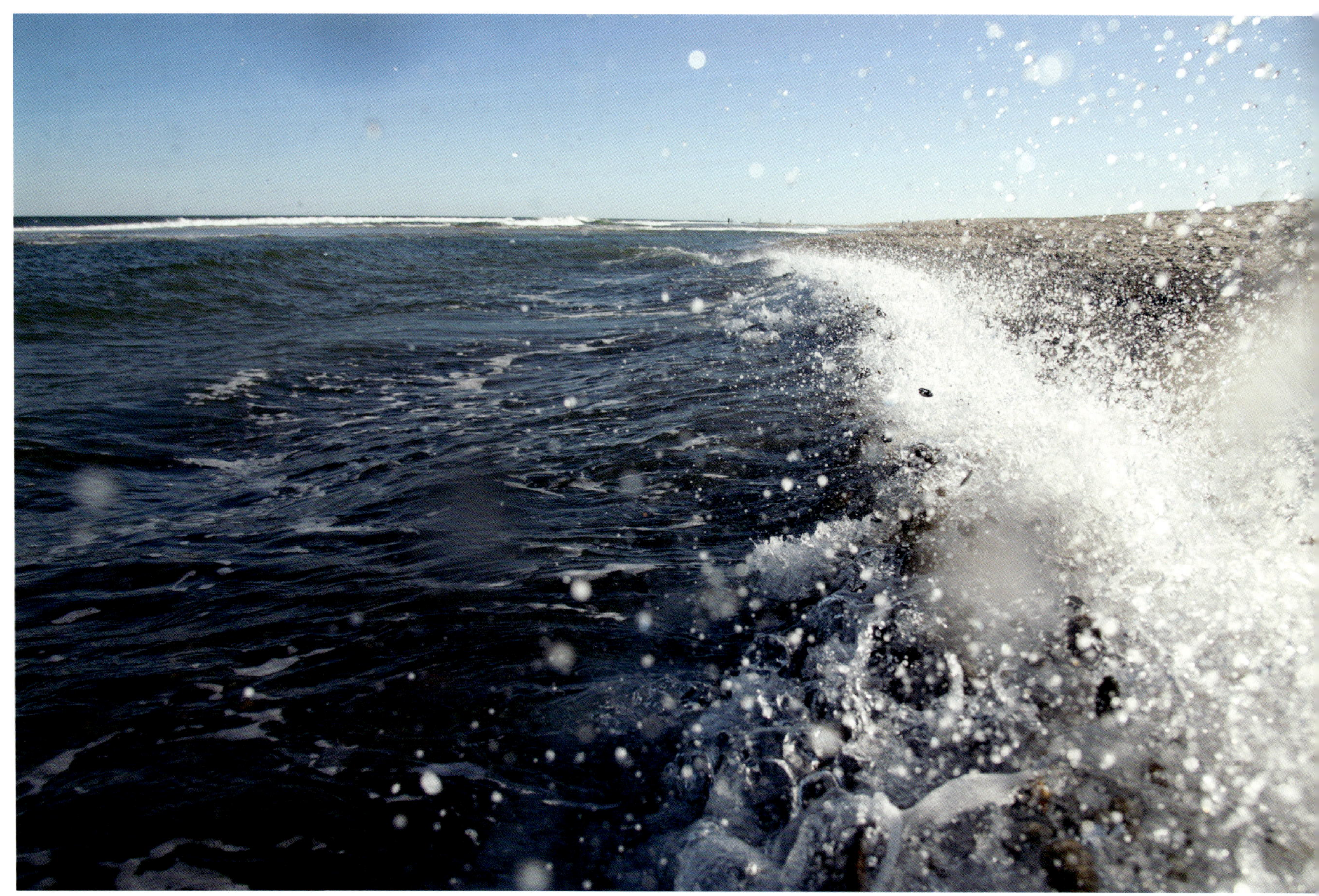

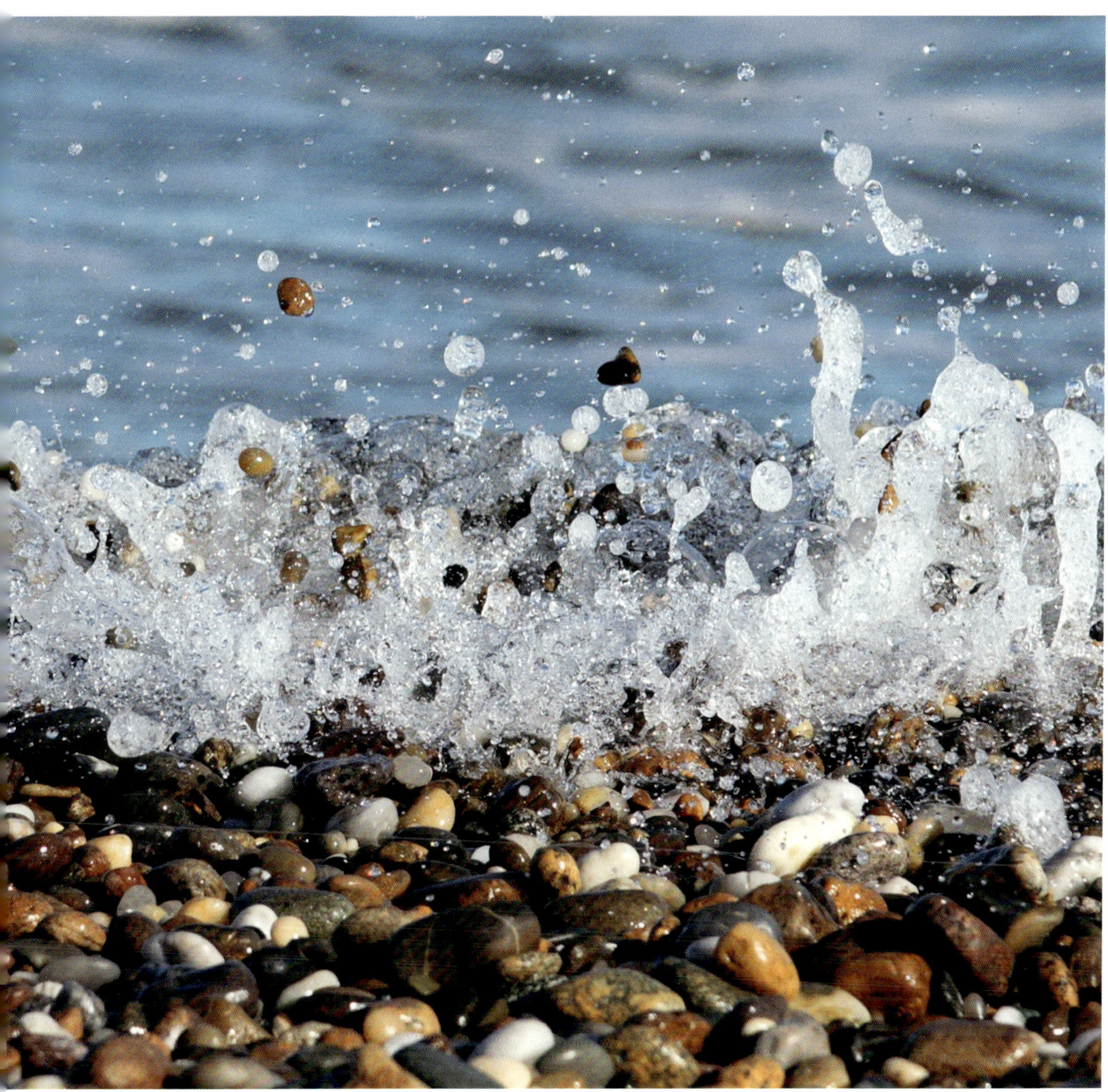

Rock Tumbler

Dancing in the surf, these beach stones demonstrate the force that creates their smooth surfaces.

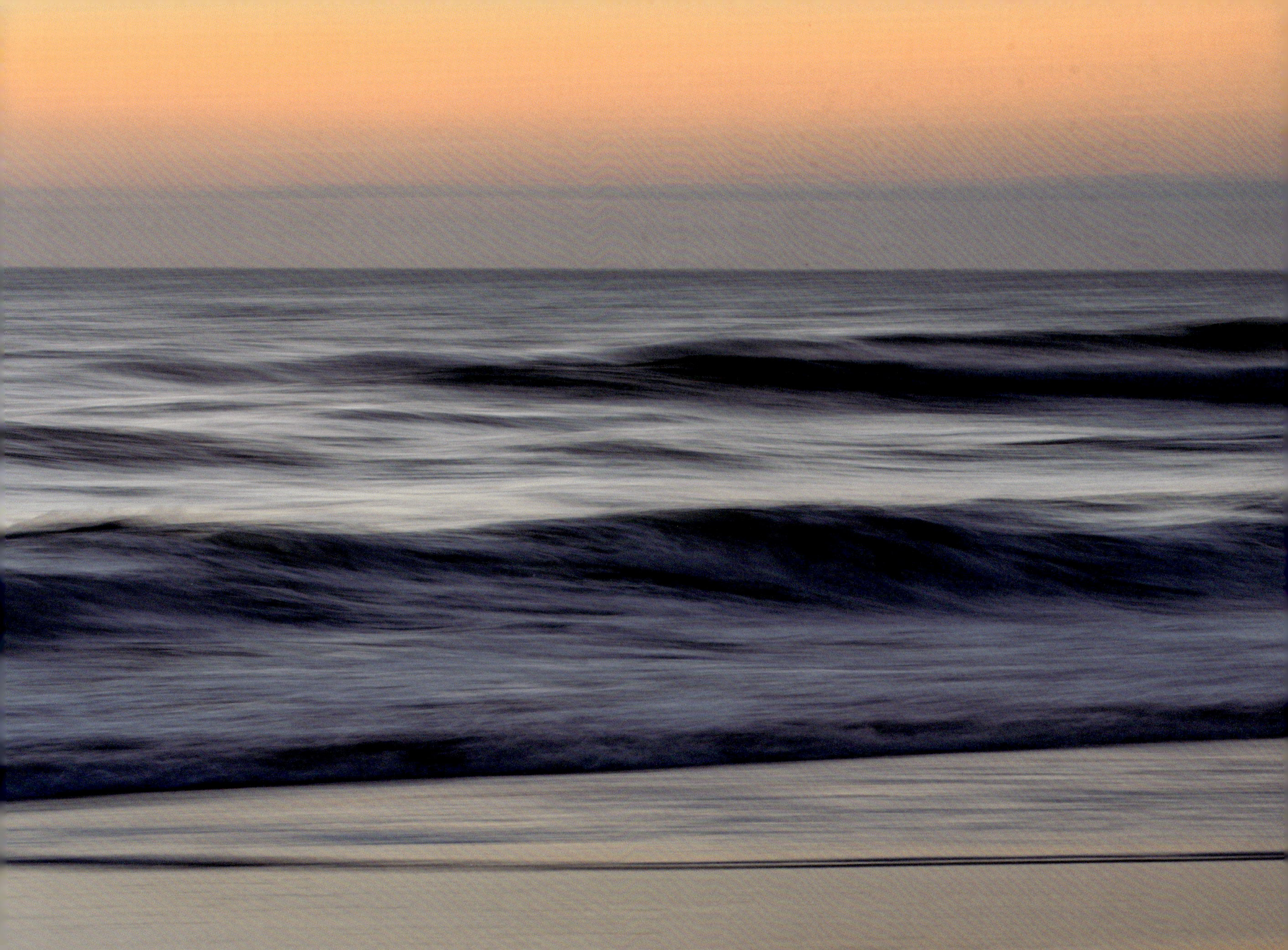

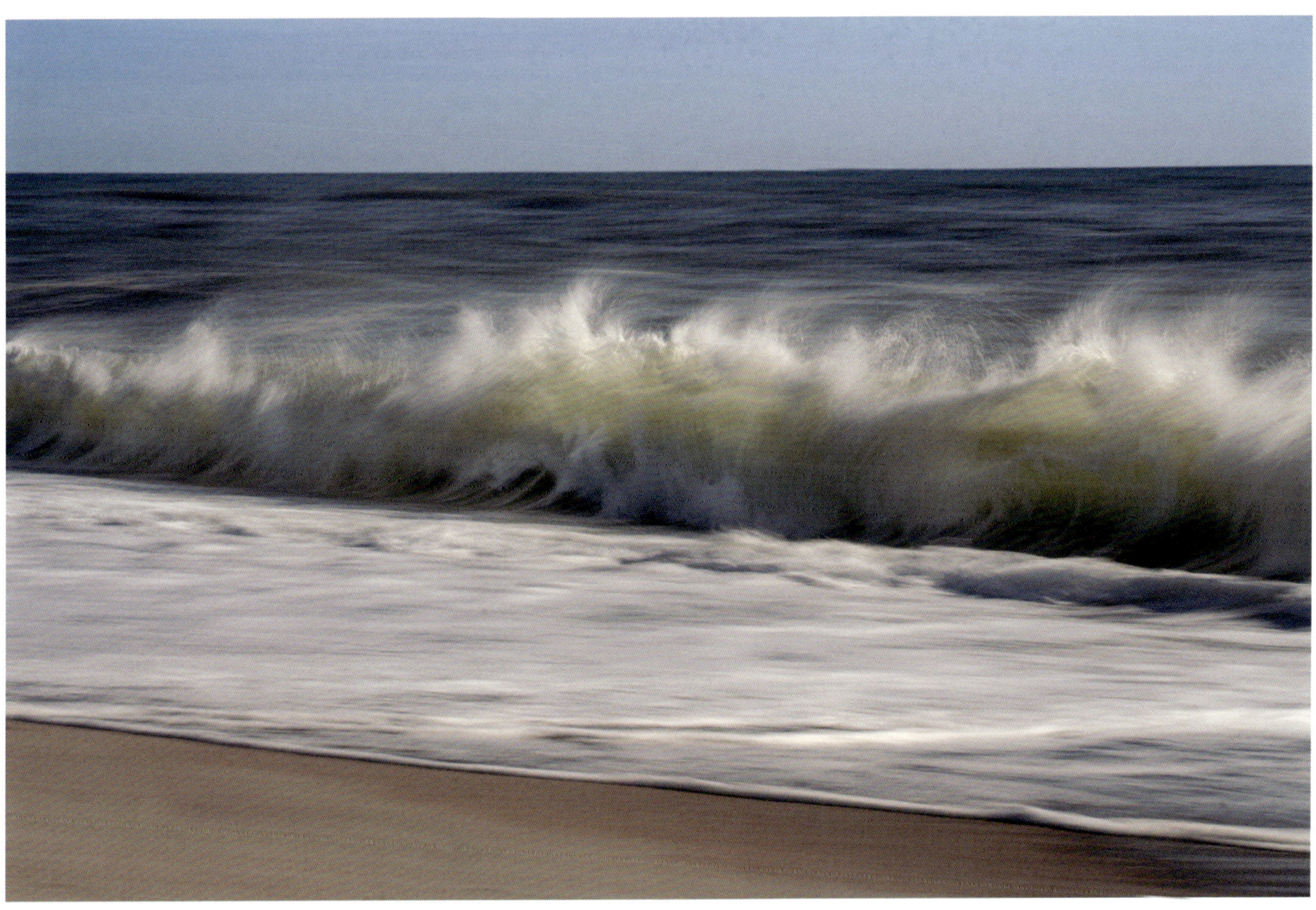

Good Morning

The beautiful, calming hues of the ocean

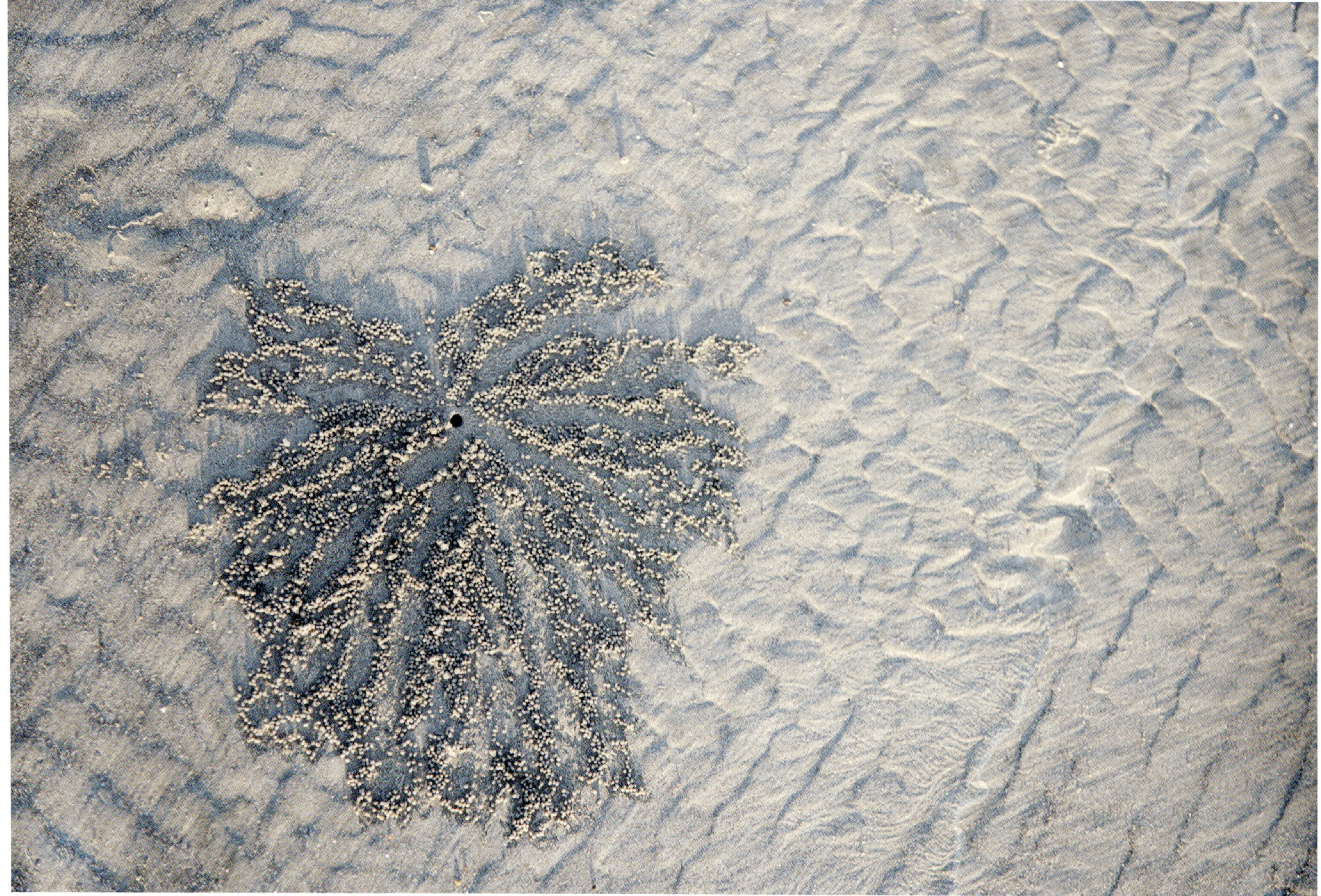

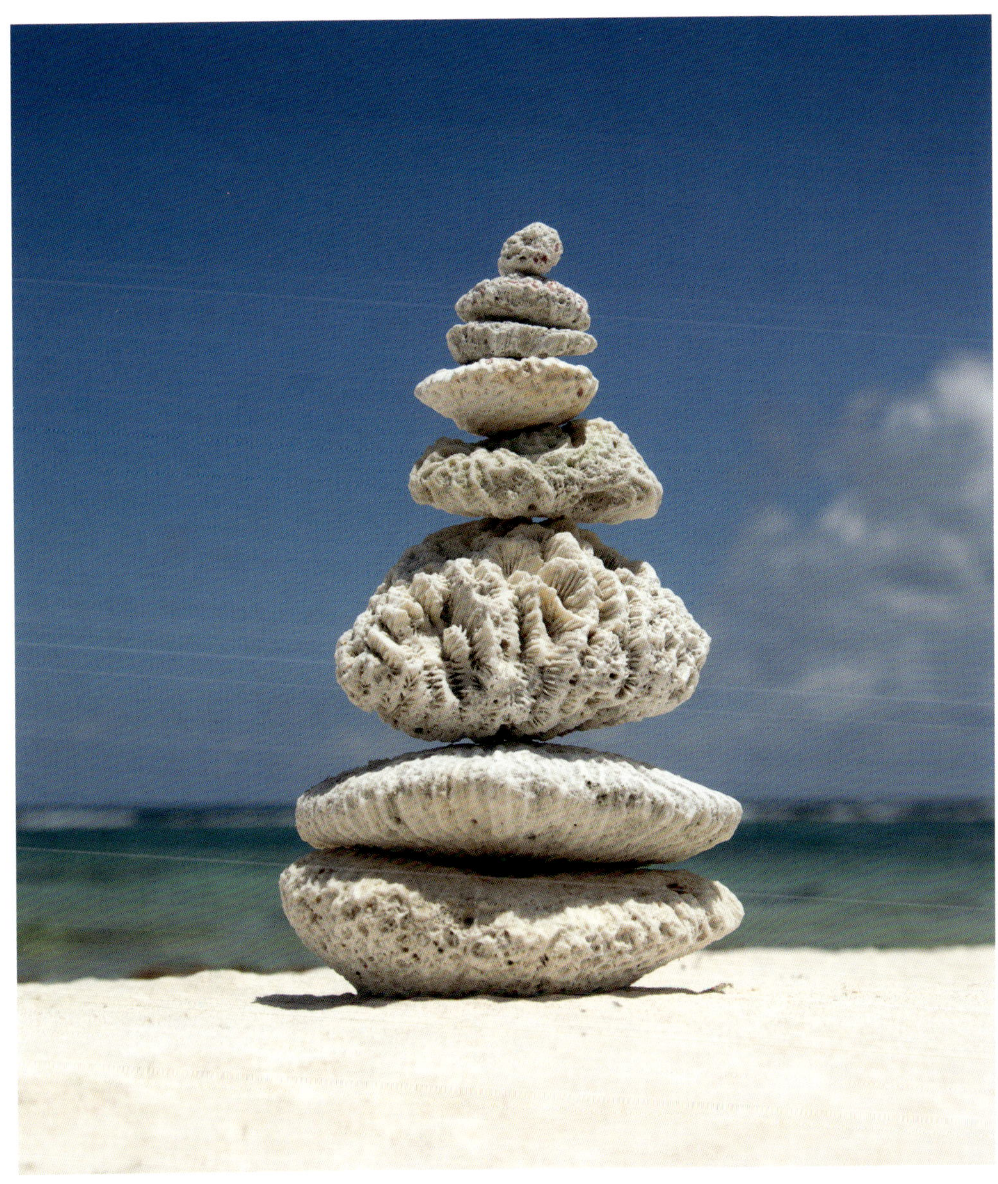

Palm Leaf

This shy beach critter created a pattern in the evening light, like a giant leaf.

Coral Cairn

Cairn-building can be a meditative exercise.

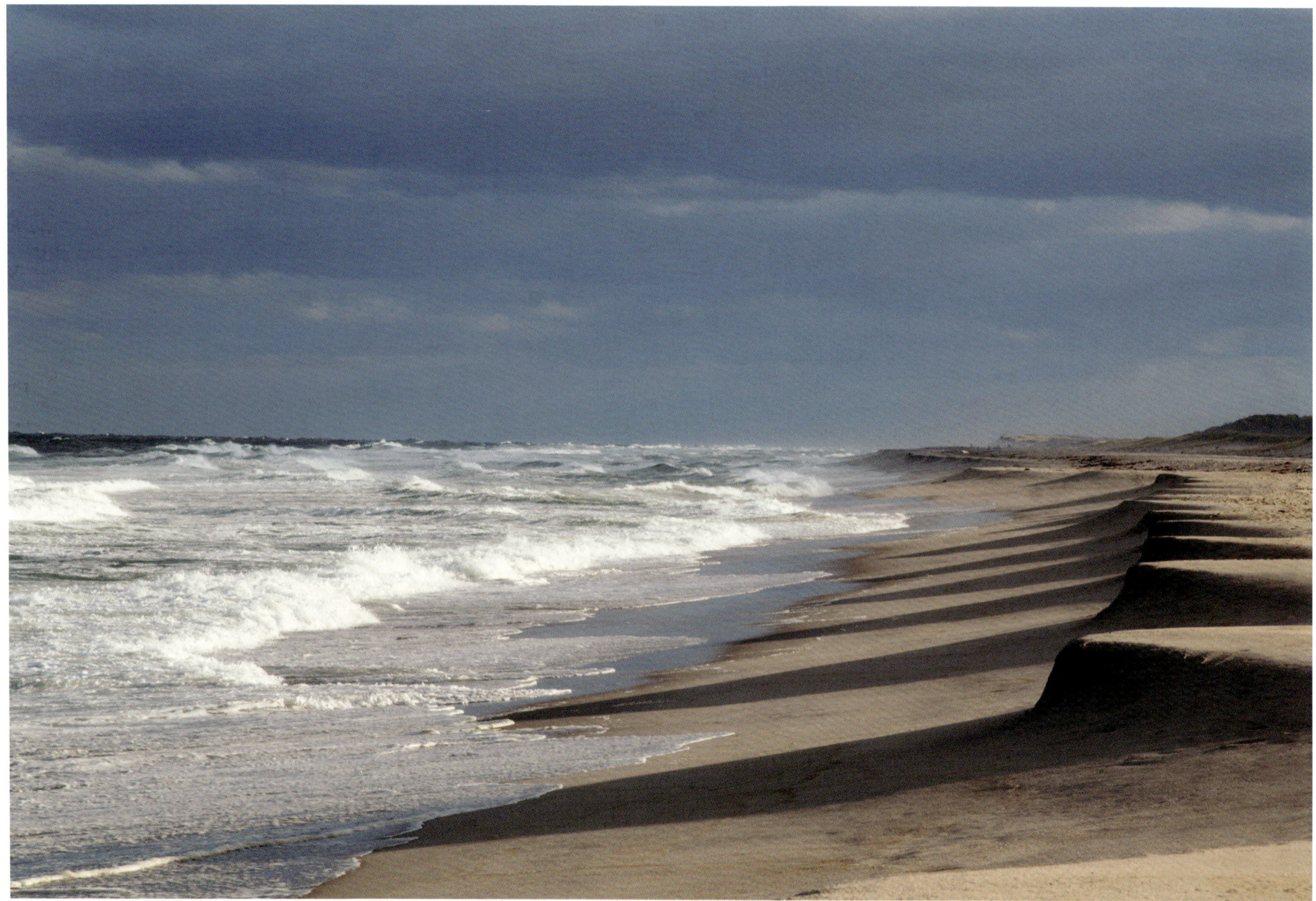

Shadow Stripes

Late daylight on Cape Cod dunes

Rainbow Rocks

Beach stones showing off: they seem so proud of their colors and patterns.

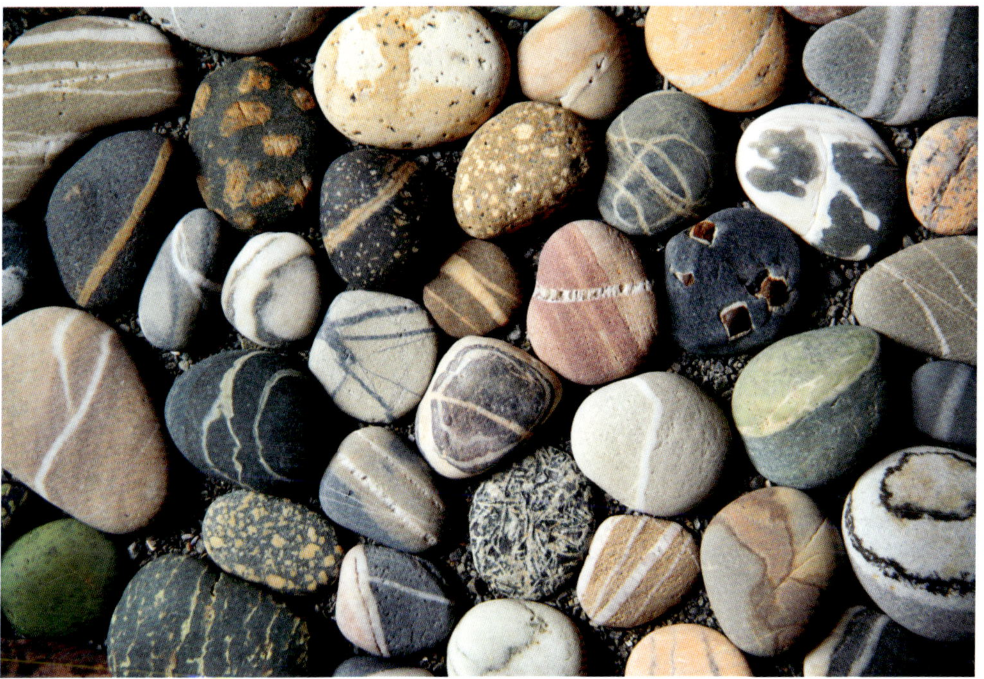

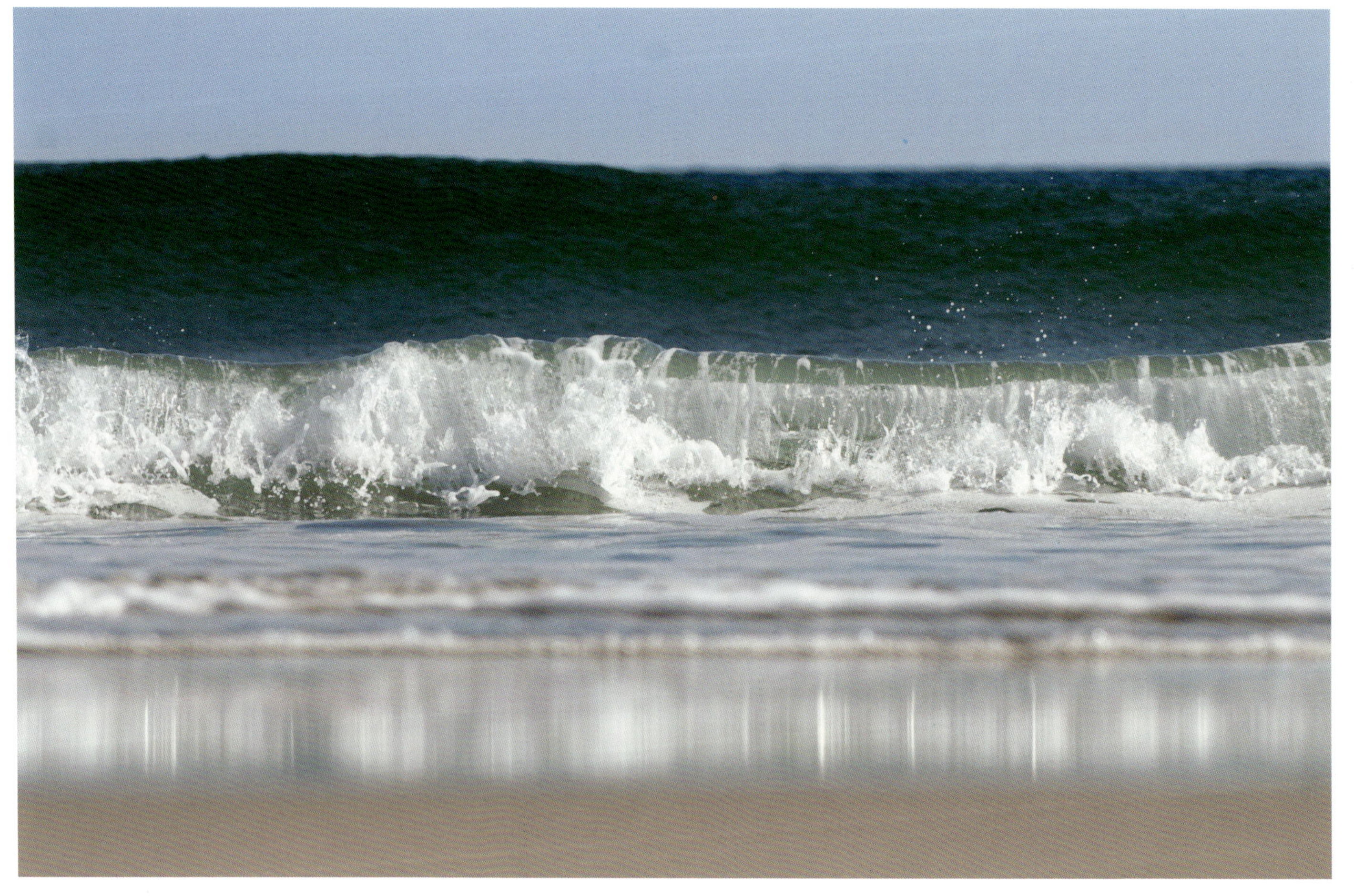

Race to the Shore

Sometimes waves hit the shore in quick succession, as though playing an endless game of tag.

Cape Cod Cumulus

Clouds cast abstract reflections on wet sand.

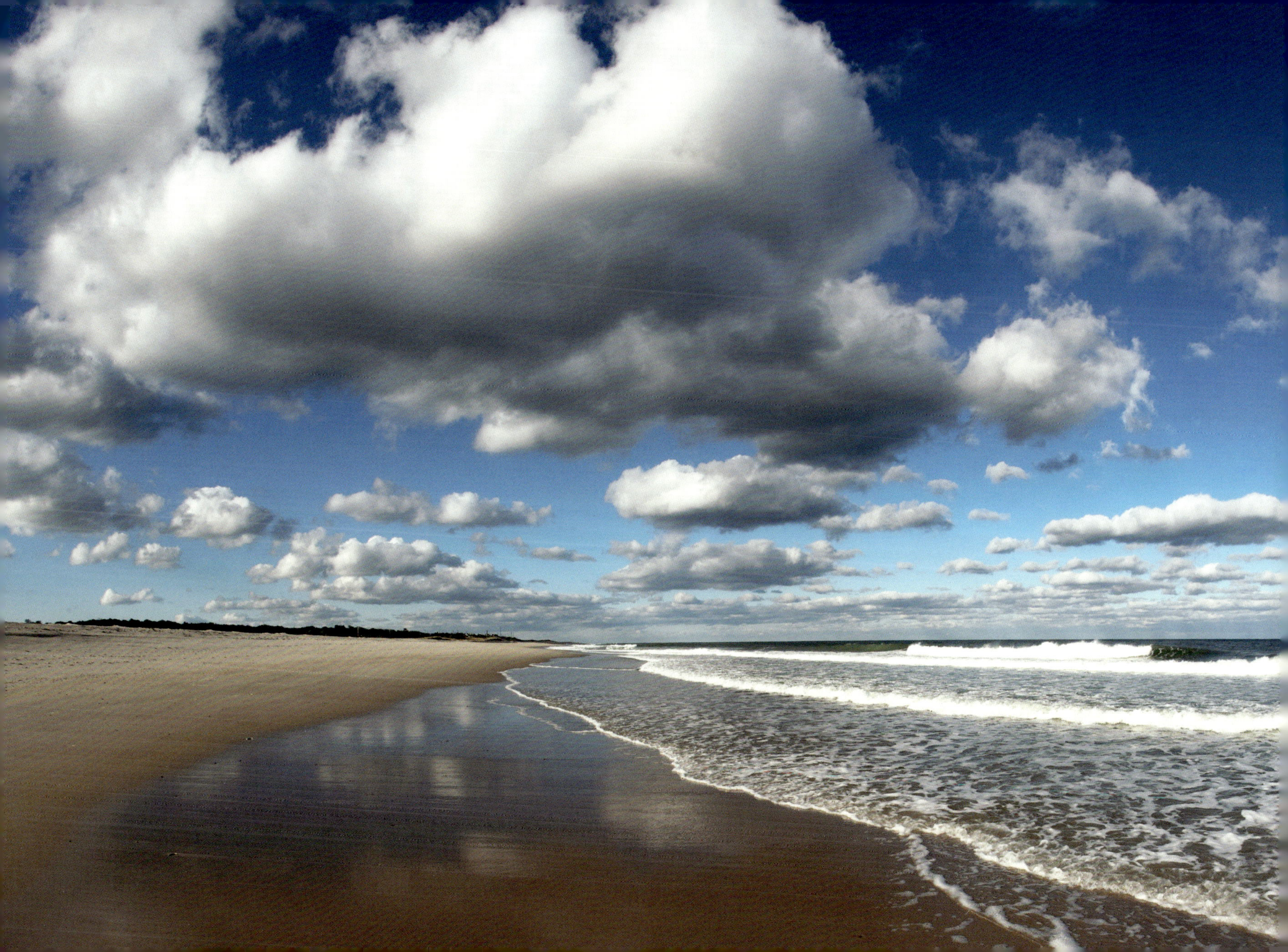

Flats Aflame

This sunset summoned many people to the beach on a gorgeous night.

Sun Bay

Double rainbows, one of nature's true wonders, on exhibit at the appropriately named Sun Bay in Vieques, Puerto Rico

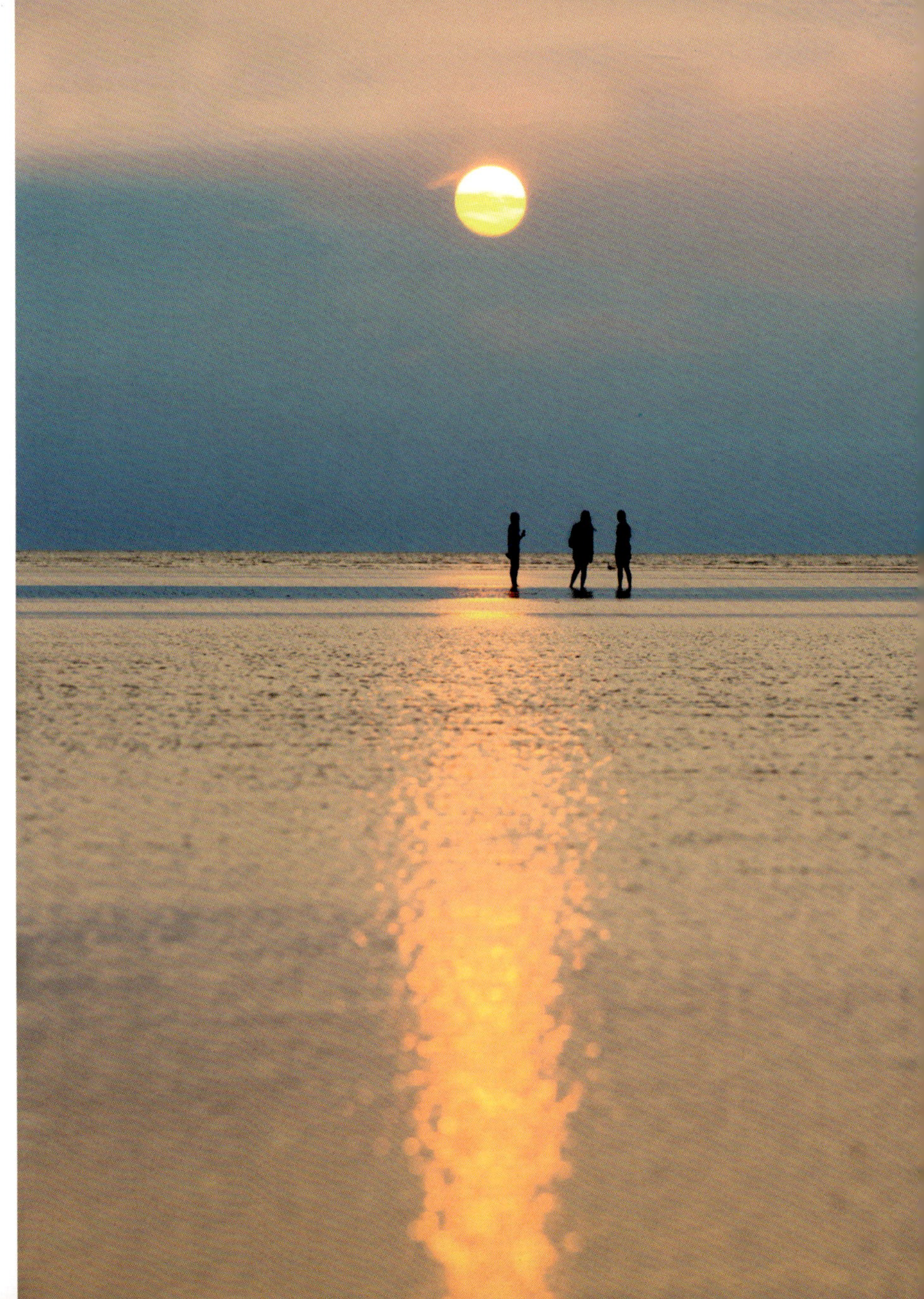

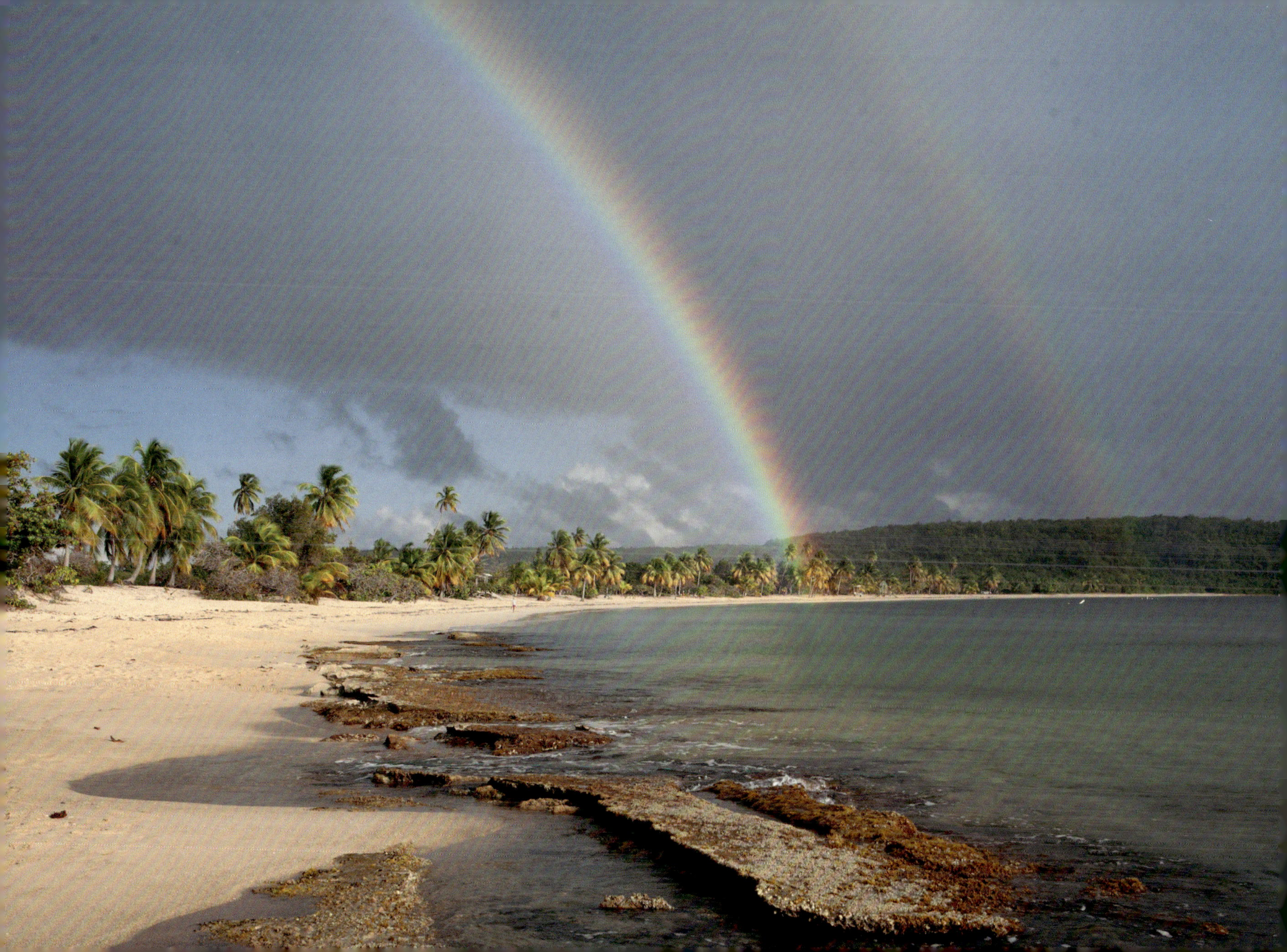

Texas Big Sky

At Padre Island National Seashore, the clouds were as intriguing as the waves.

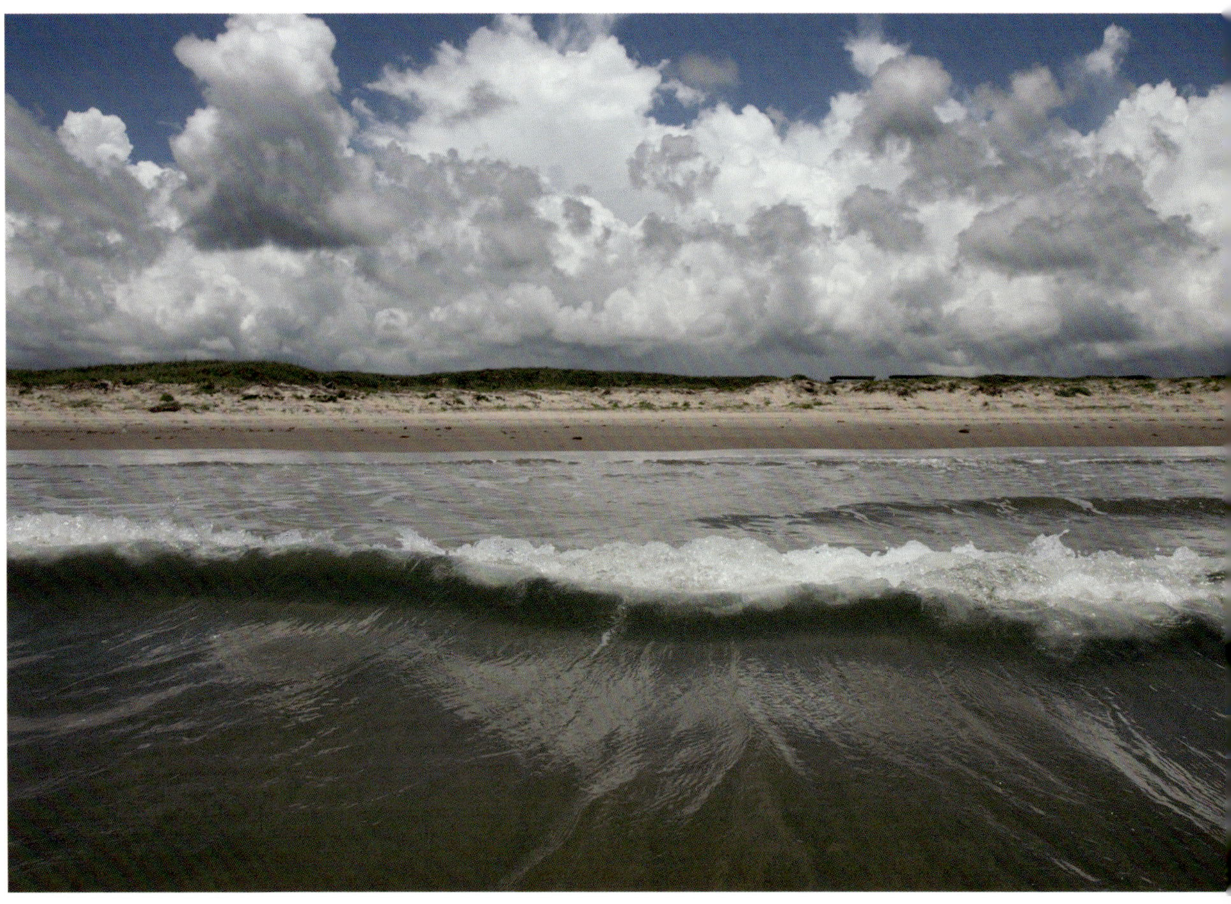

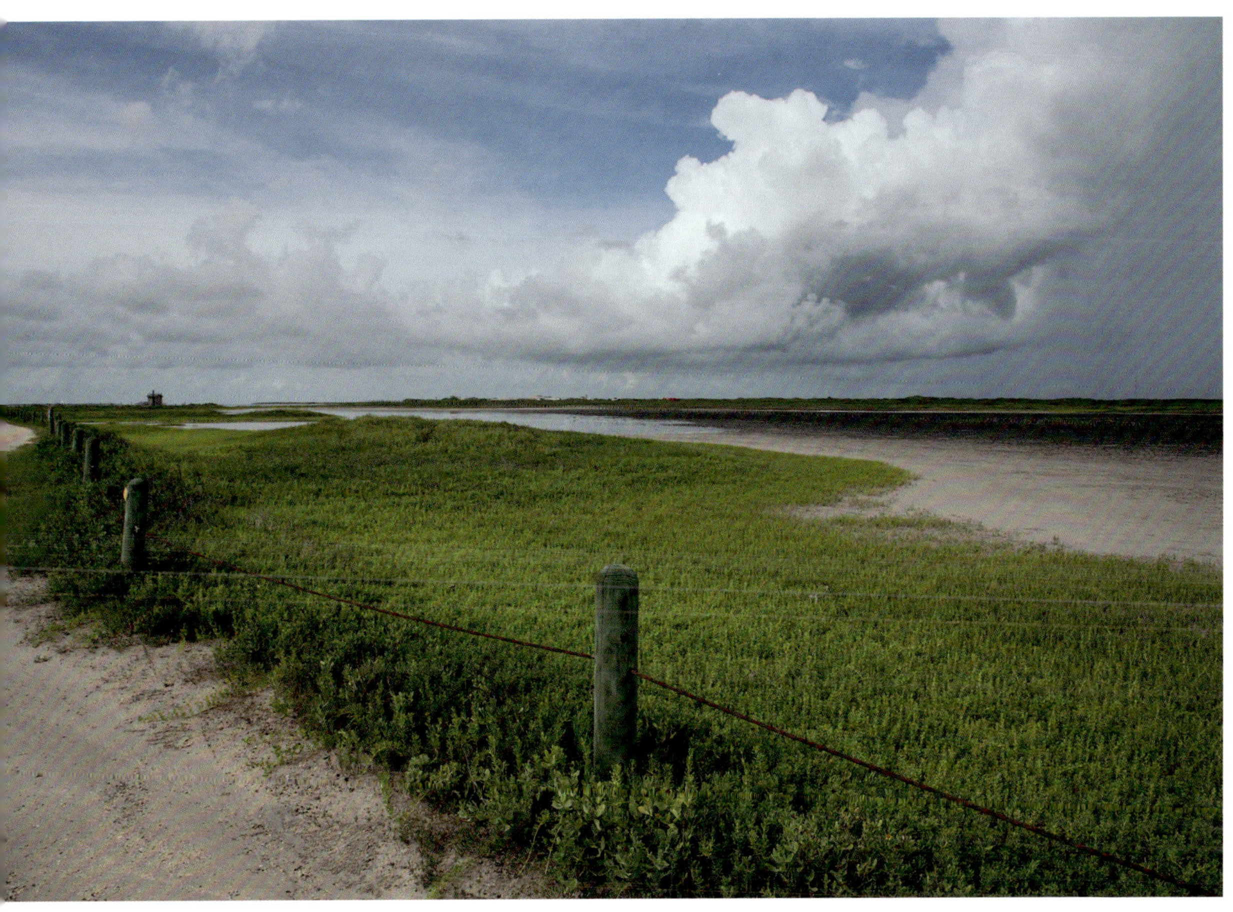

Texas Palette

Texas skies have an intensity in springtime.

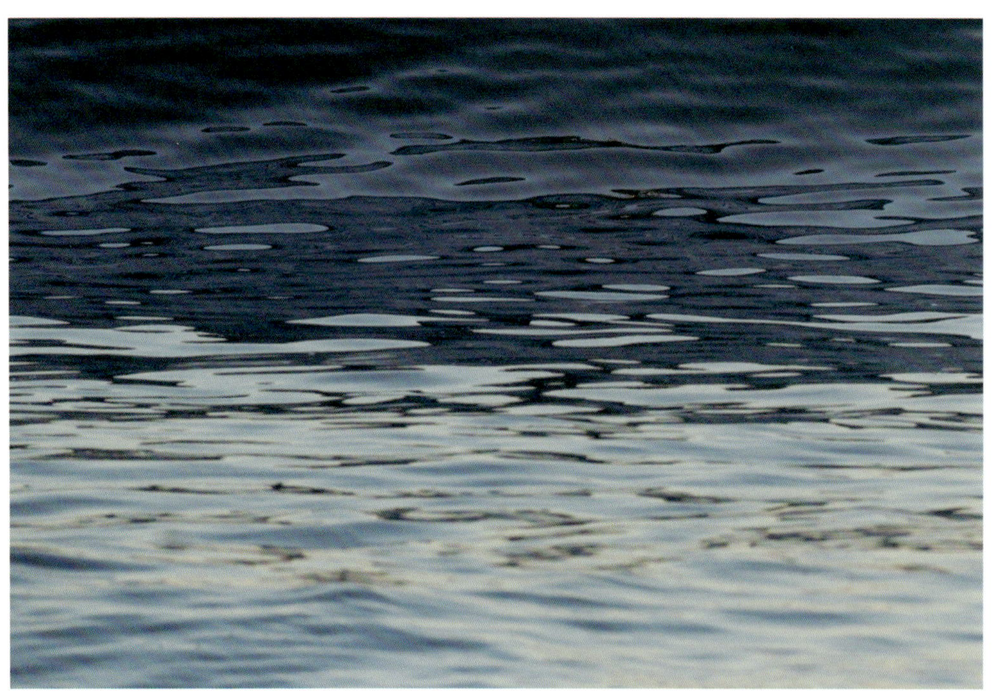

Ocean Blues

Curling to reach the shore, a wave shows off its varied blues.

Jade

This wave reminds me of gorgeous green jade.

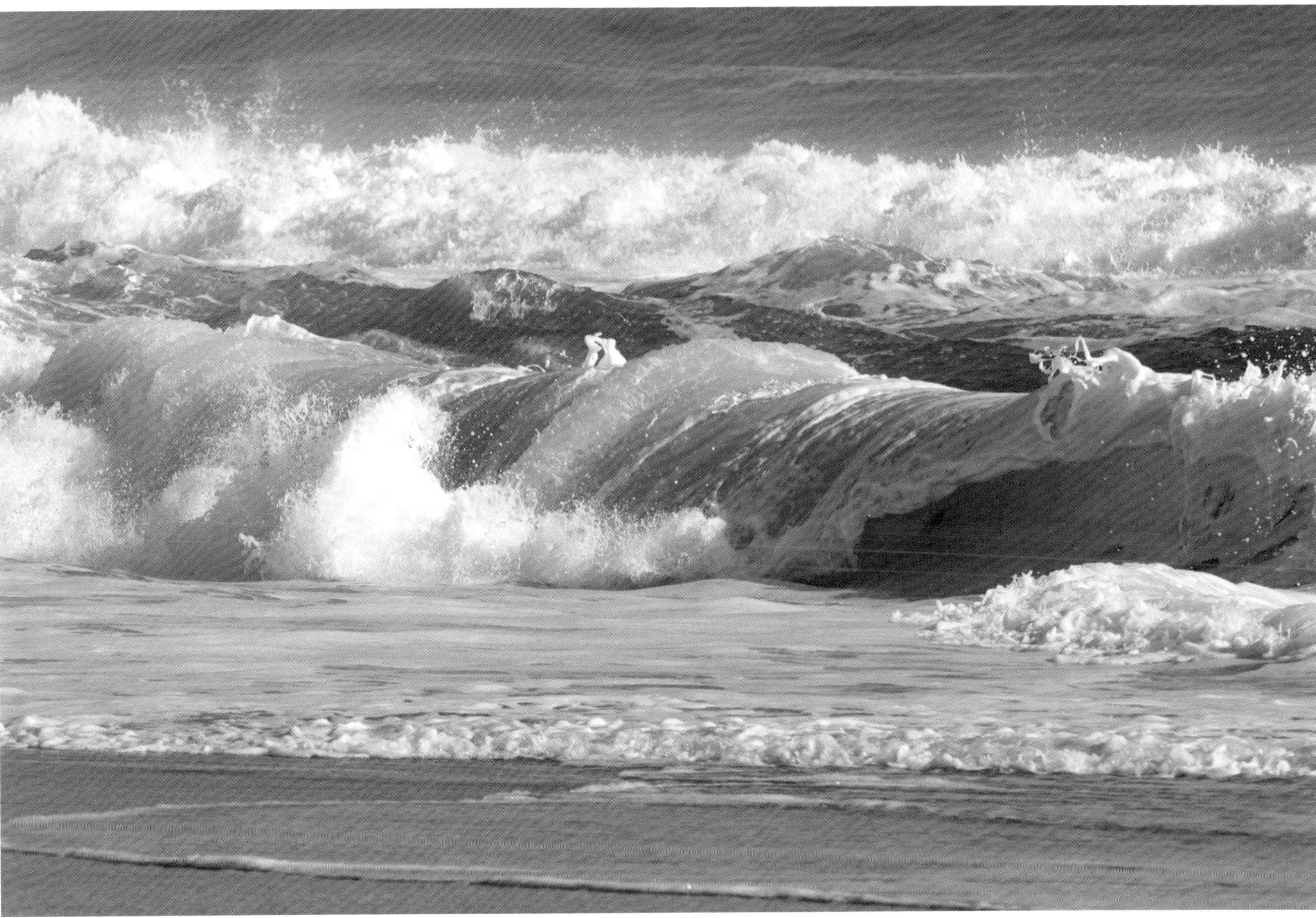

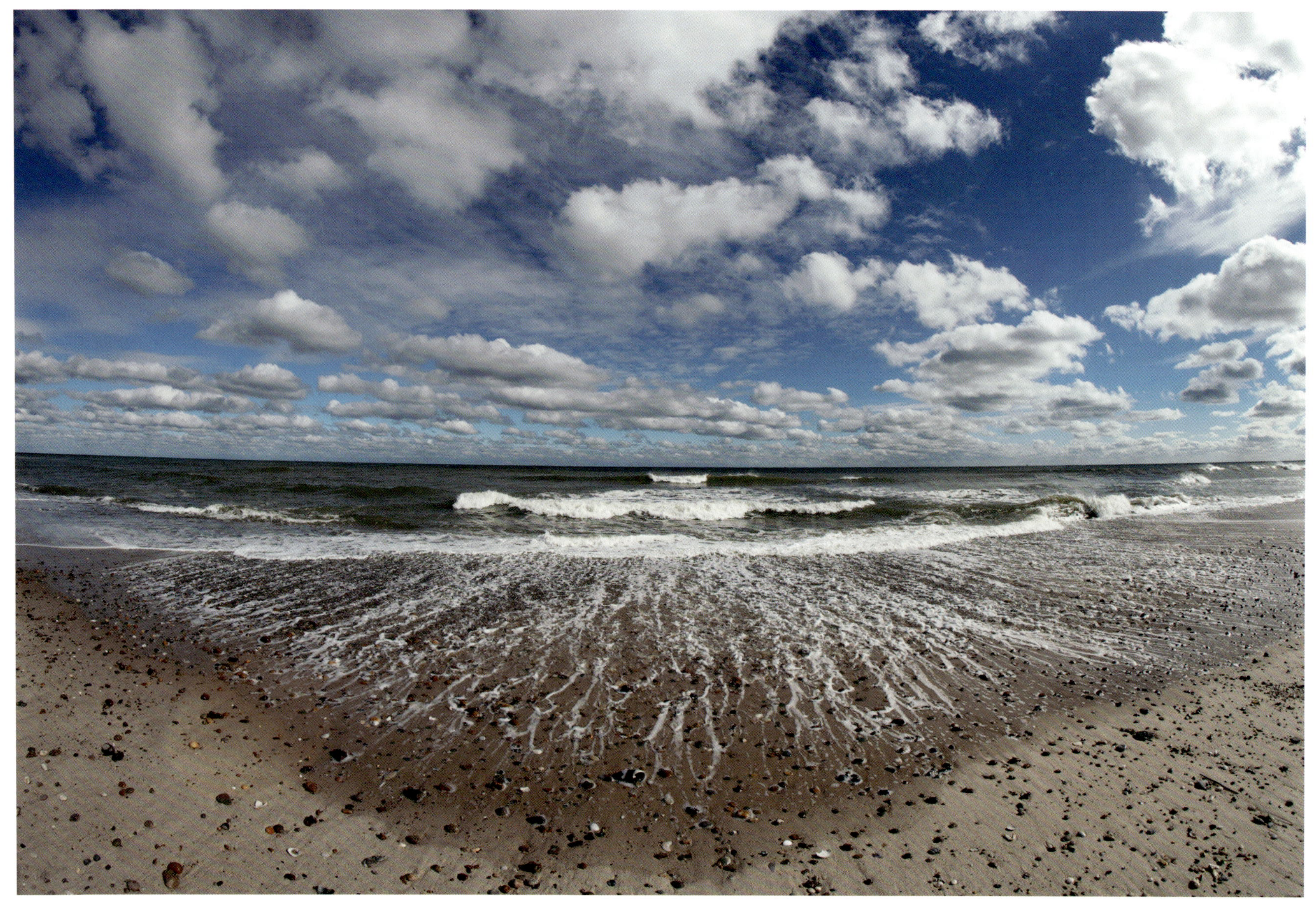

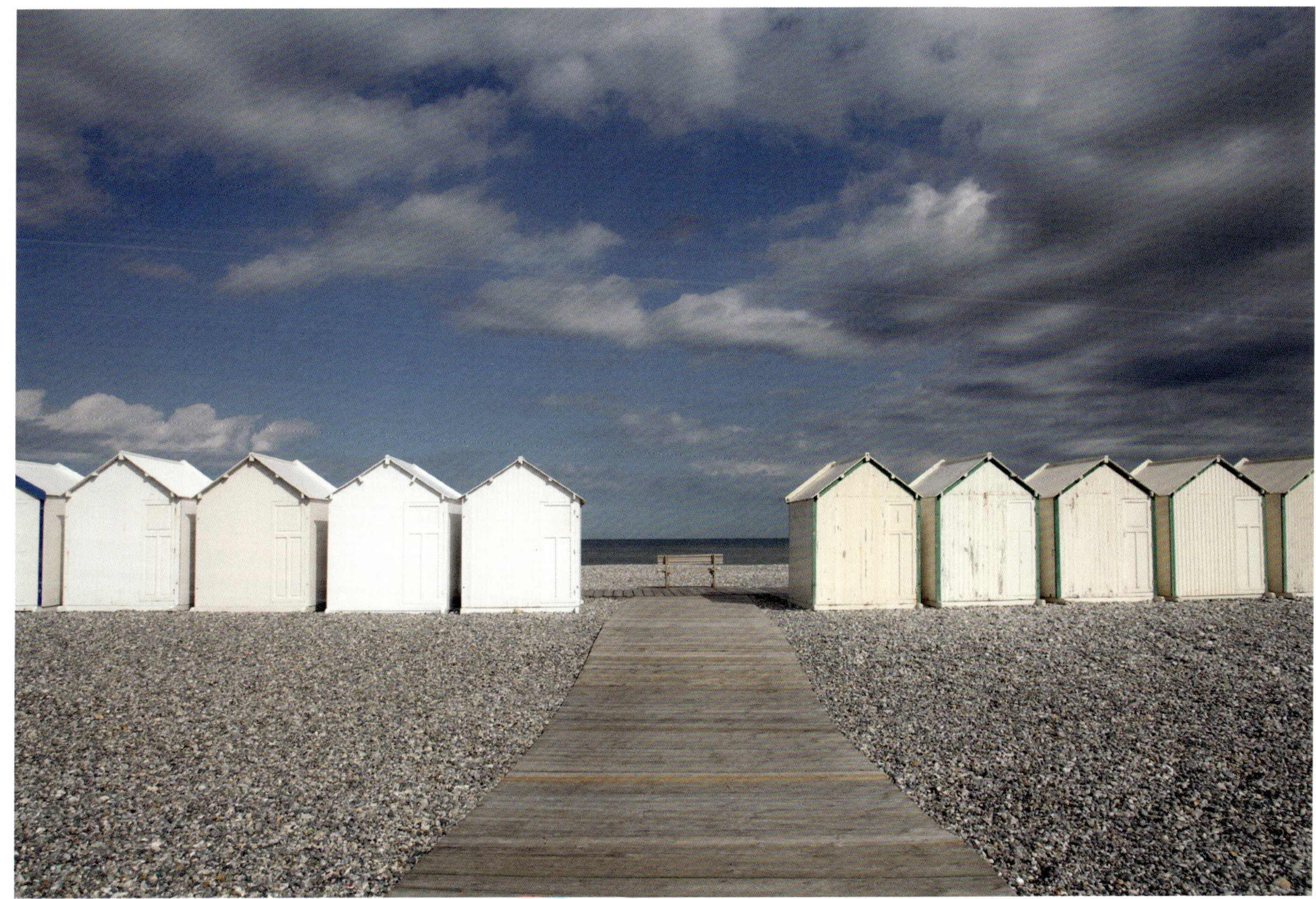

Wave Out

An ebbing wave is as beautiful as a breaking one.

Heaven

Beach huts hunker down along France's English Channel.

Hidden Stones

Beaches may be sandy, but the surf hides many stones. These images simultaneously capture the stones from below and above the water, slowly being reduced to new sand.

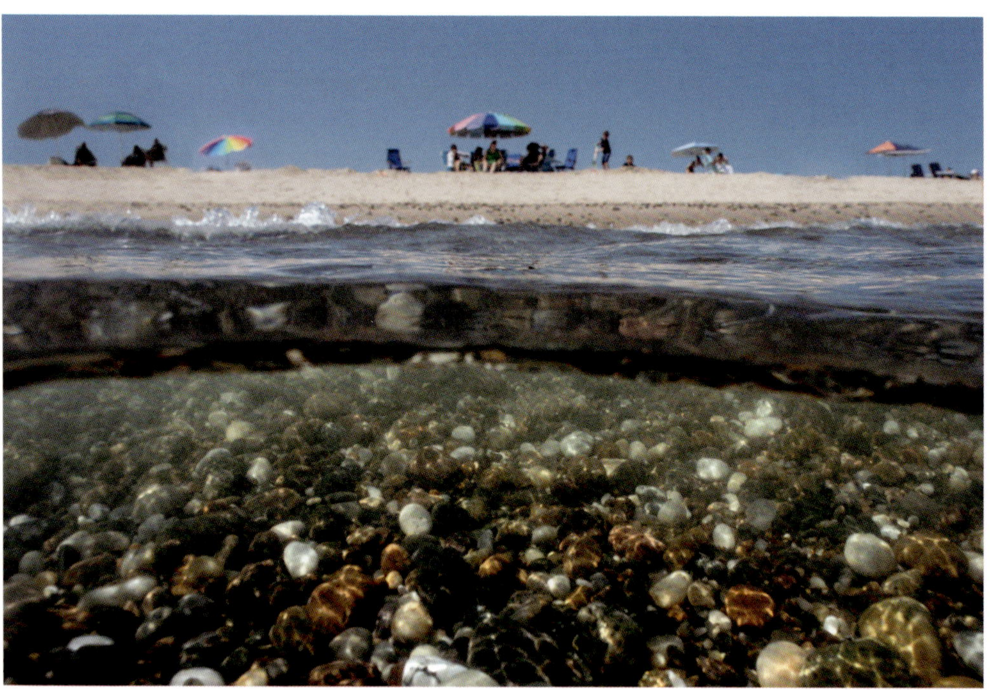

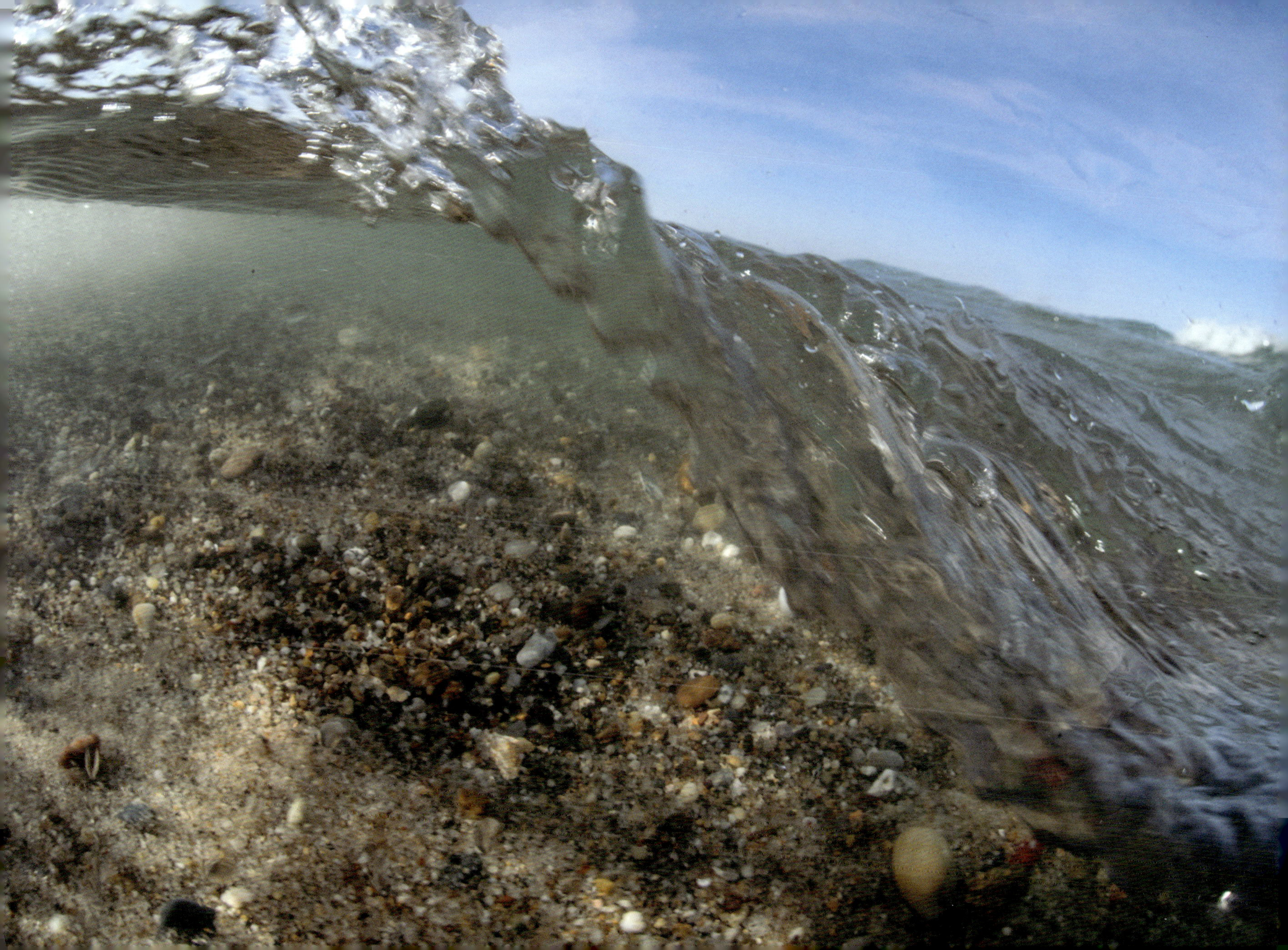

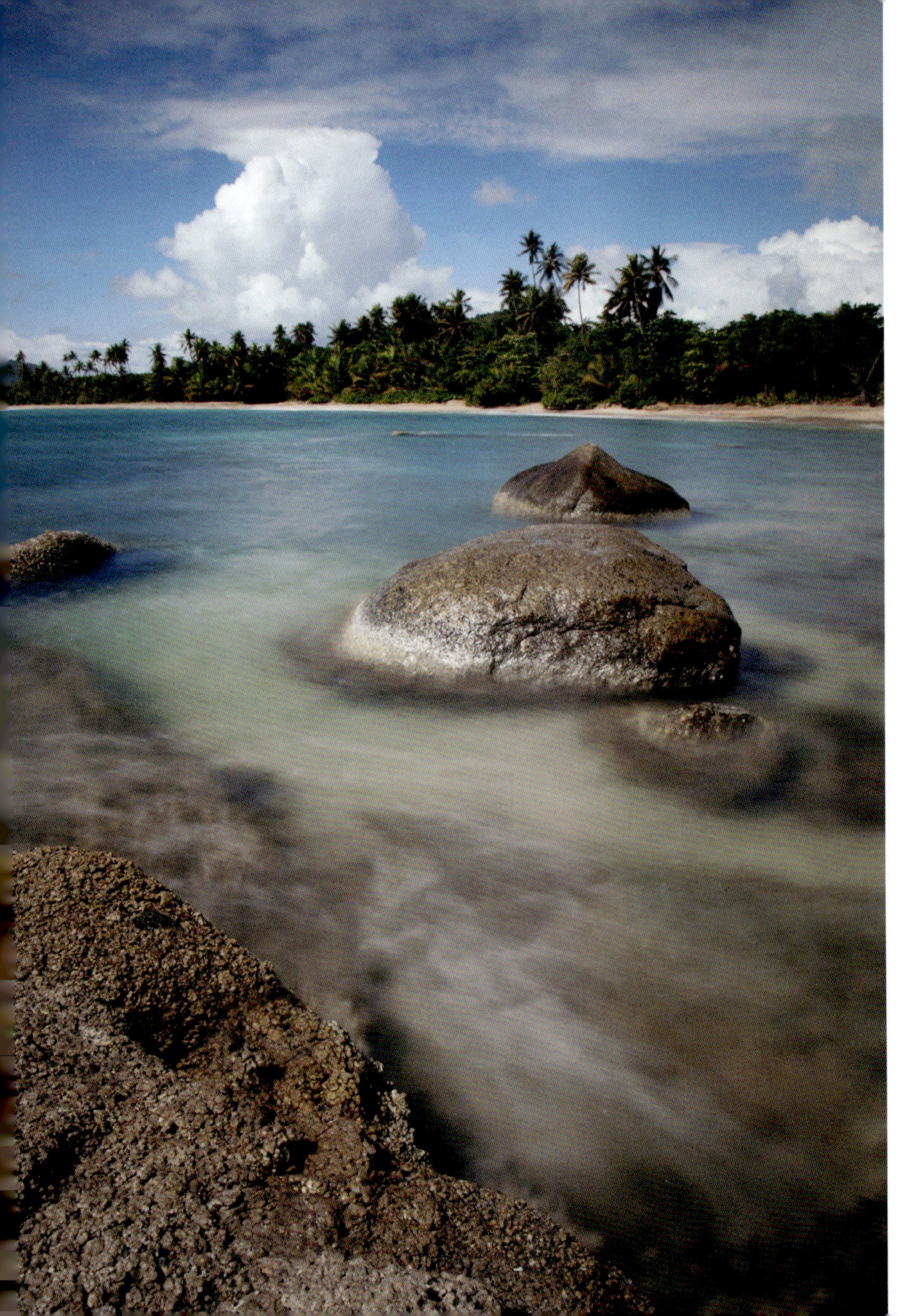

Coconut Beach

Countless coconut trees dot this gorgeous beach in Vieques, giving it its name. The name could also have been prompted by the curious coconut-like boulders.

Leading Lines

Lapping waves create ephemeral sand ripples.

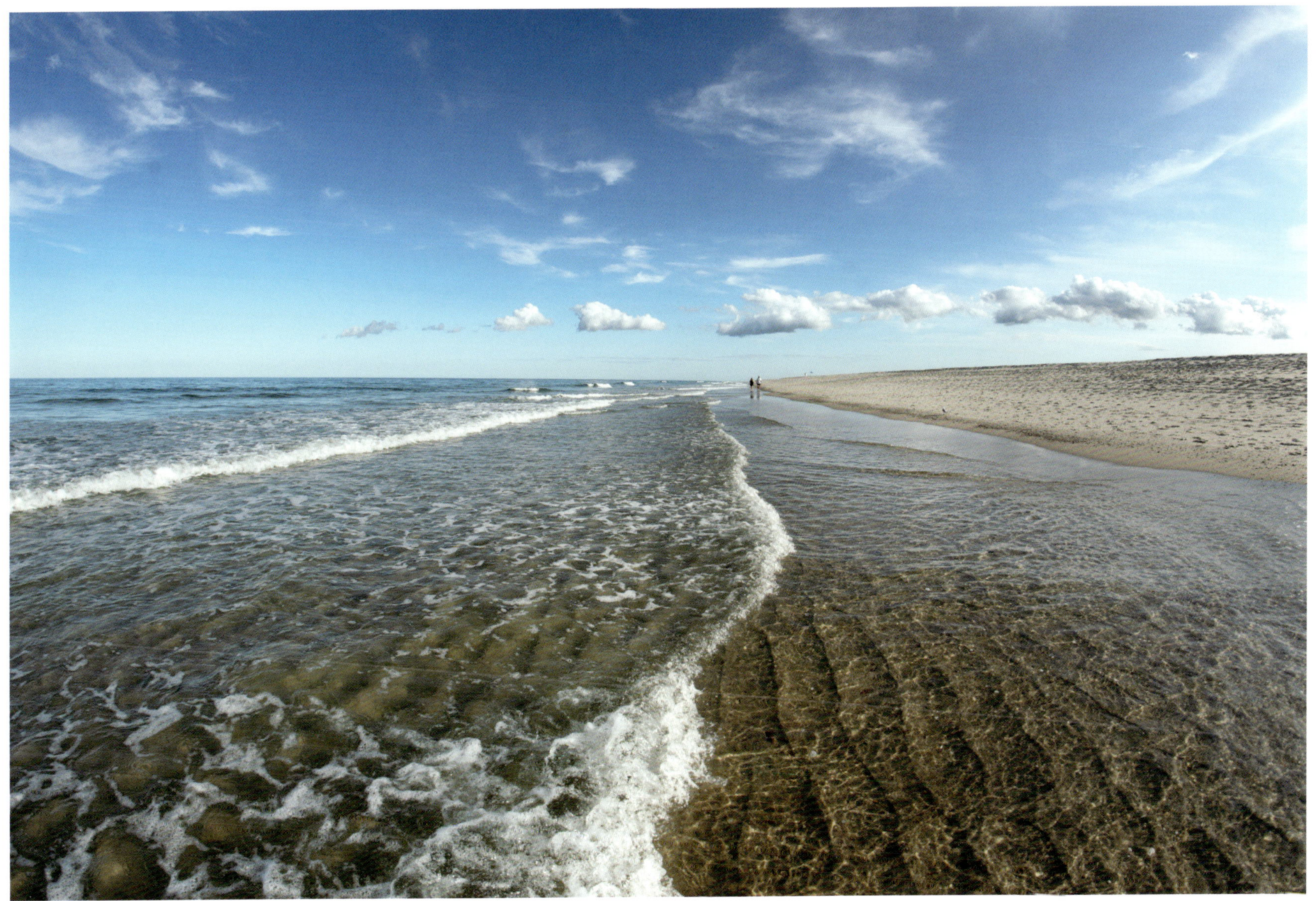

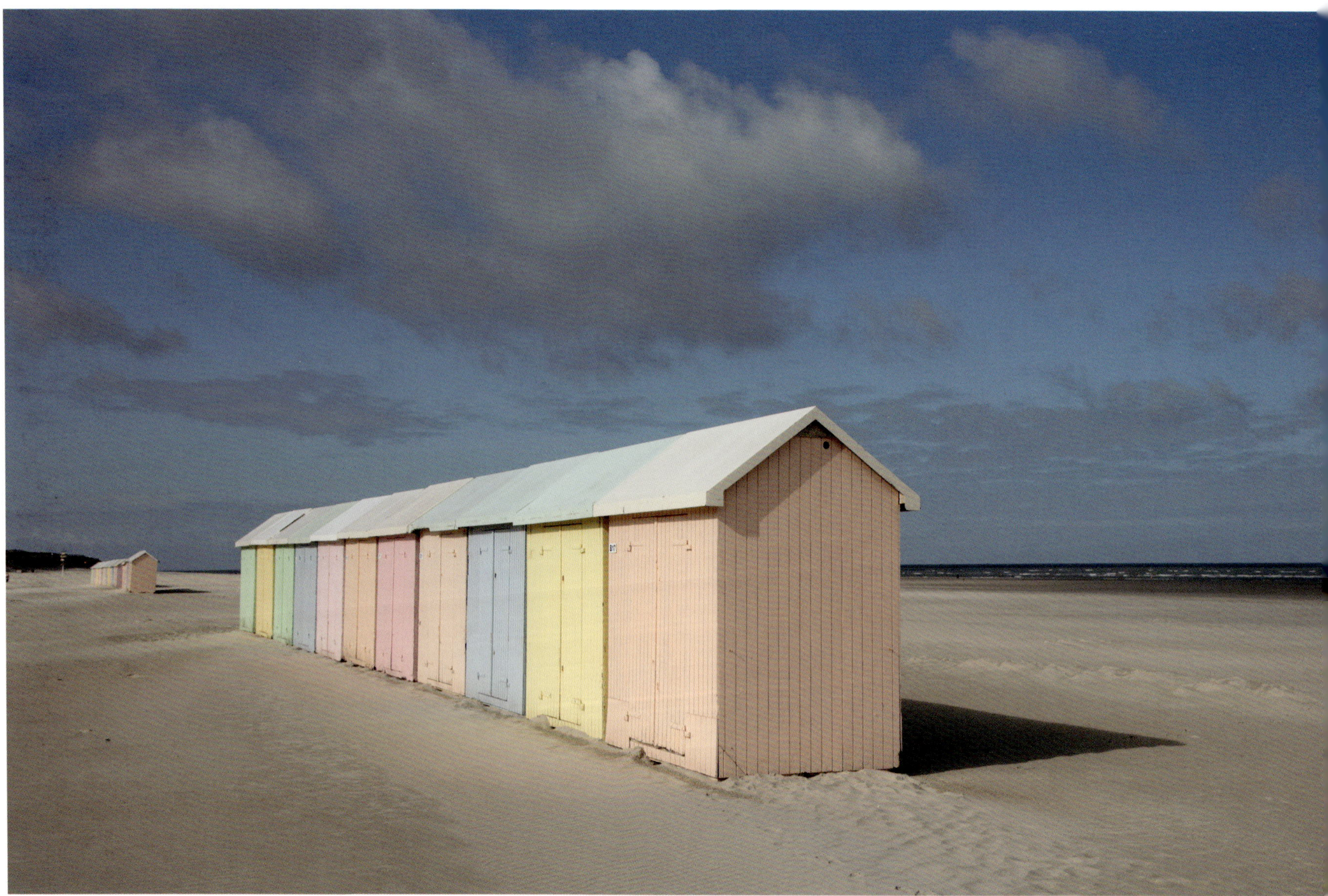

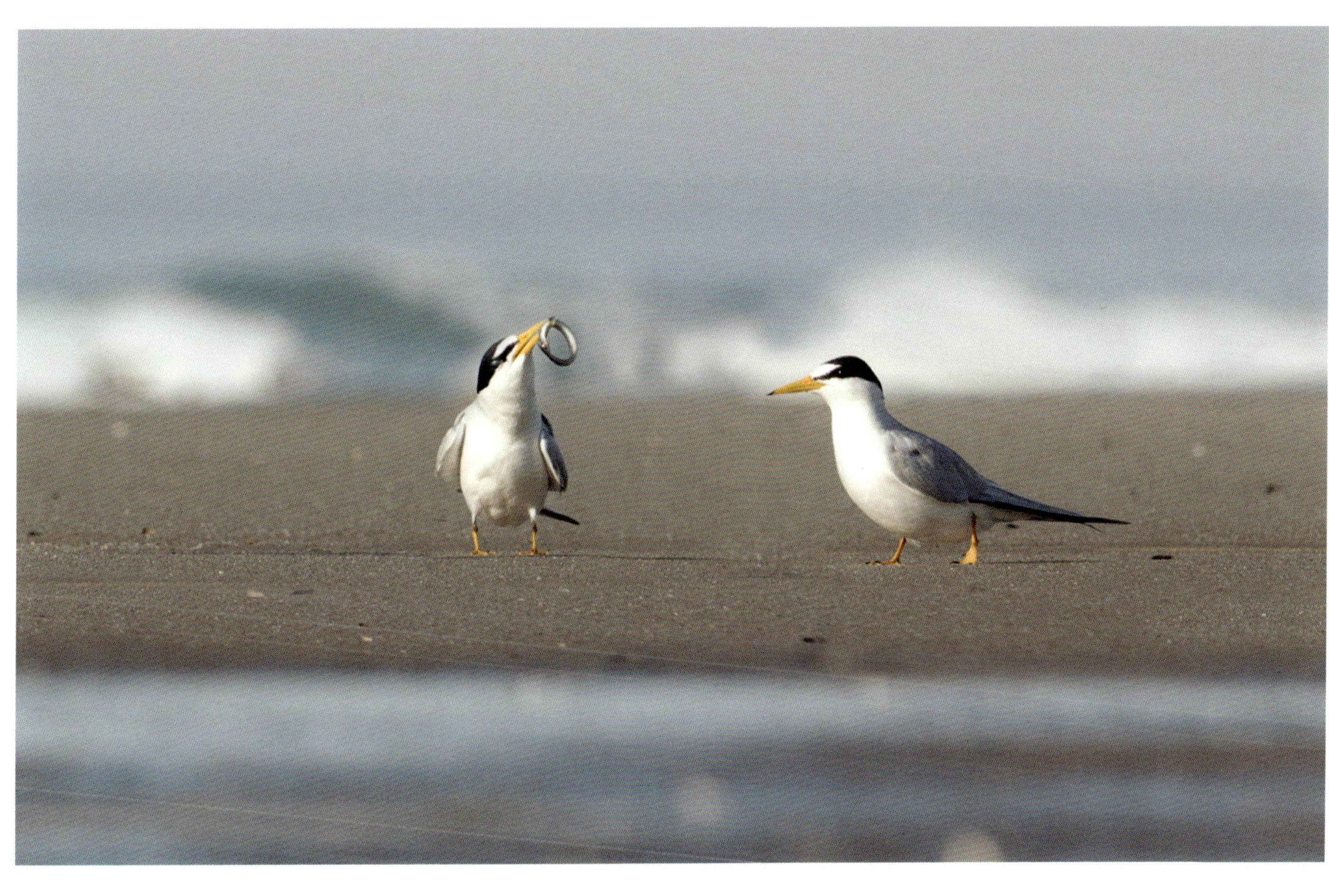

Sherbet Boxes

Pastel sheds bring to mind frozen treats.

Proposal

As part of the tern courtship ritual, the male presents the female with a fish, usually displayed crosswise in his mouth. This male tern may not have gotten it exactly right, but I think the female got the idea.

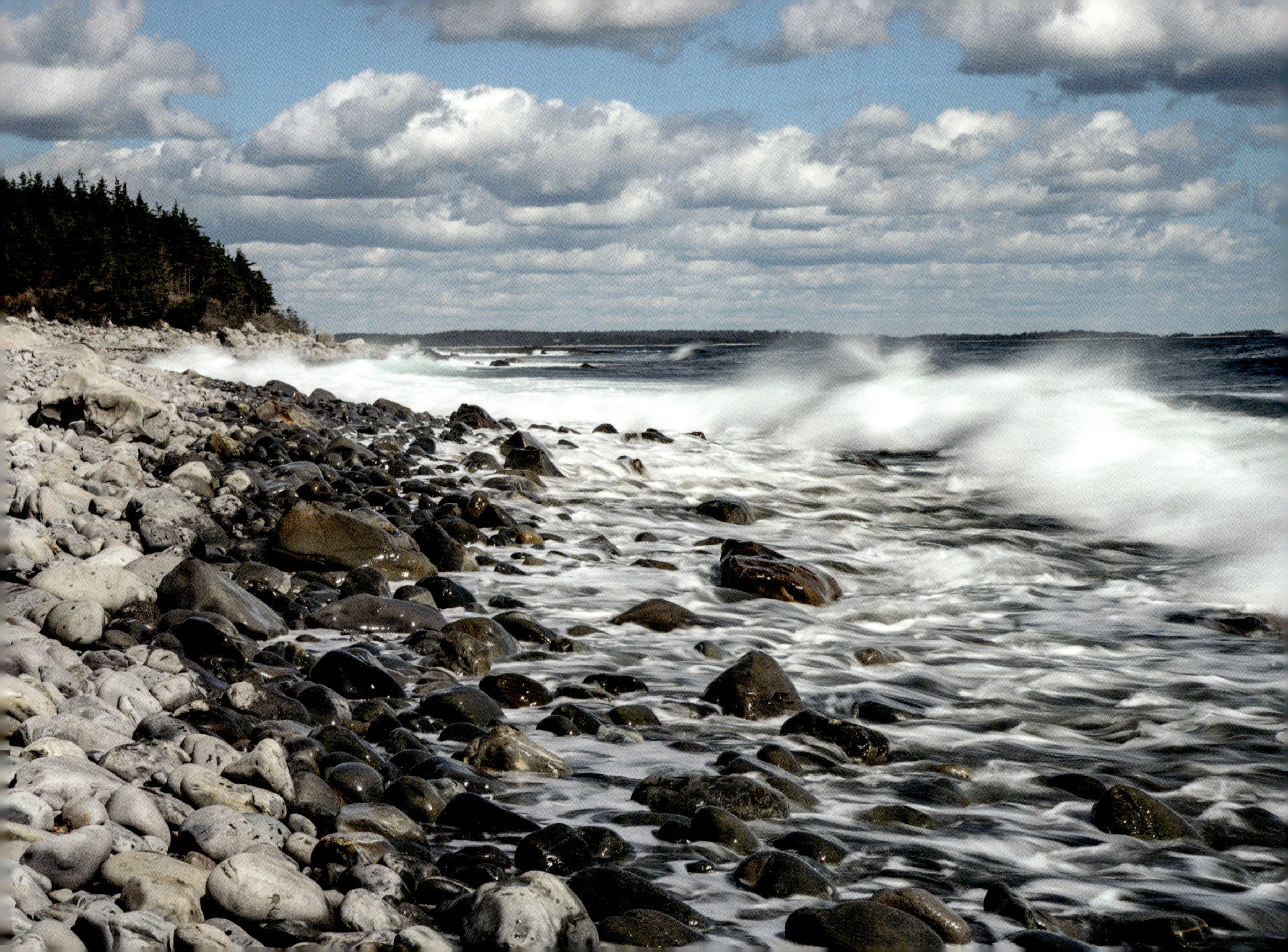

Clickity Clack

I have always been entranced by the sound of the water moving through rocks when a wave recedes from shore. Sometimes the clickety clack of rocks becomes a roar.

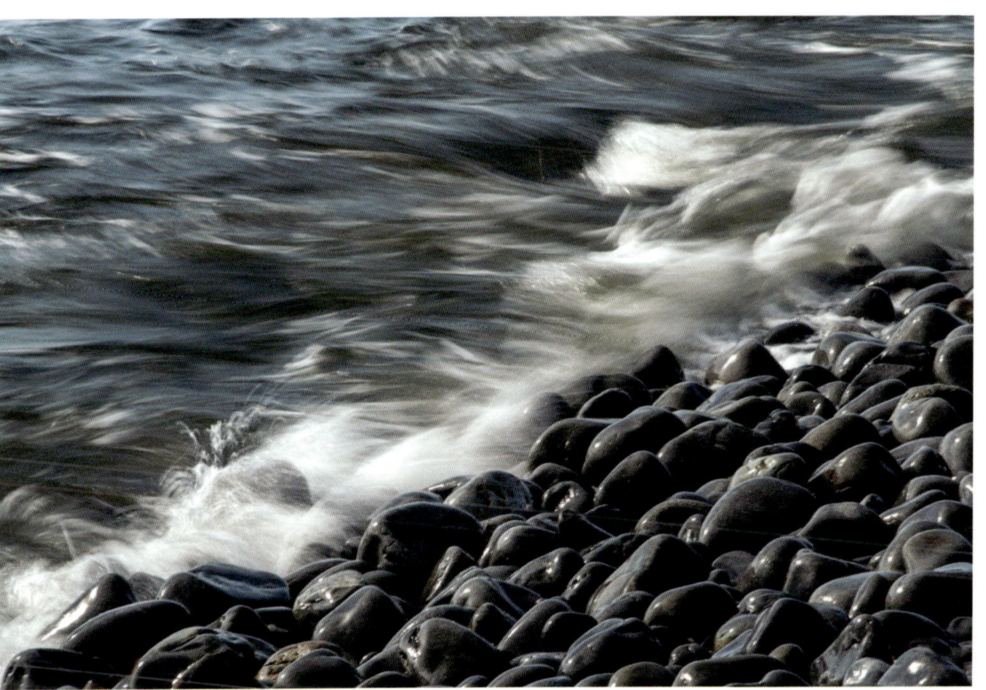

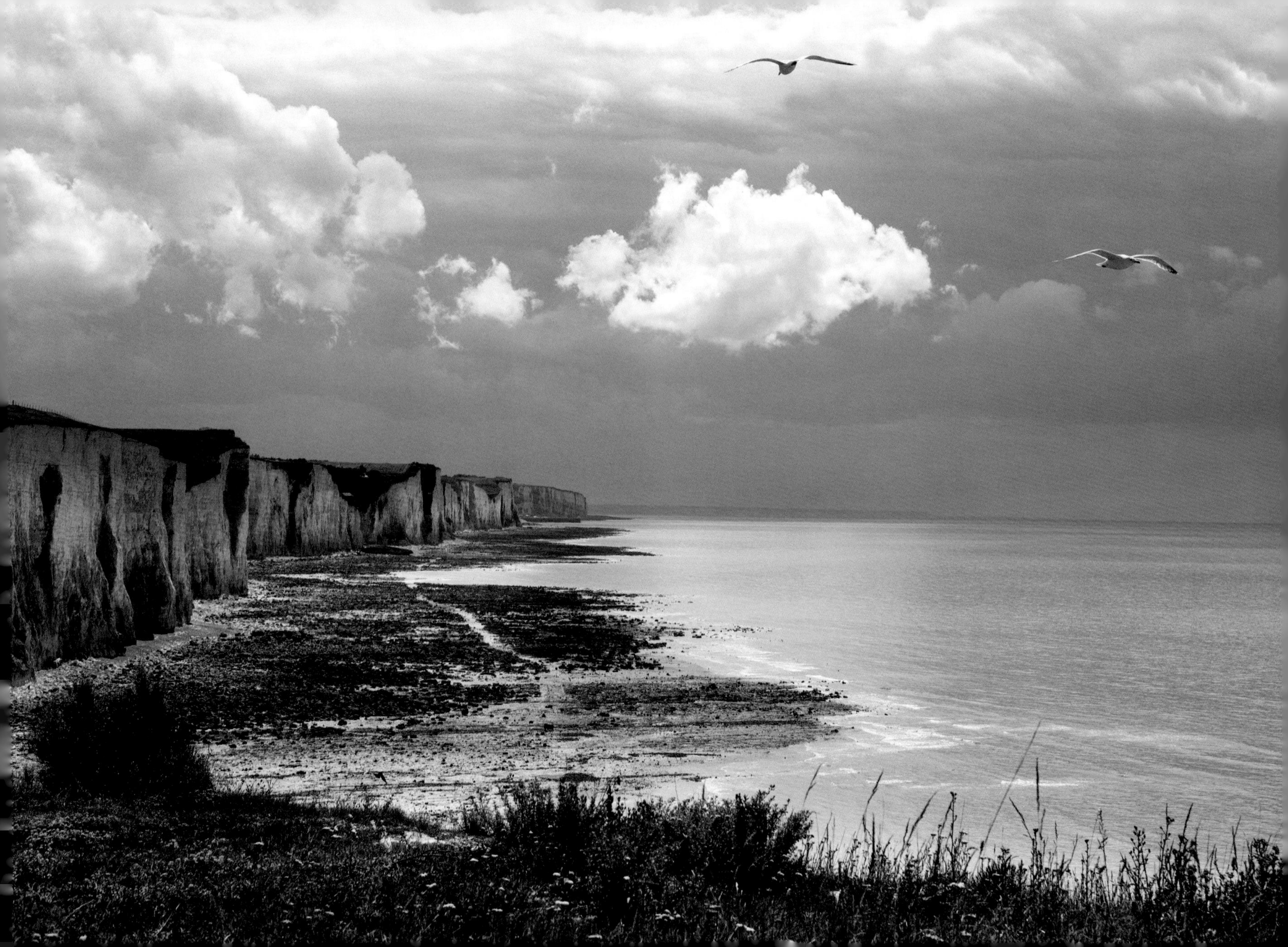

Dream Come True

The white cliffs of Dover have long been on my bucket list. We didn't make it to the UK, but the west coast of France was the perfect substitute. Its cliffs are the same as those across the channel.

Cape Cod Bay

A Cape Cod Bay sunset draws brushstrokes through the sand and surf.

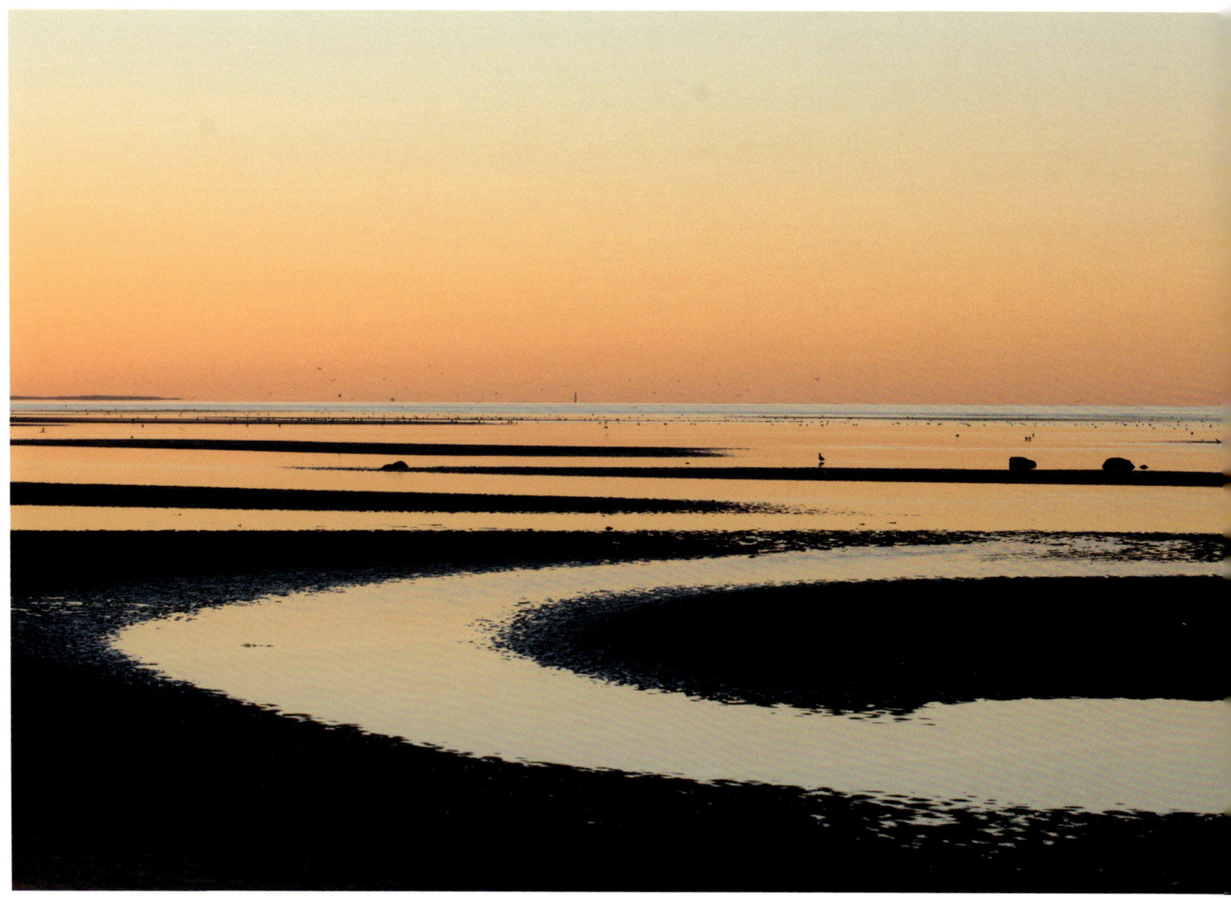

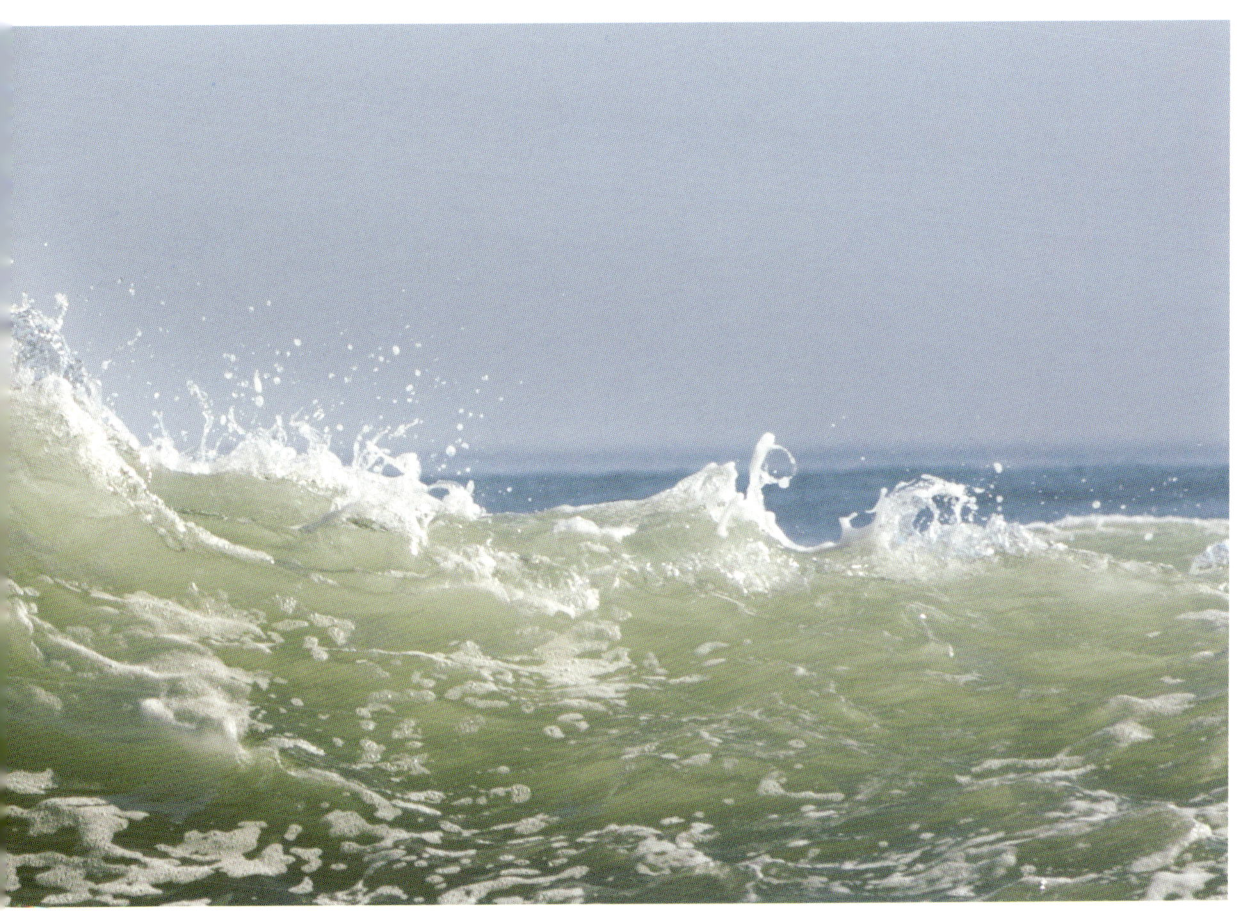

Crest of the Wave

The wave's spray dances in the morning light.

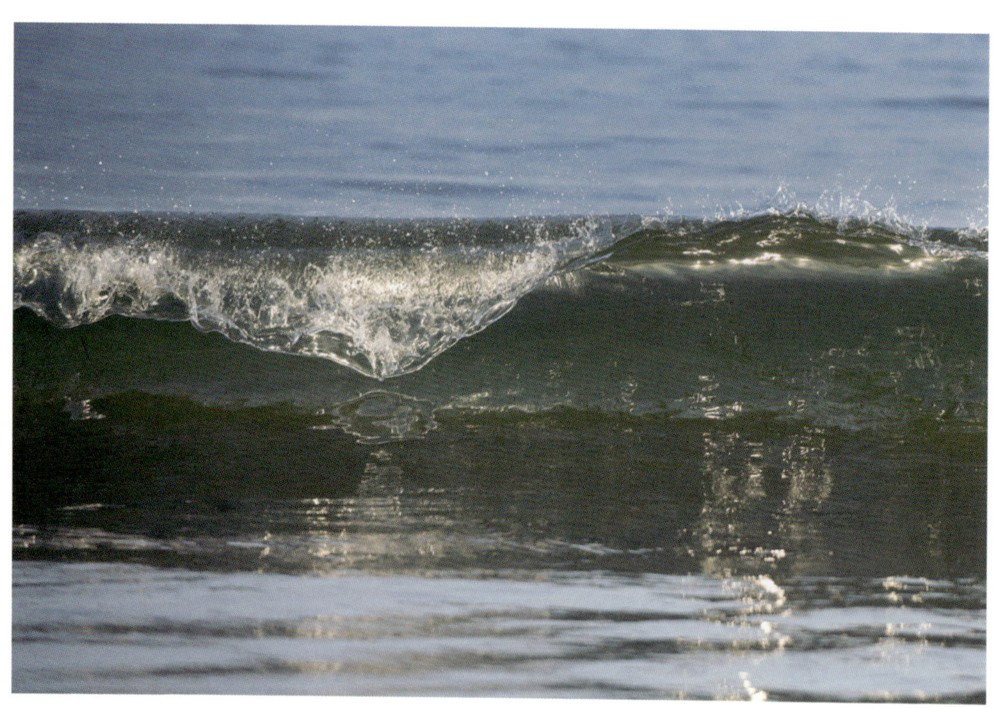

Ice

A wave, frozen in time, resembles ice.

Altocumulus Display

This checkerboard covered the entire sky, as though the beach had its own tiled ceiling.

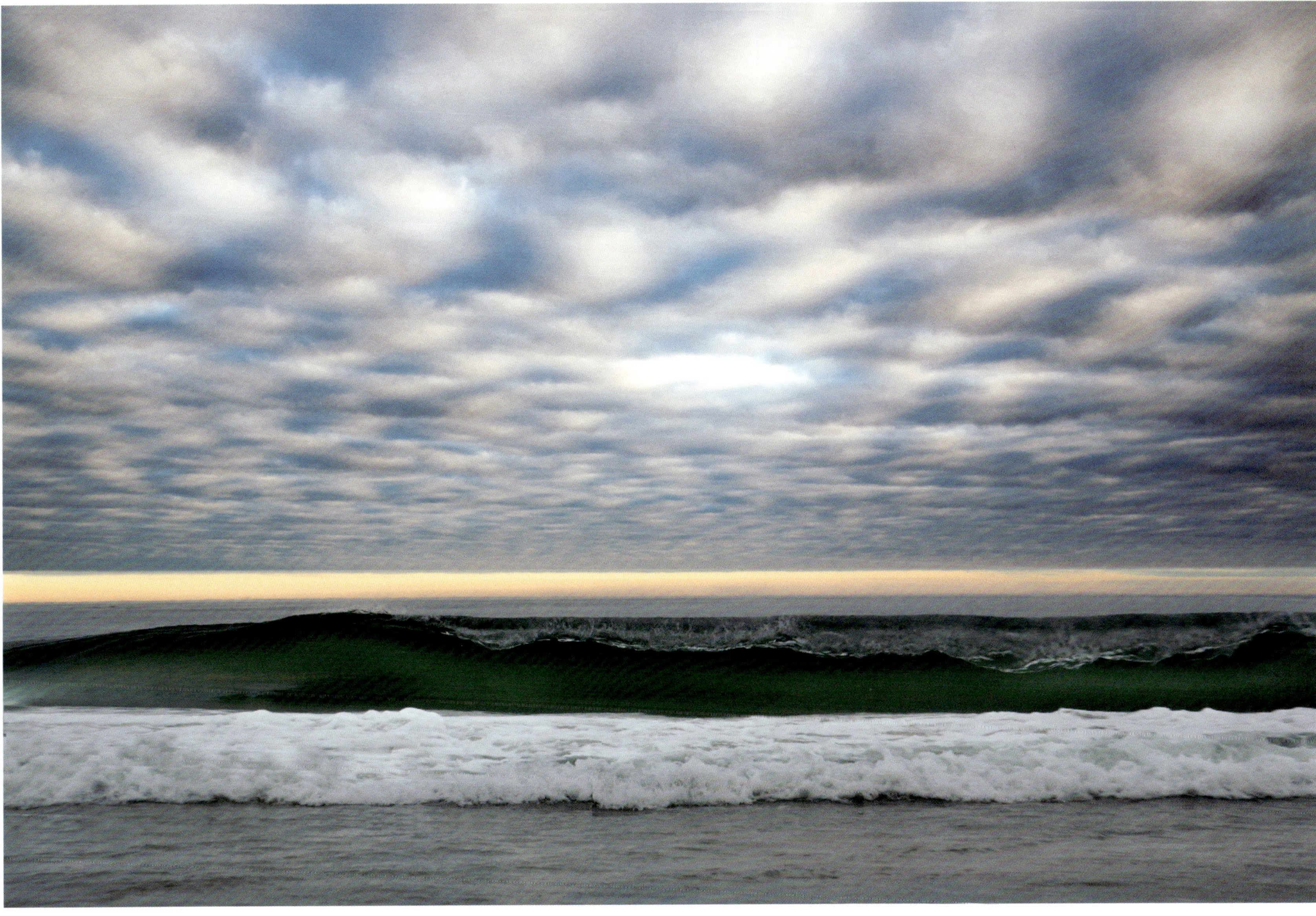

Sky and Sea

A Caribbean wave imitates the cloud above it.

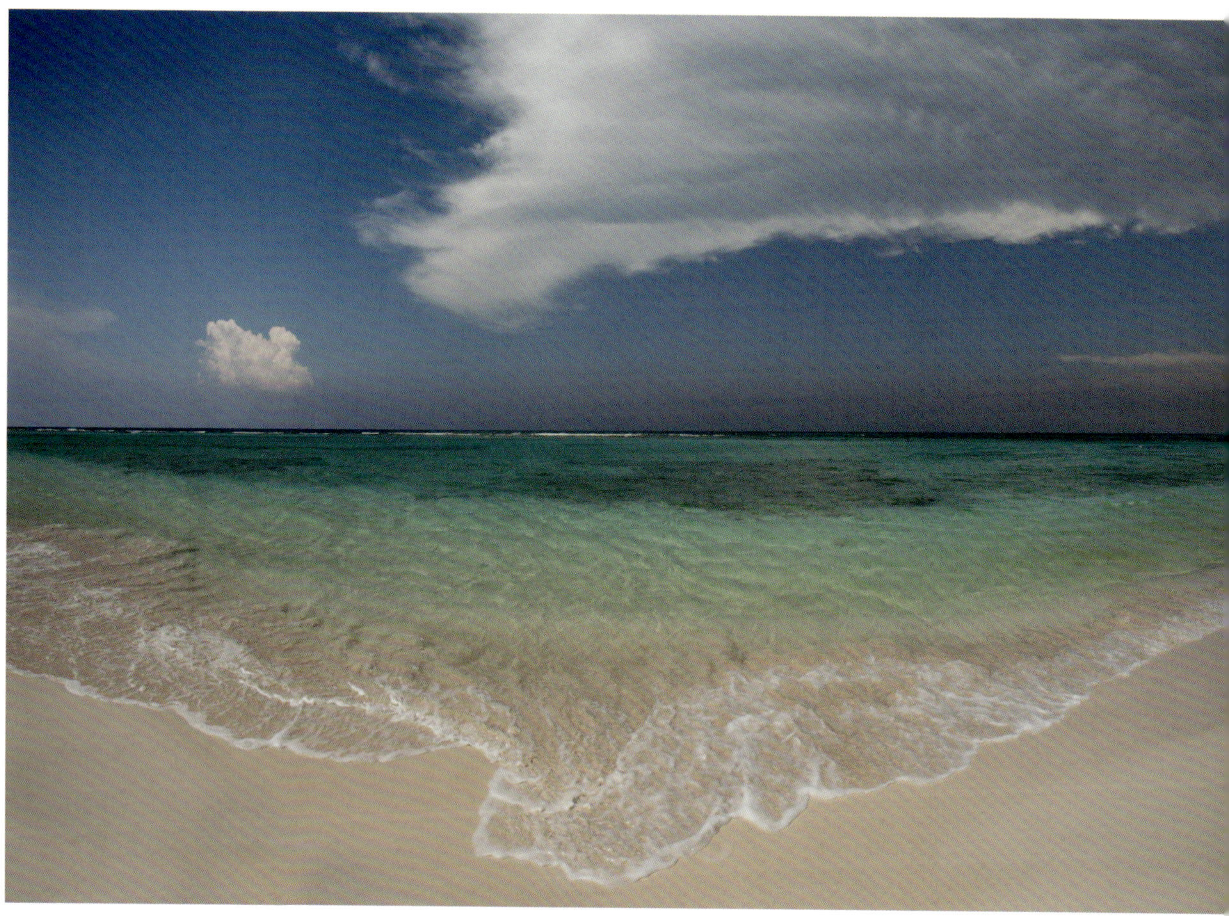

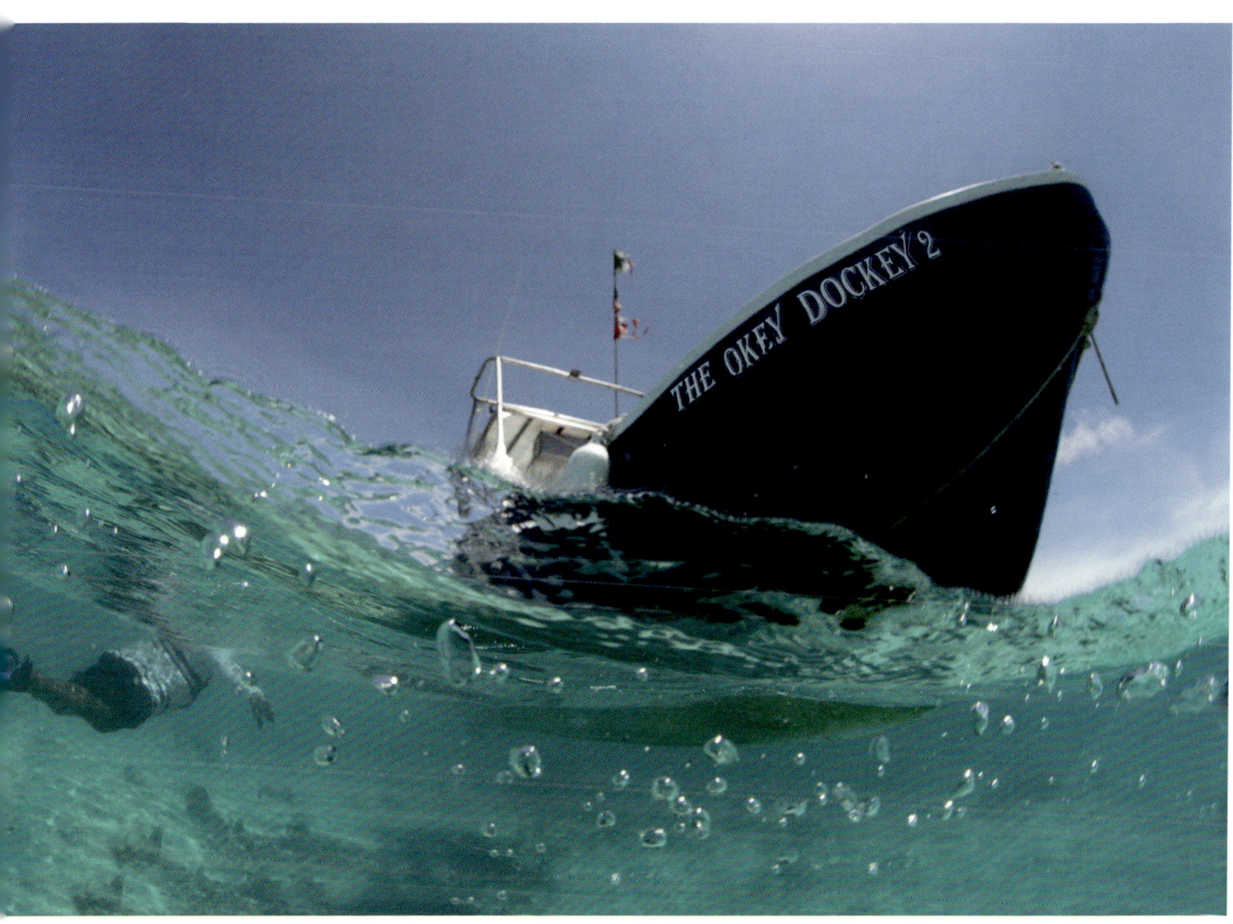

It's Okey Dokey

Floating alongside this ship in a warm-water bay was definitely "okey dokey."

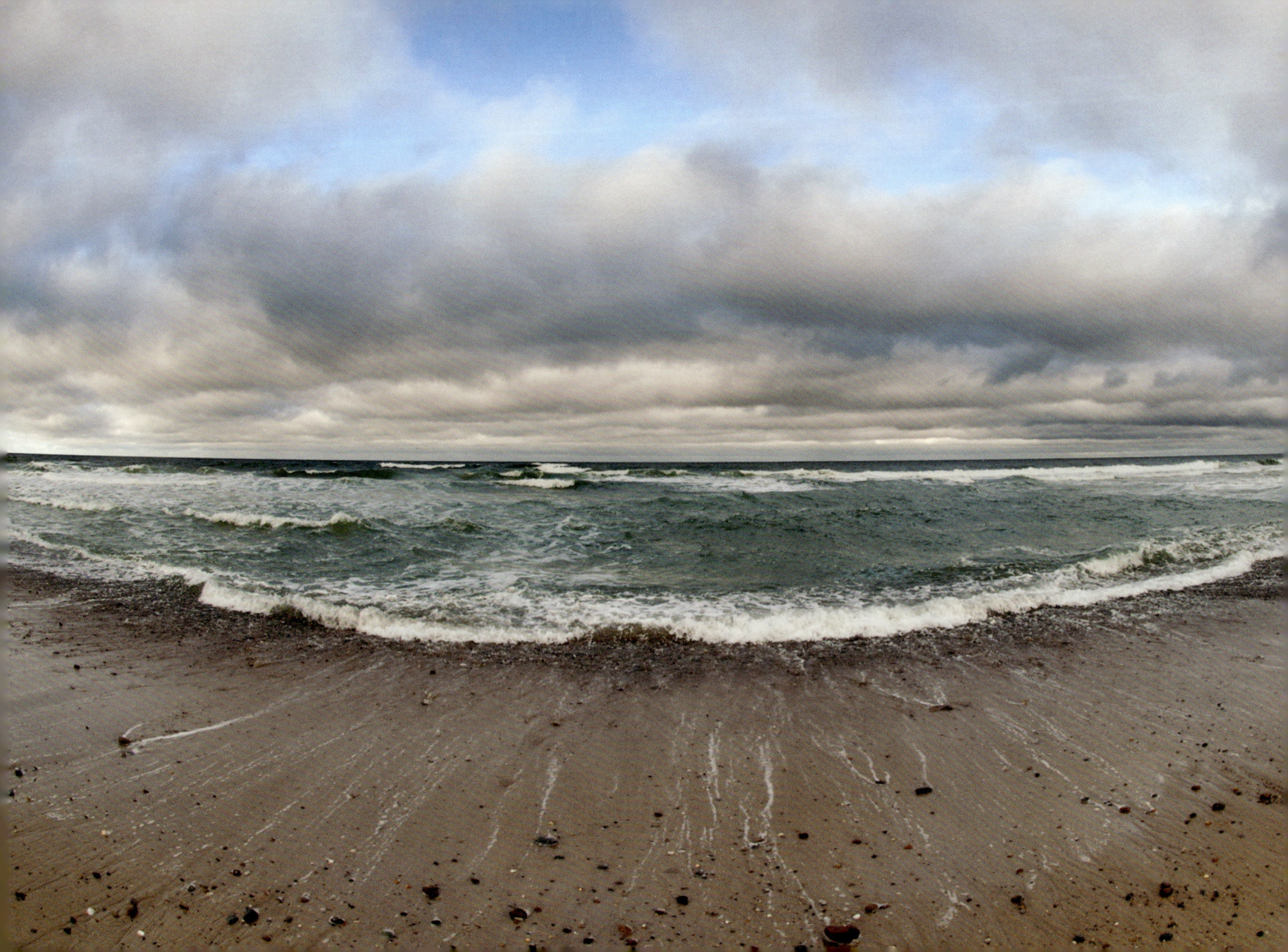

Ebbing Wave

Soft blues and greens lend a sense of peace and place on an evening walk.

Sand and Sea Storm

This wild storm brought many onlookers to the beach, but not many wandered down to the water's edge. The sand was whipping and the wind made standing difficult. Many thanks to the kindred soul who provided a scale marker for my photo while taking his own.

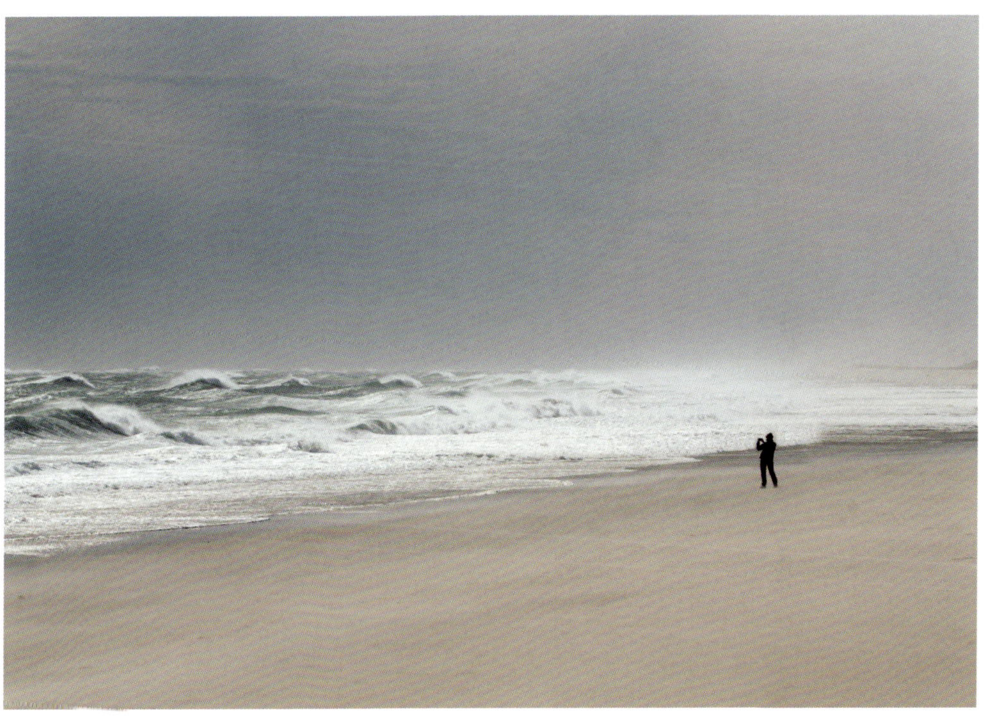

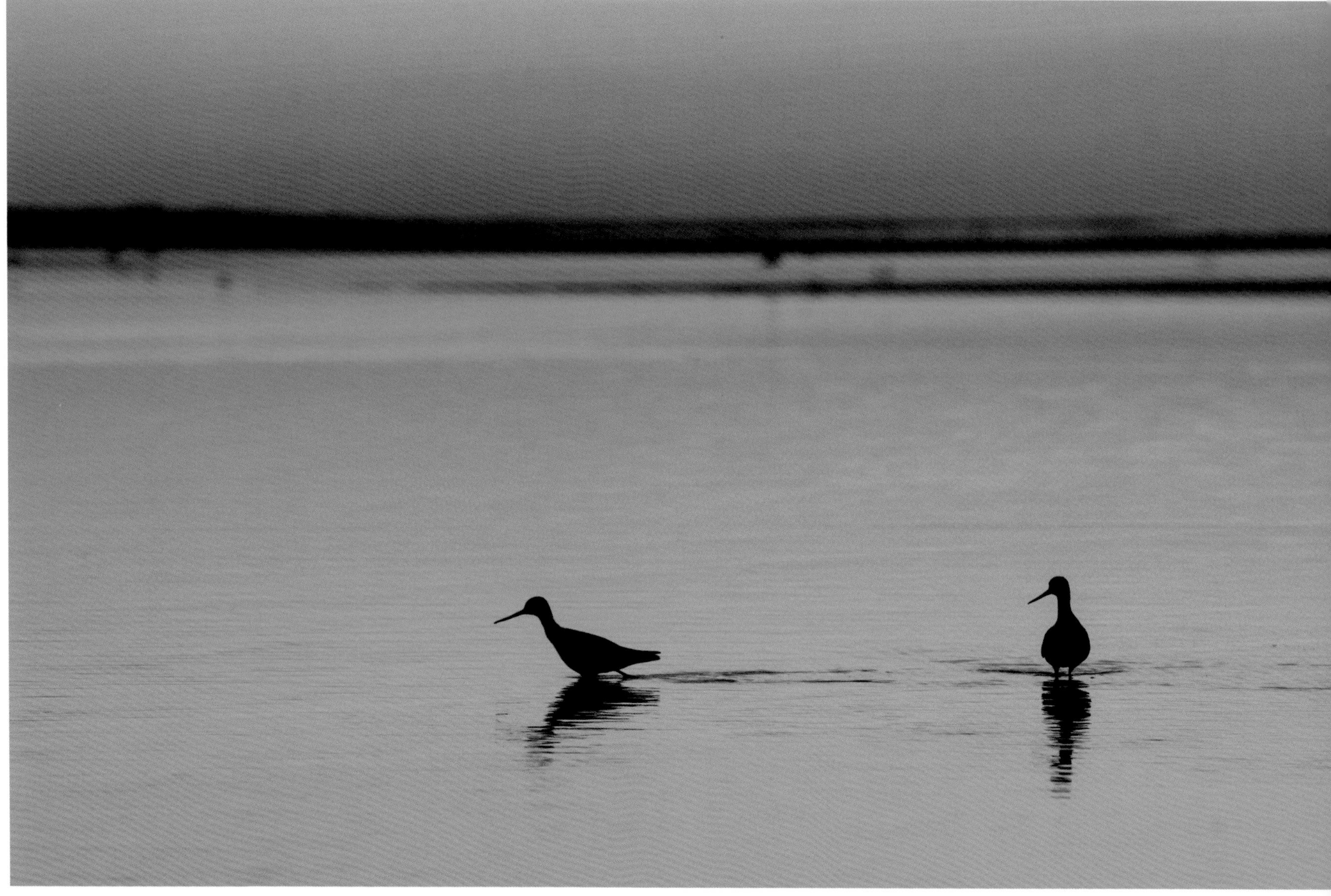

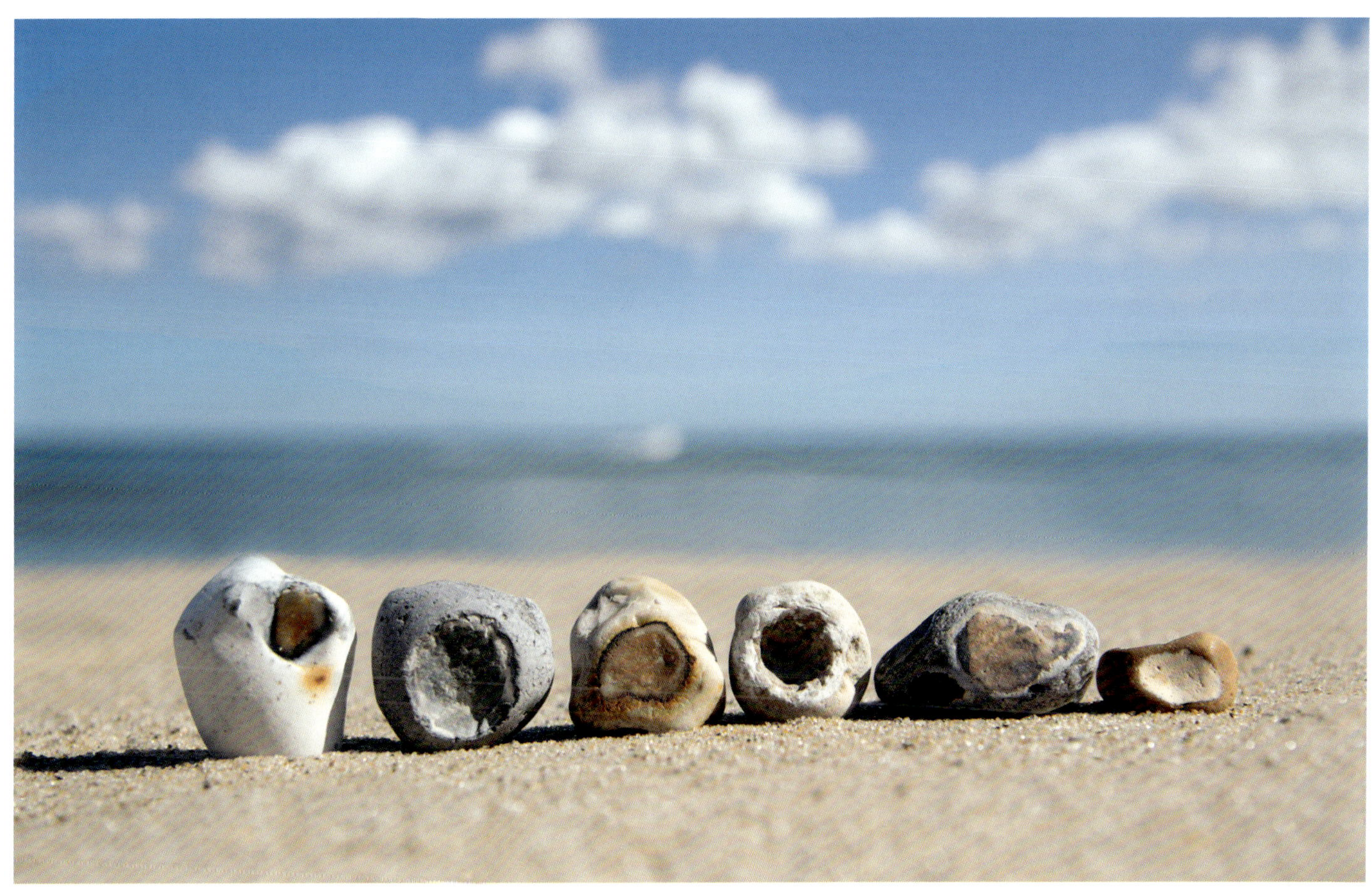

Something I Said?

It's fun to create captions for this one. Make up one of your own!

Western France

One of the best things about traveling to beaches far afield is discovering the geological diversity of the world's minerals.

Beach Glass Barrel

A bottle-green wave delivers a flawless barrel as it hits the shore. It resembles beach glass that appears frosted, the result of endless tumbling in the sand. This image helps settle the argument that the sea is not blue or green, but both.

Peaceful Evening

There's nothing like an evening walk at low tide. The clouds agree.

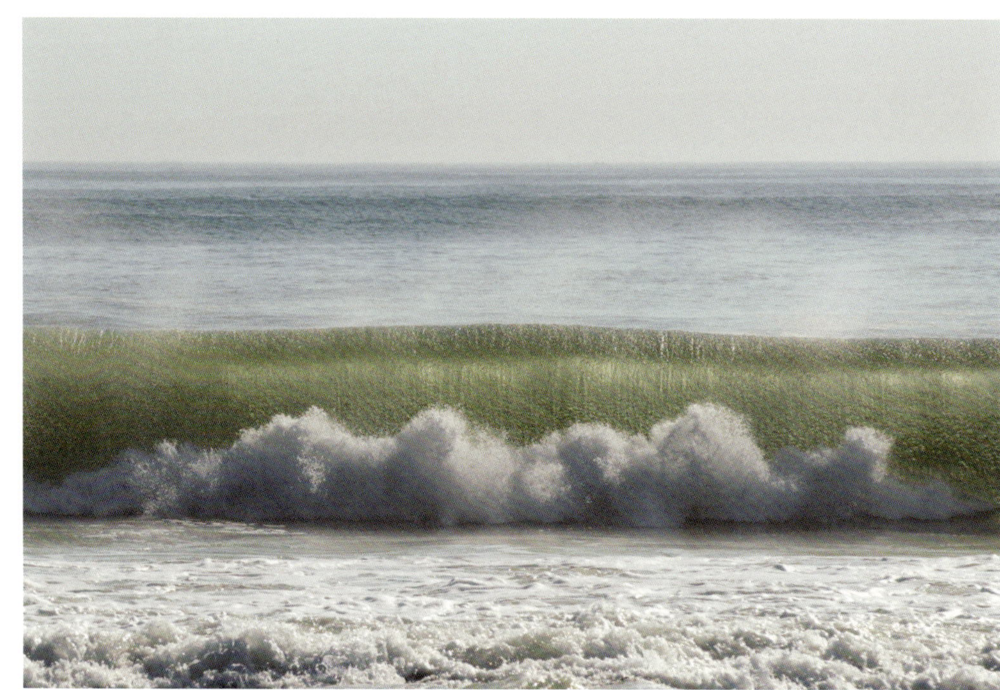

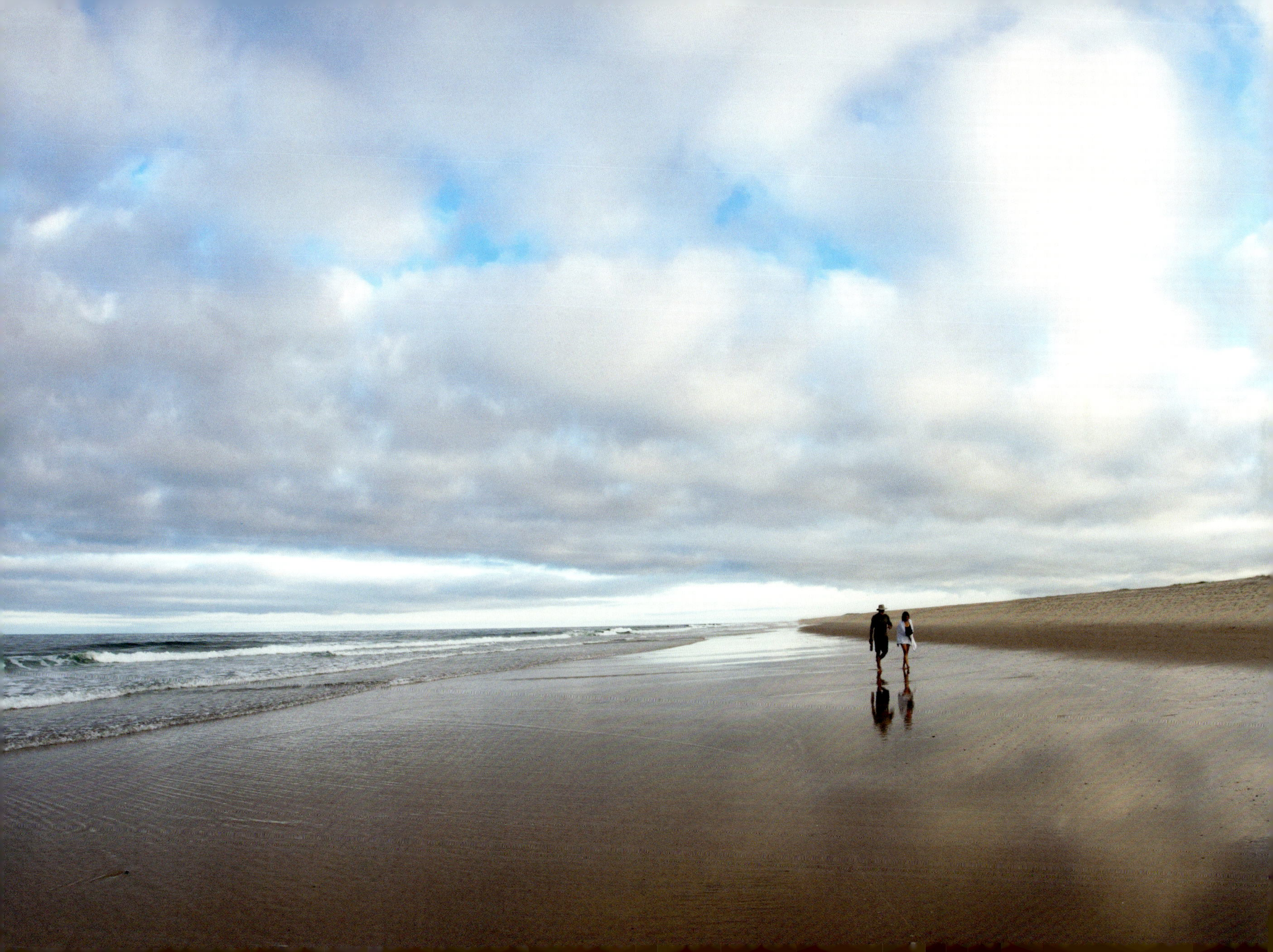

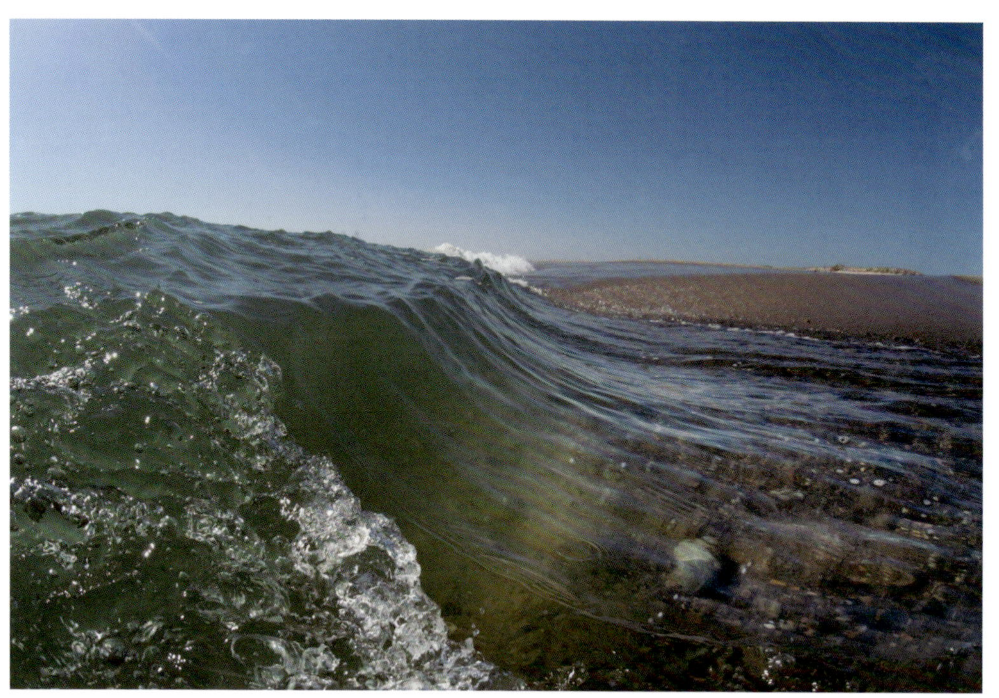

Hidden Heart

A watery view enhances beach stones' colors and shapes.

LOVE

Nauset Beach shares the love. Letters are awaiting discovery among the stones.

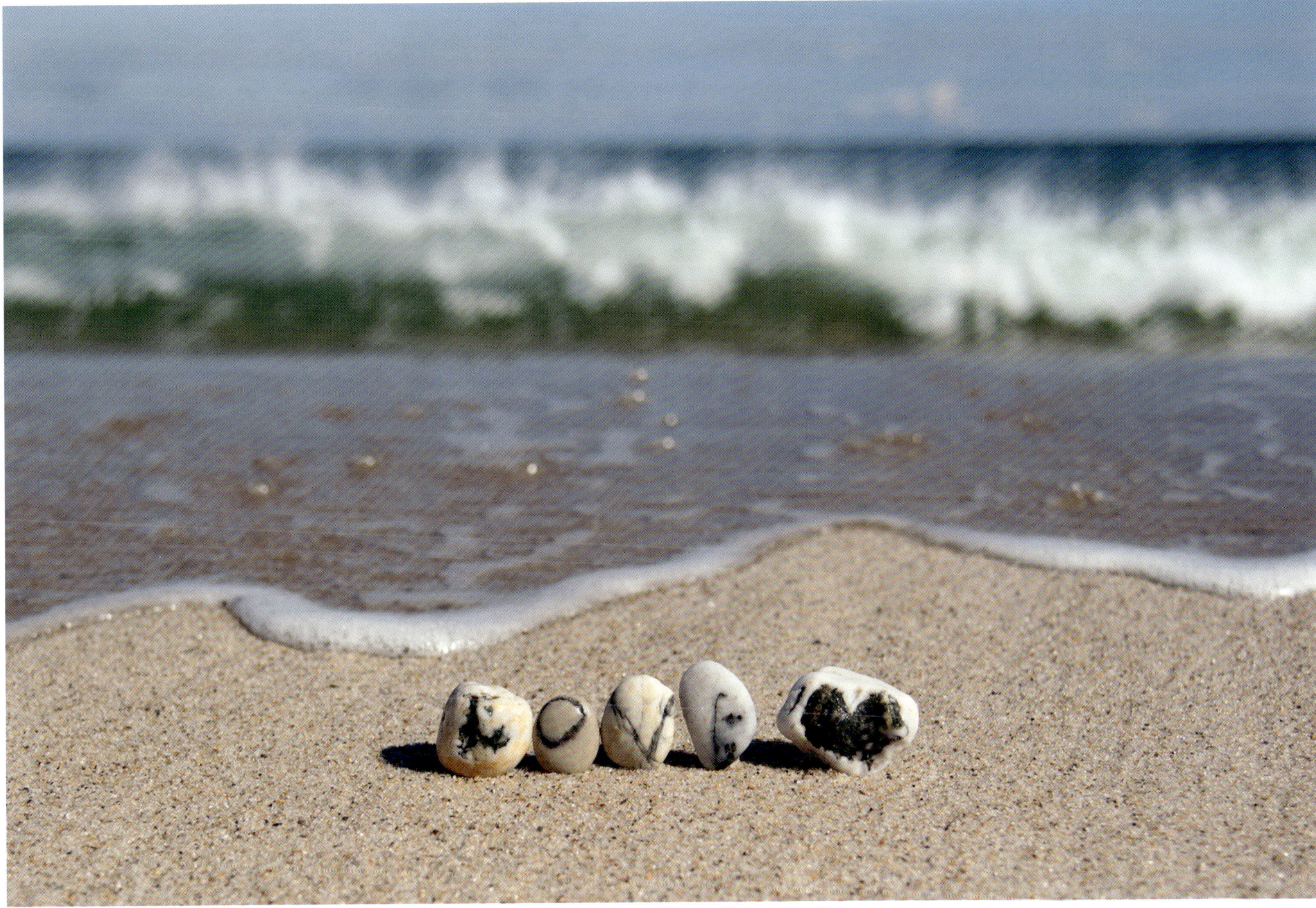

Foamy Morning

Water, endlessly shaken and stirred, like a milkshake

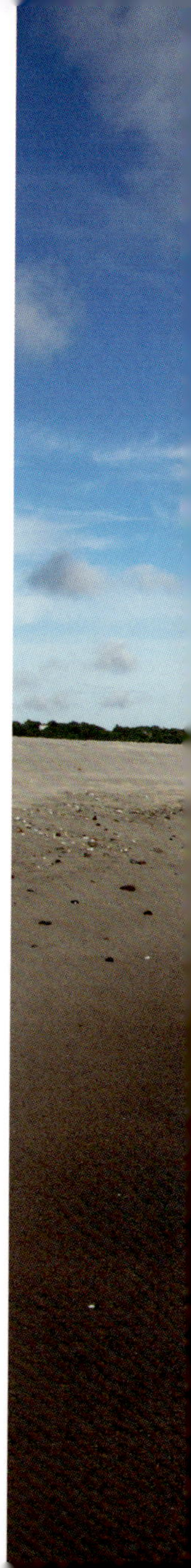

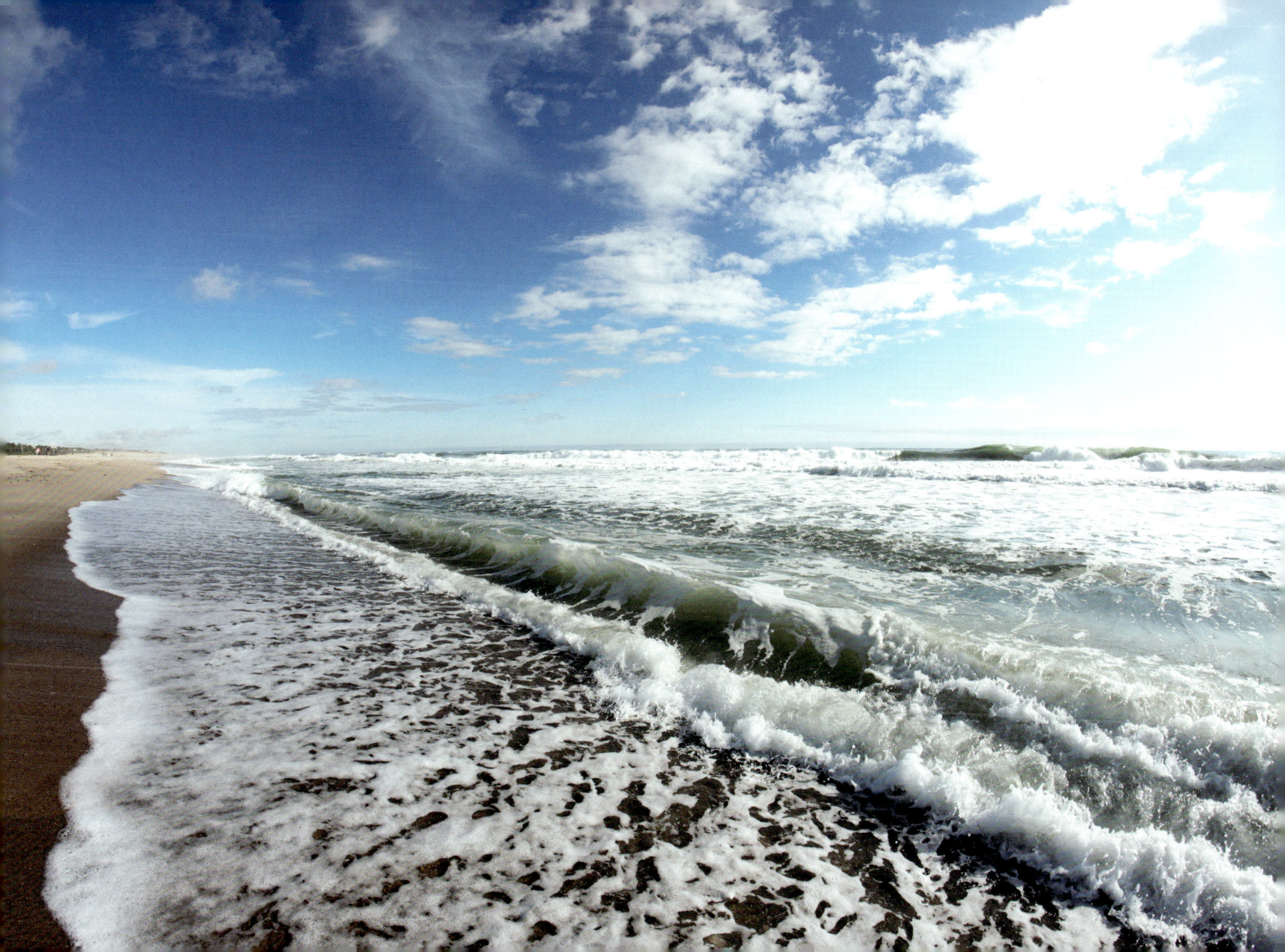

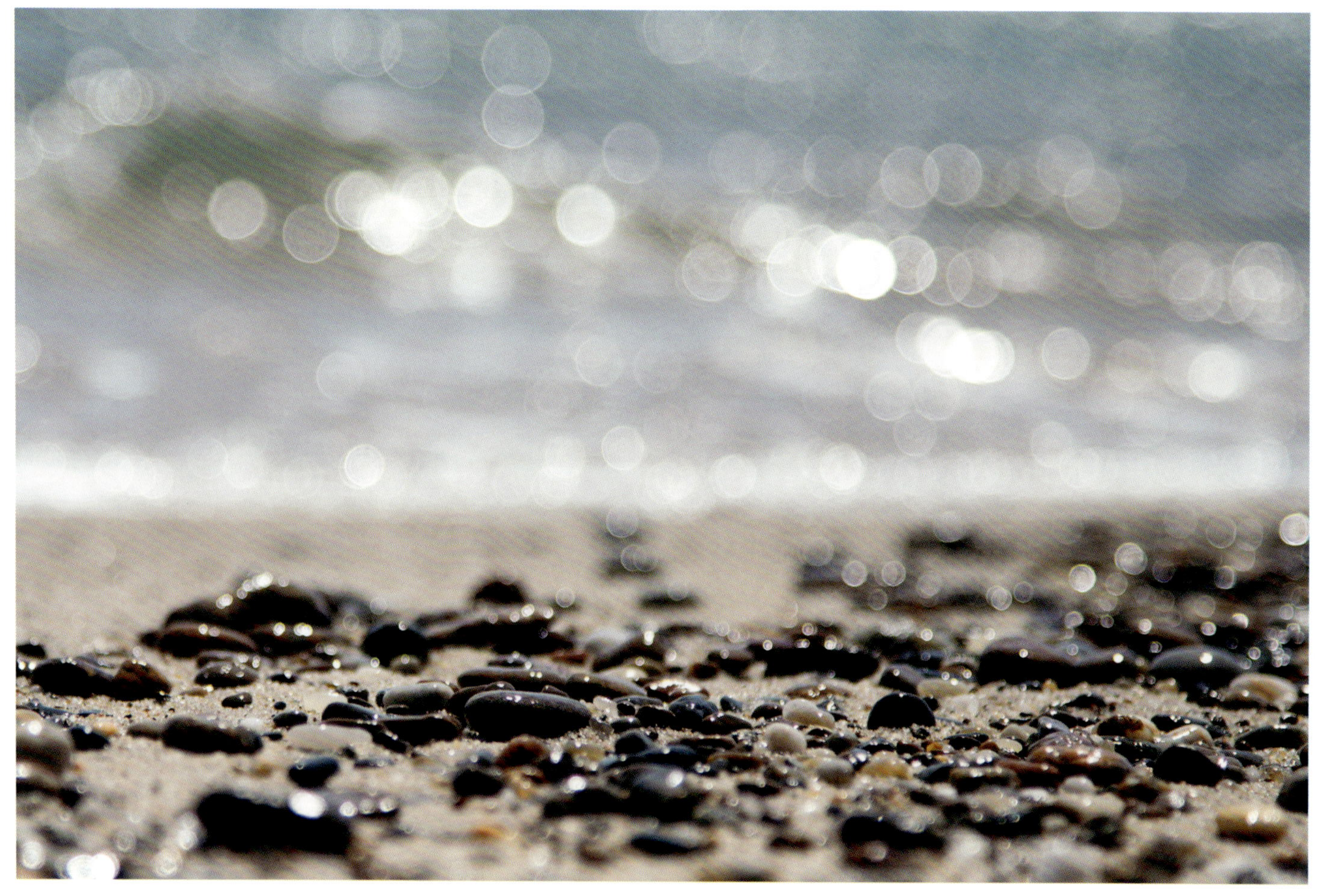

Specular Highlights

A low angle captures the light at its finest. These rocks may not be gemstones, but they sparkle nevertheless.

Wave Cross-Section

This beach in Mexico drew me with its clear, warm water. Spending time in the serene waves was a joy.

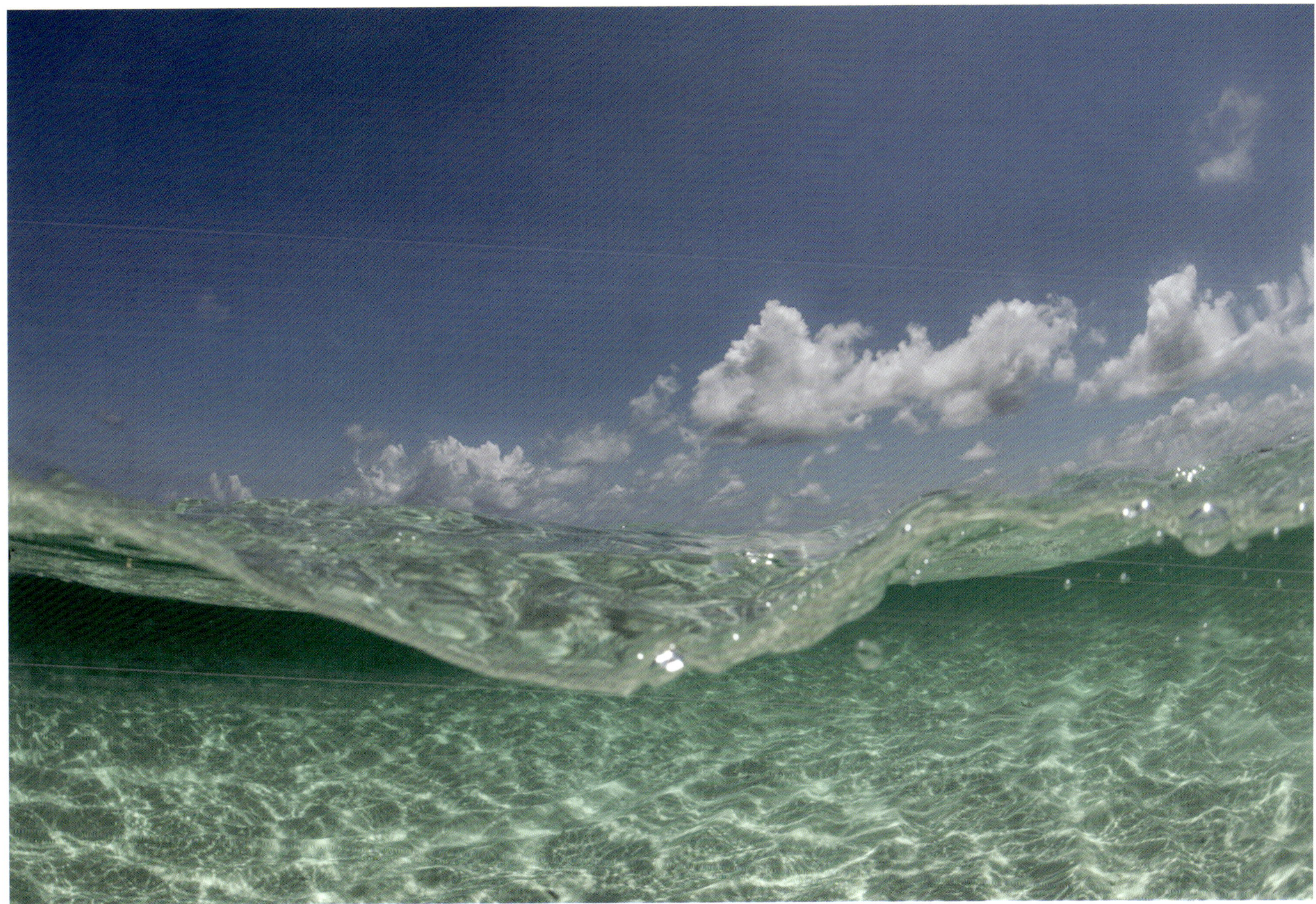

Morning Light

Morning light filters through the waves.

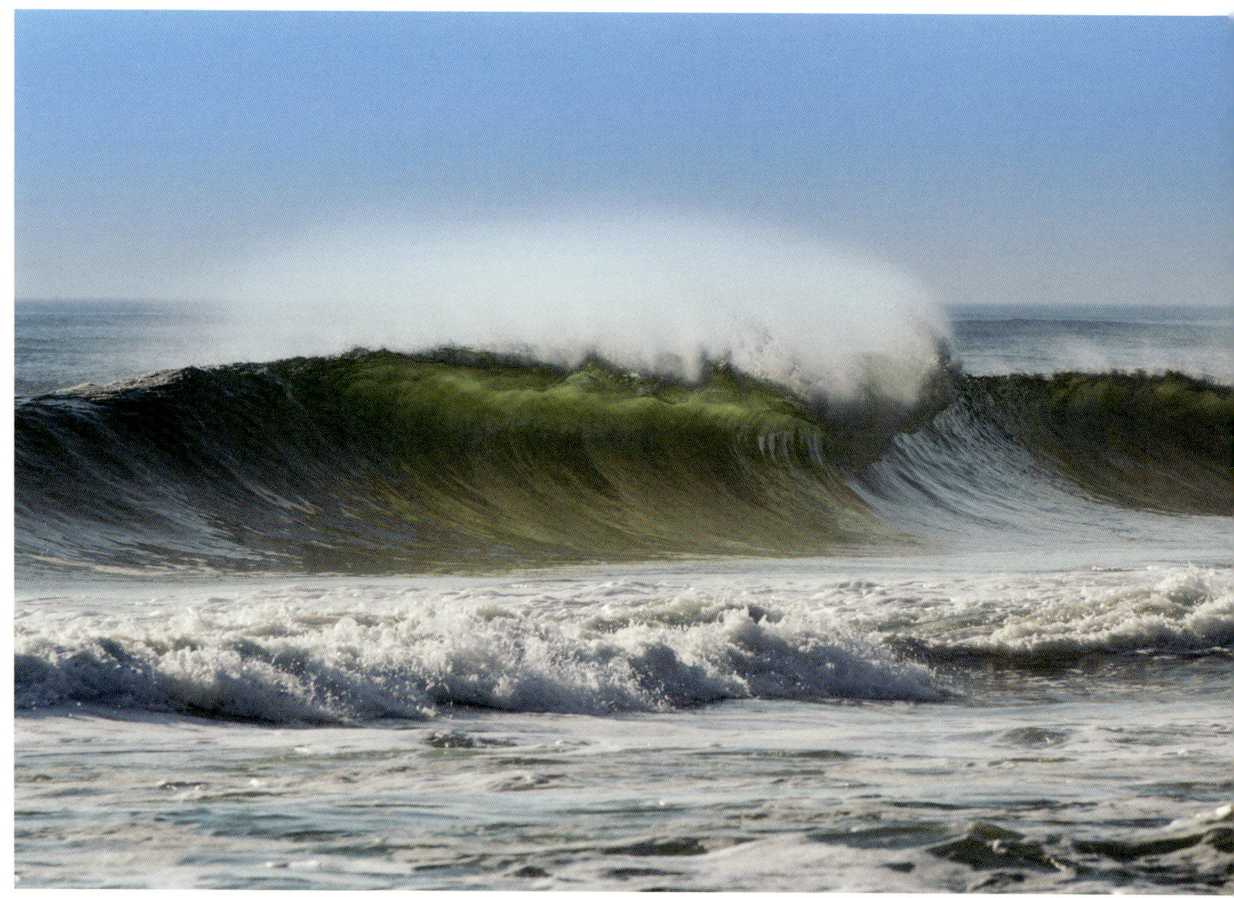

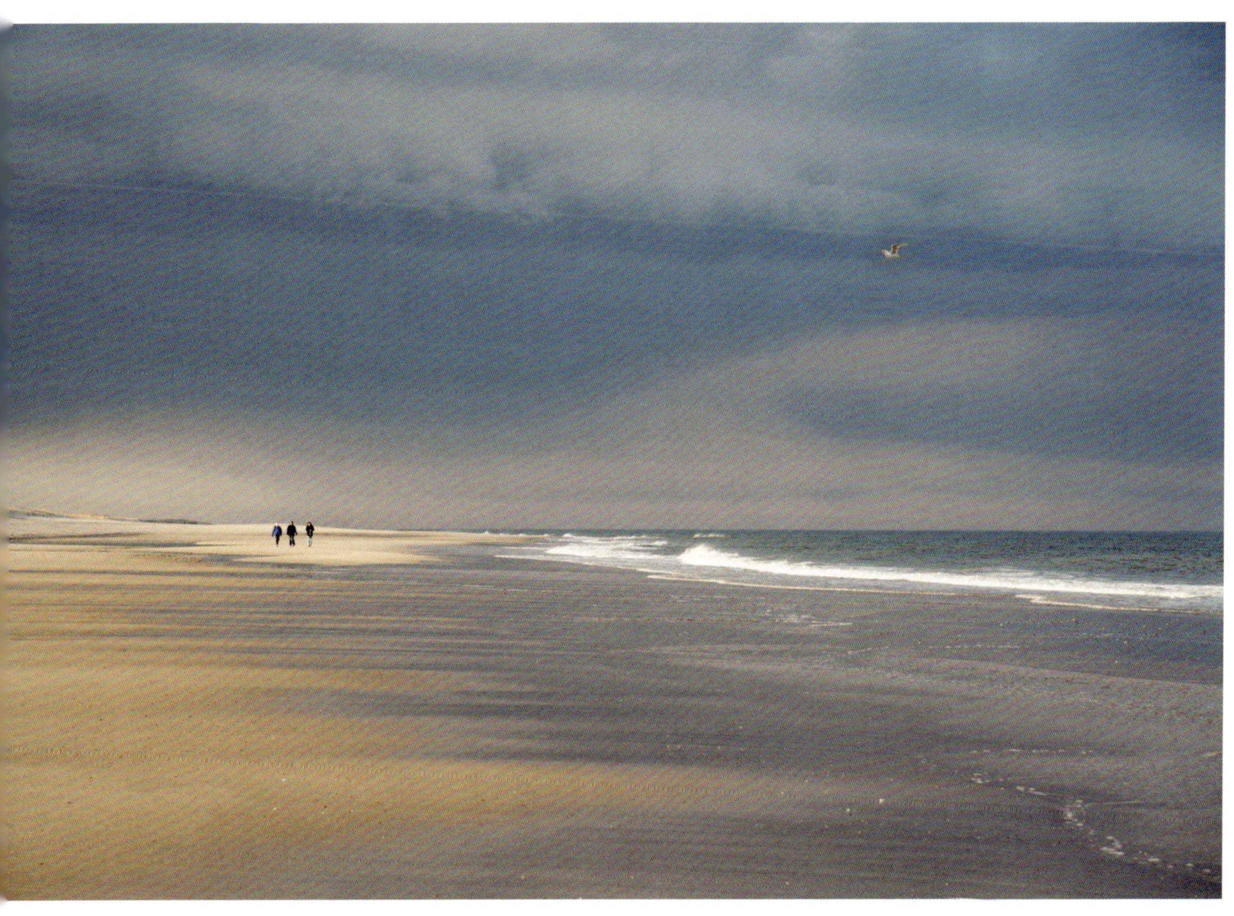

Family of Three

An overcast but colorful sky

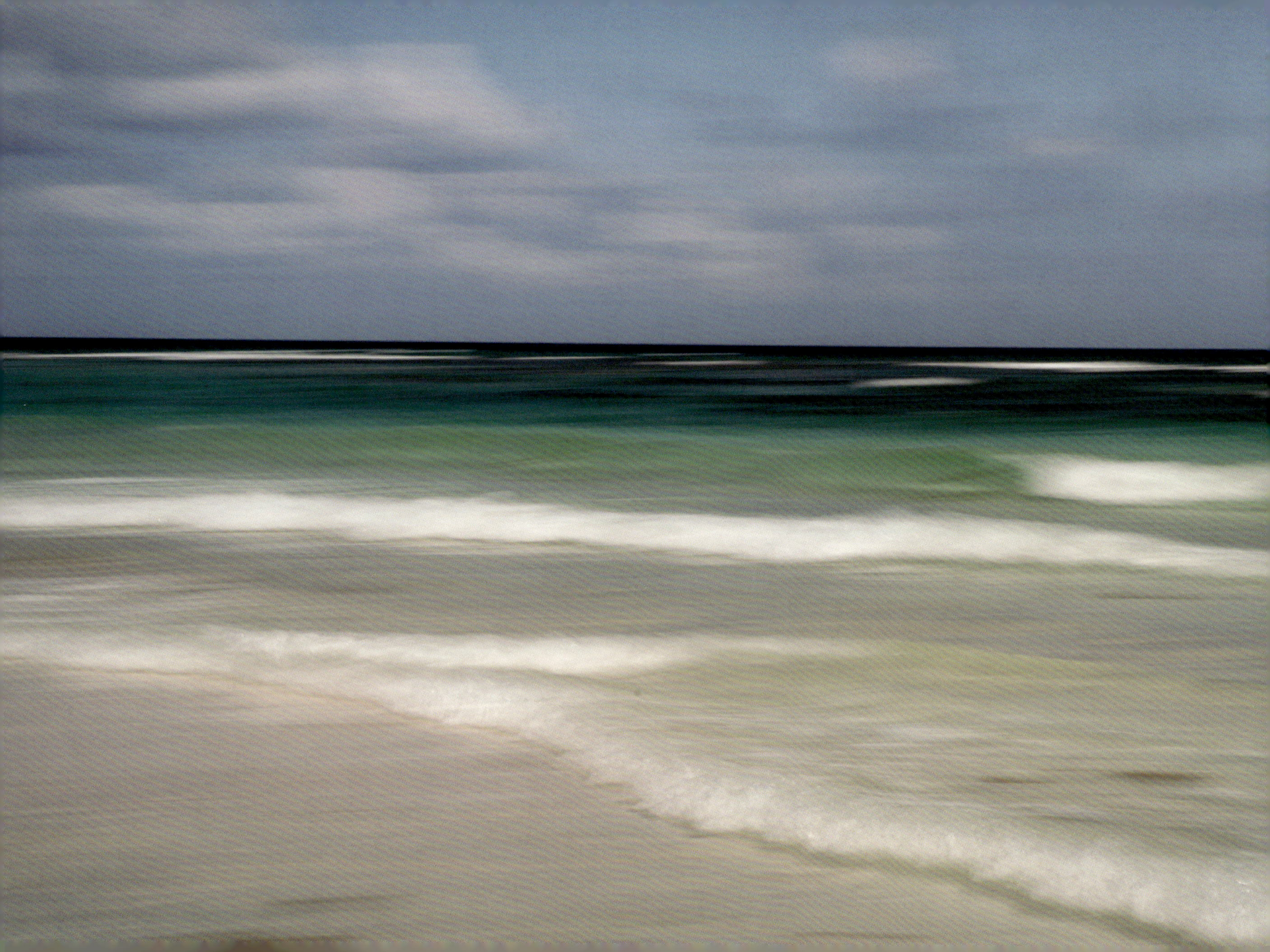

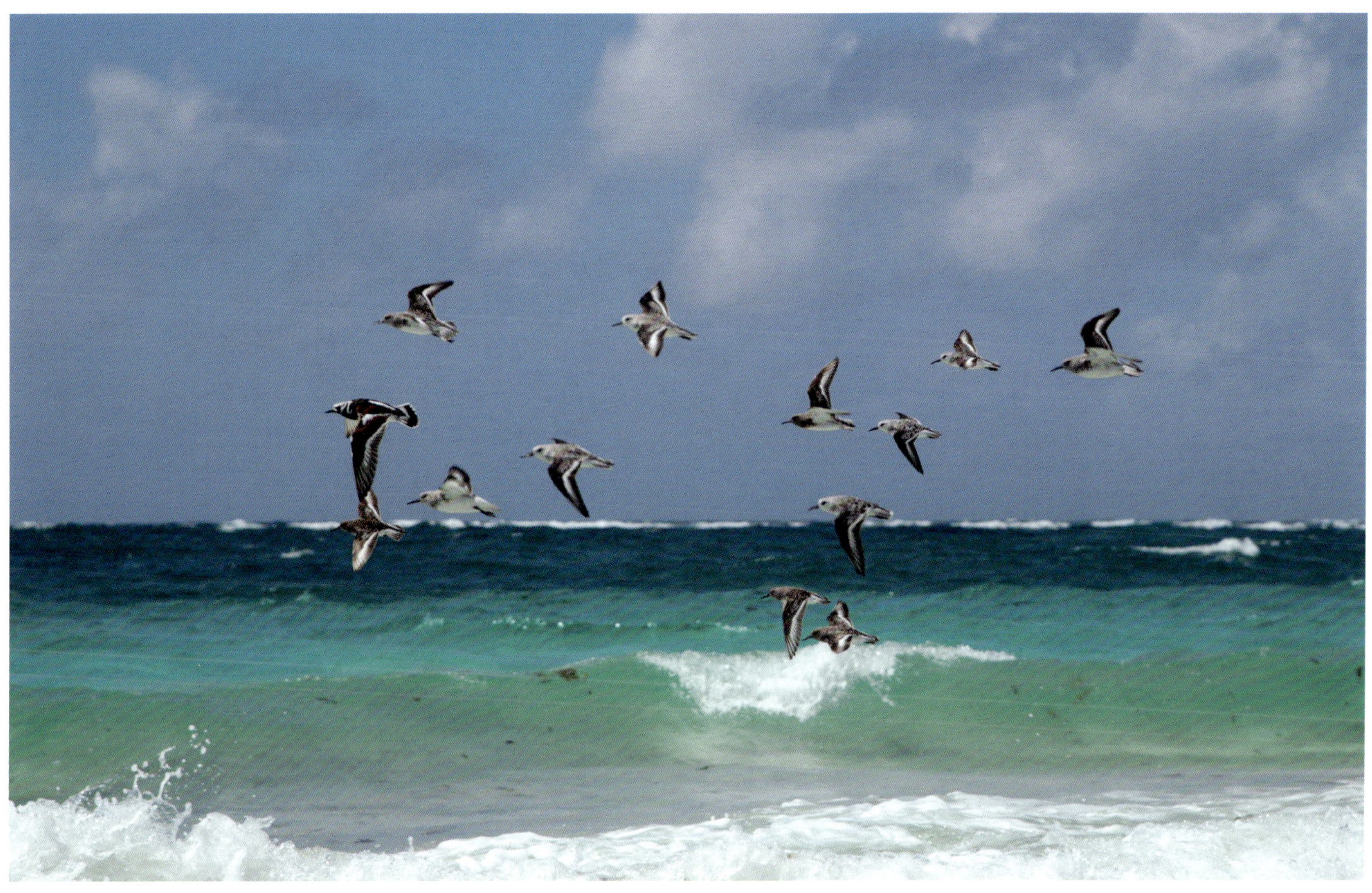

Tropical Ocean Colors

There is nothing quite like the variety and intensity of the Caribbean Sea's colors.

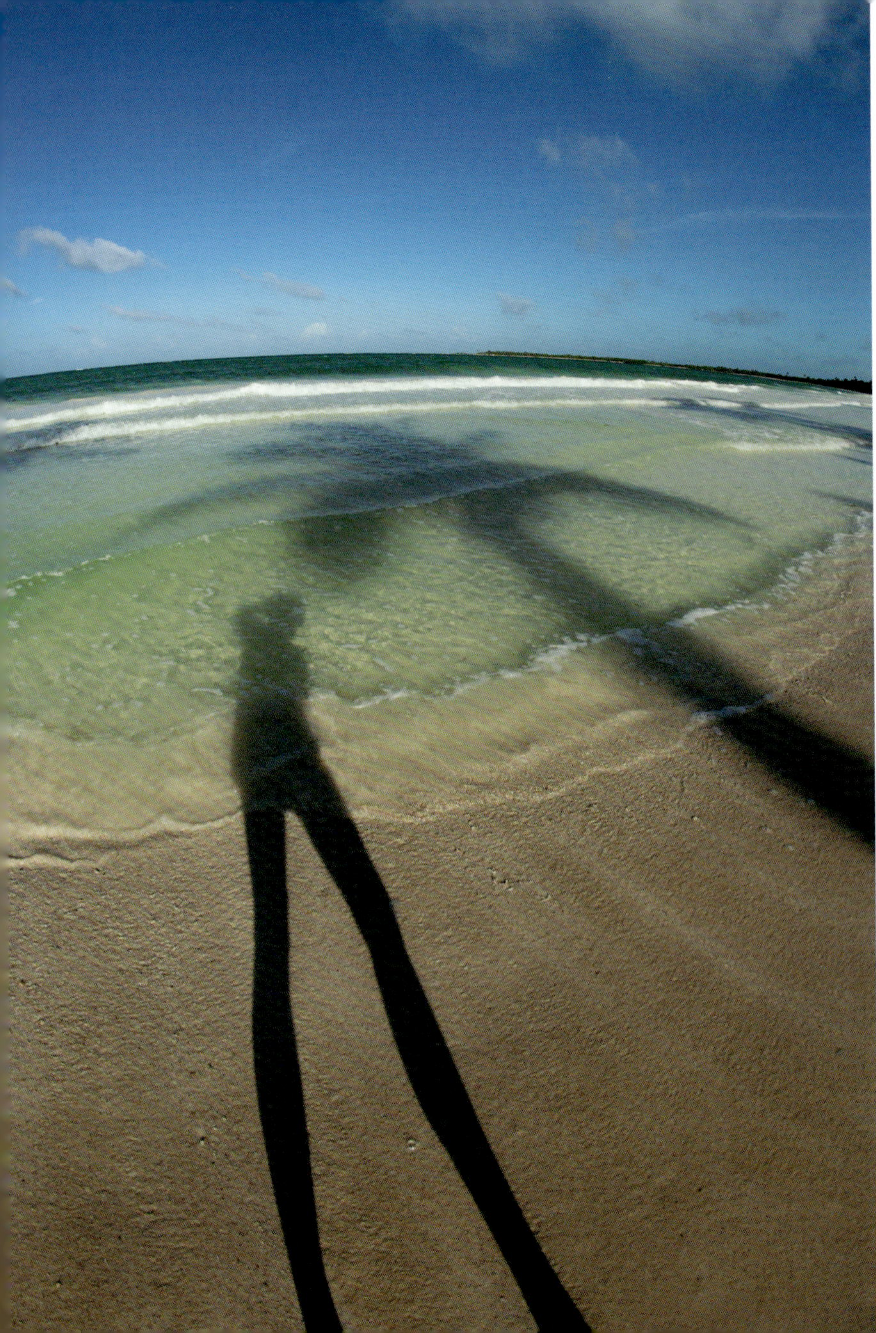

Soliltude

Happiness is a remote tropical beach.

Doggy Paddle

This was puppy Winston's very first swim, and he seemed thrilled to be in the water. In case you're wondering, he's a Havanese.

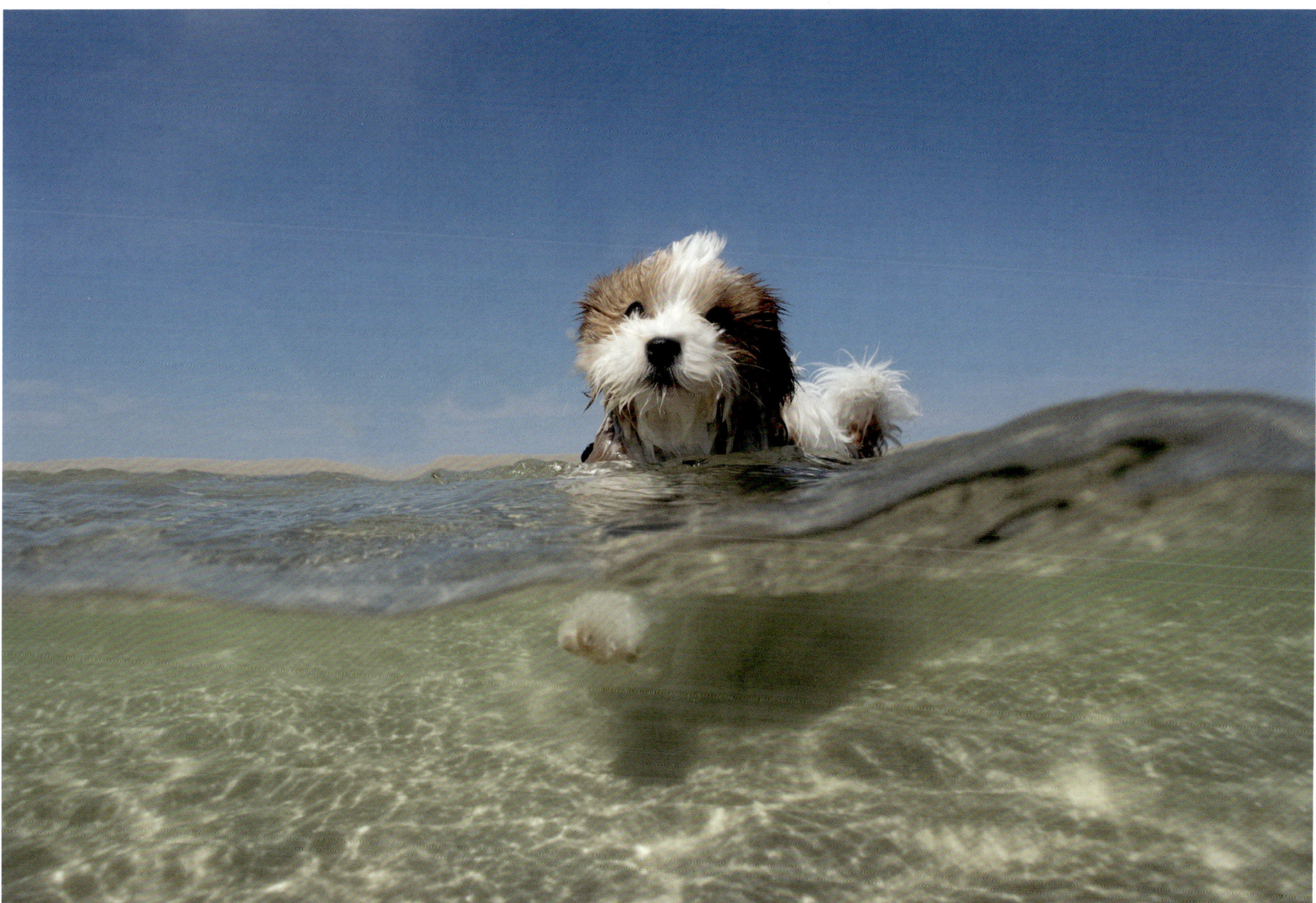

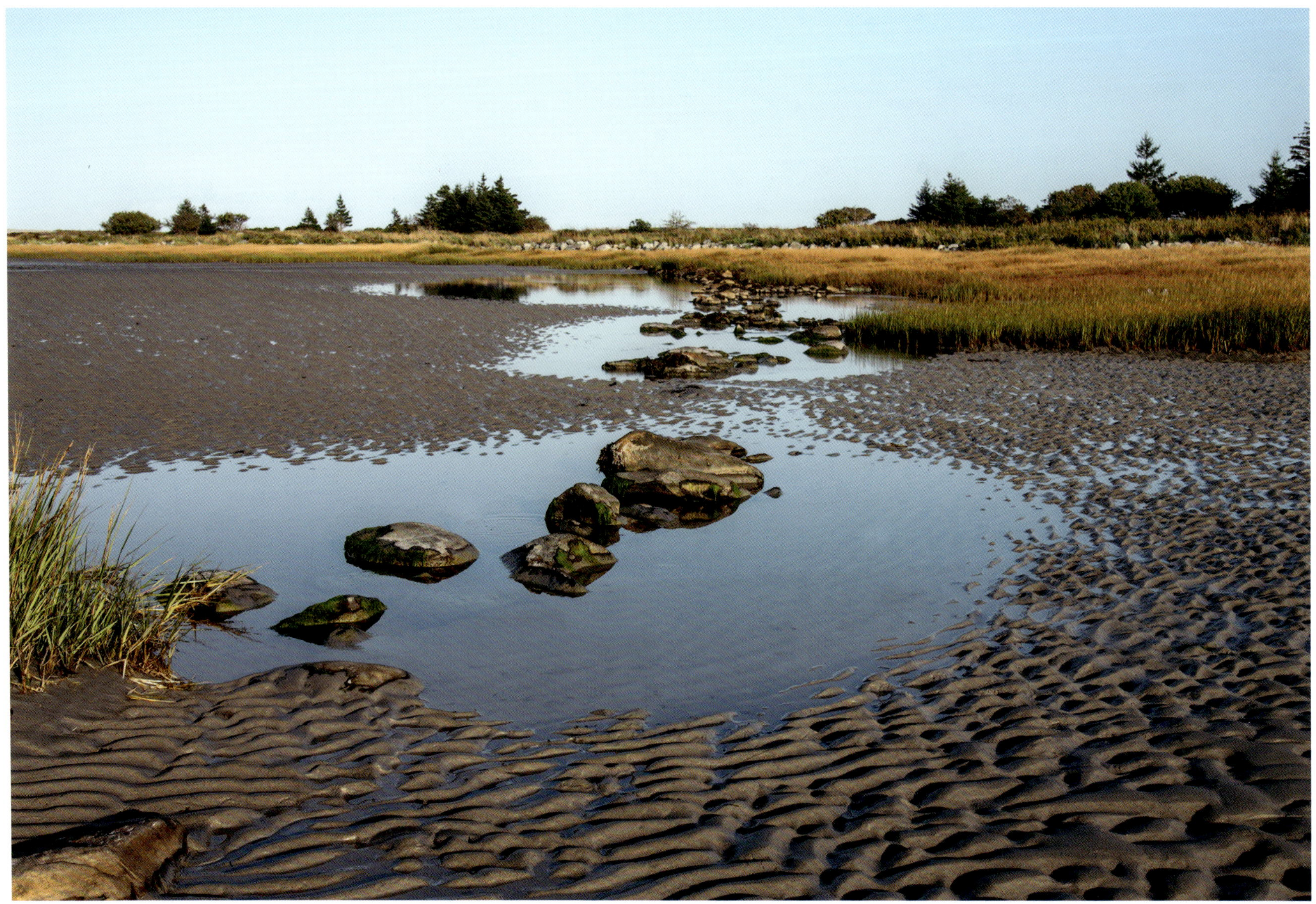

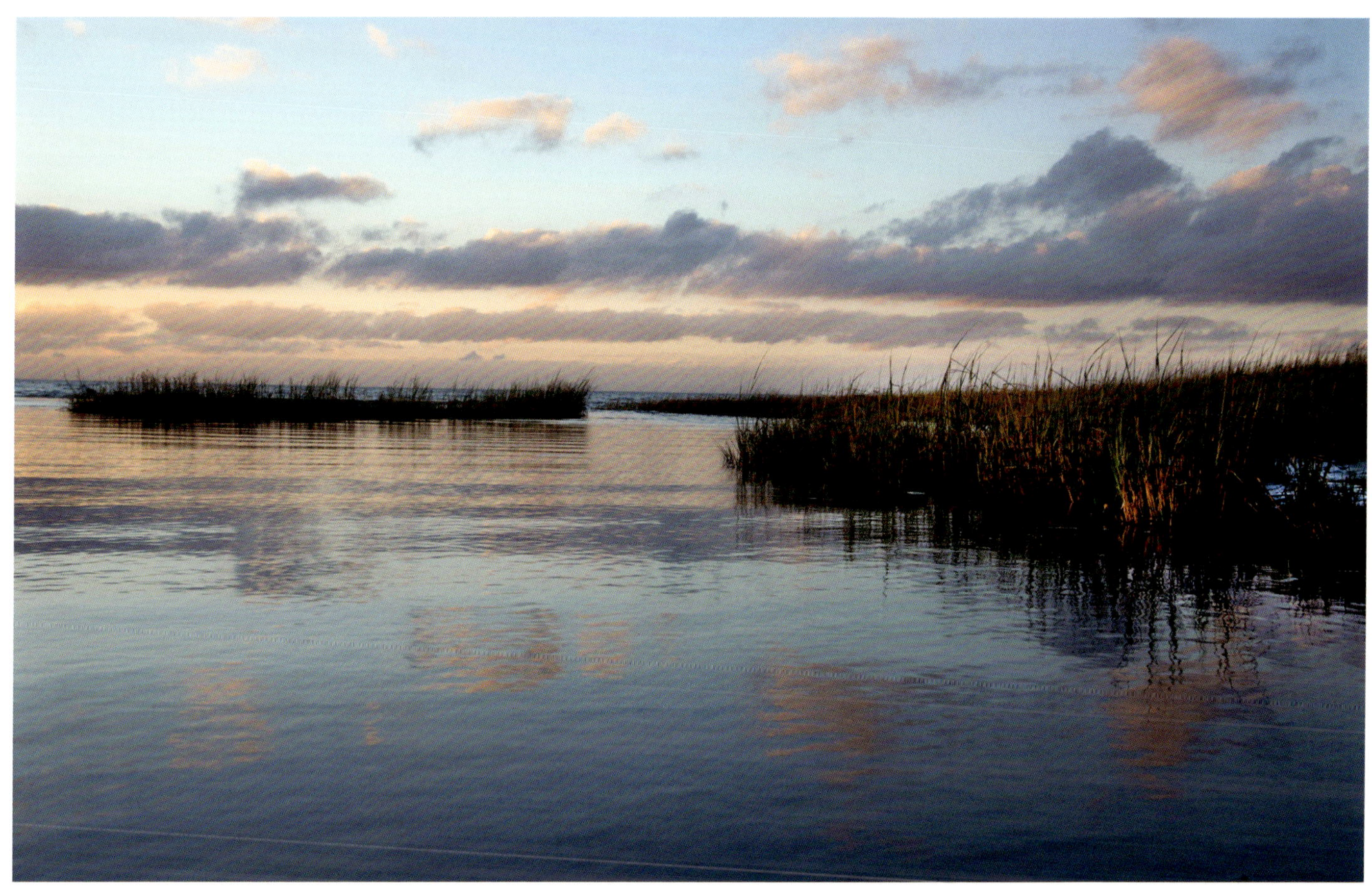

Evening Calm

Watery reflections on a peaceful autumn evening

Tropical Tide Pool

A small coral heart emerged in this tidal pool in Costa Rica.

Fantasy

This quintessential tropical beach is the very image of midwinter daydreams.

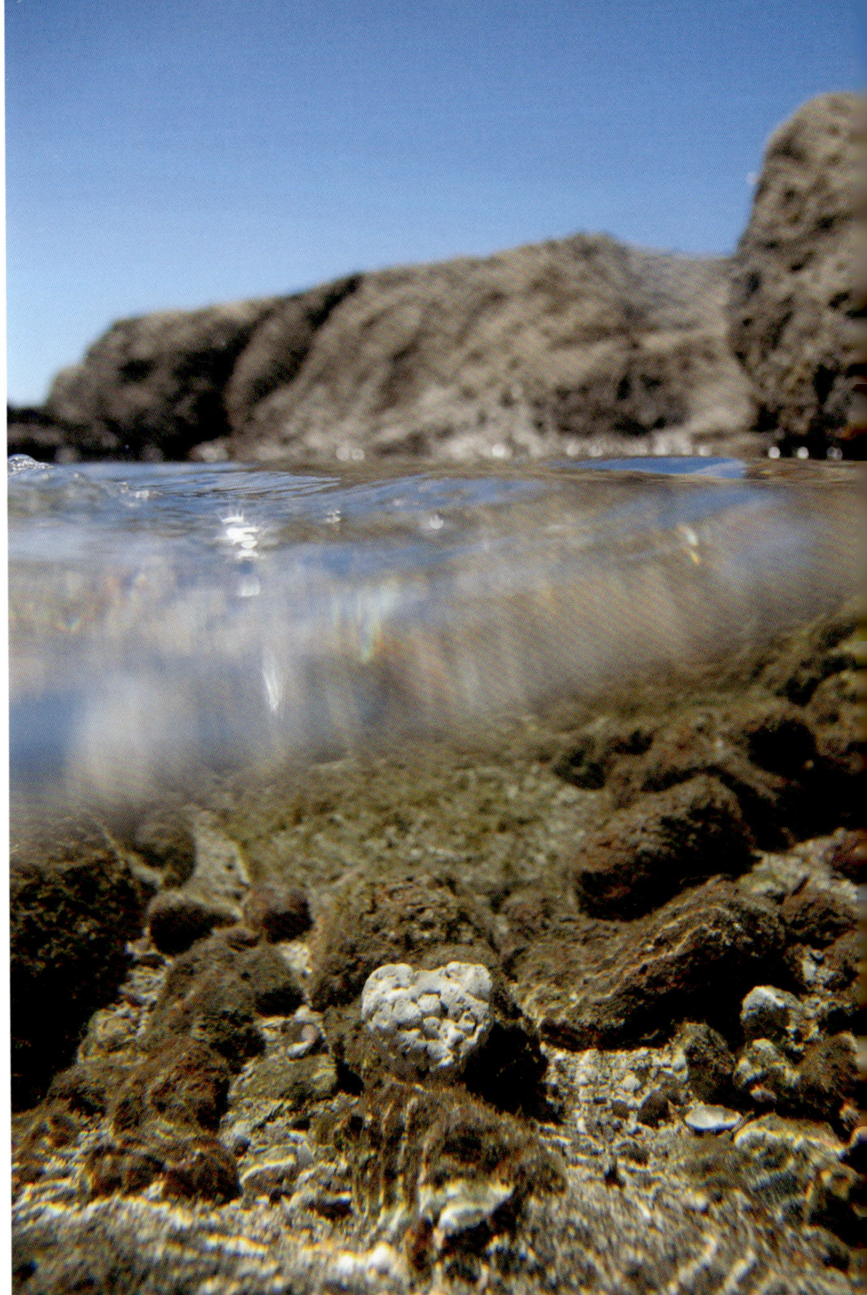

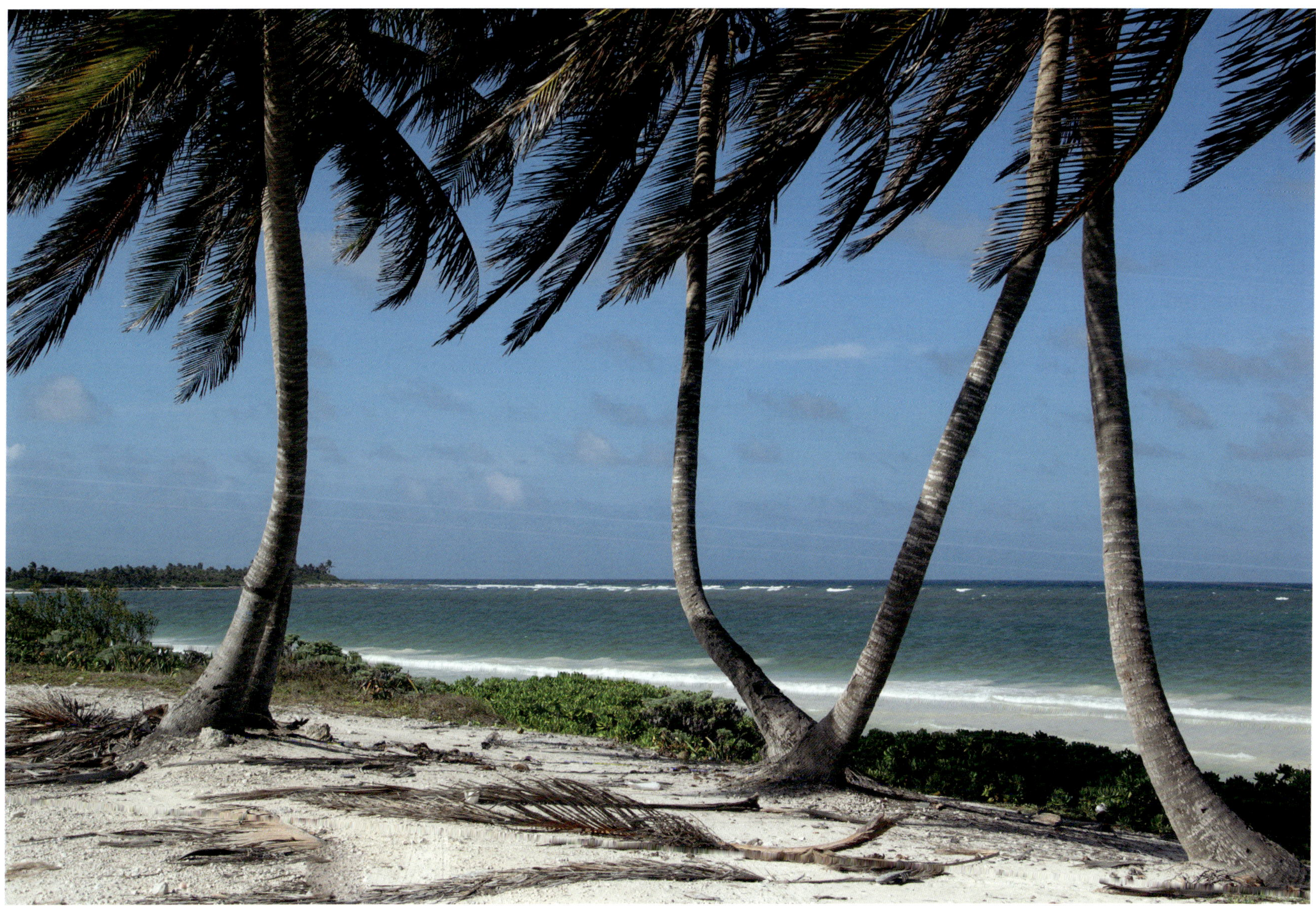

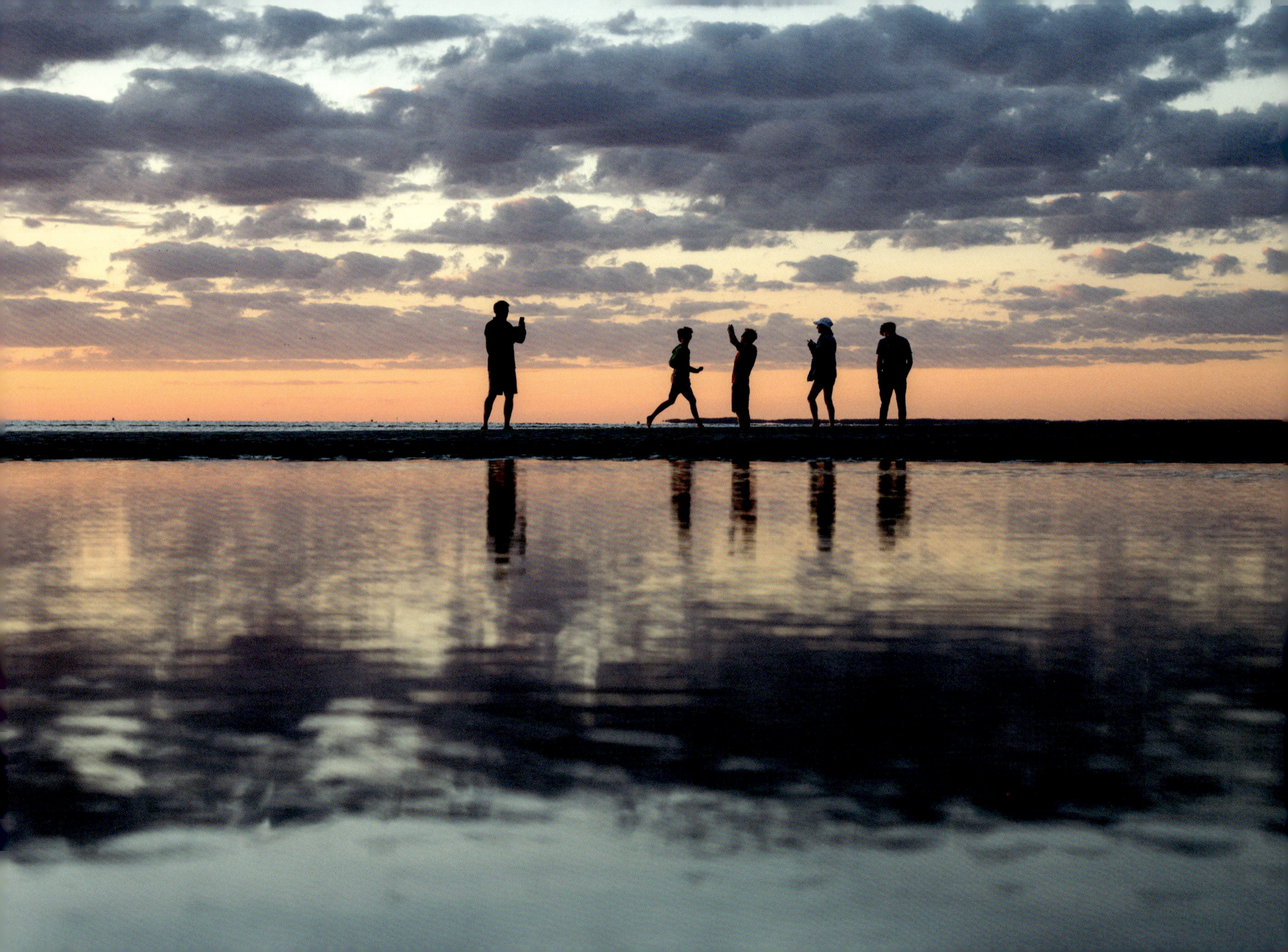

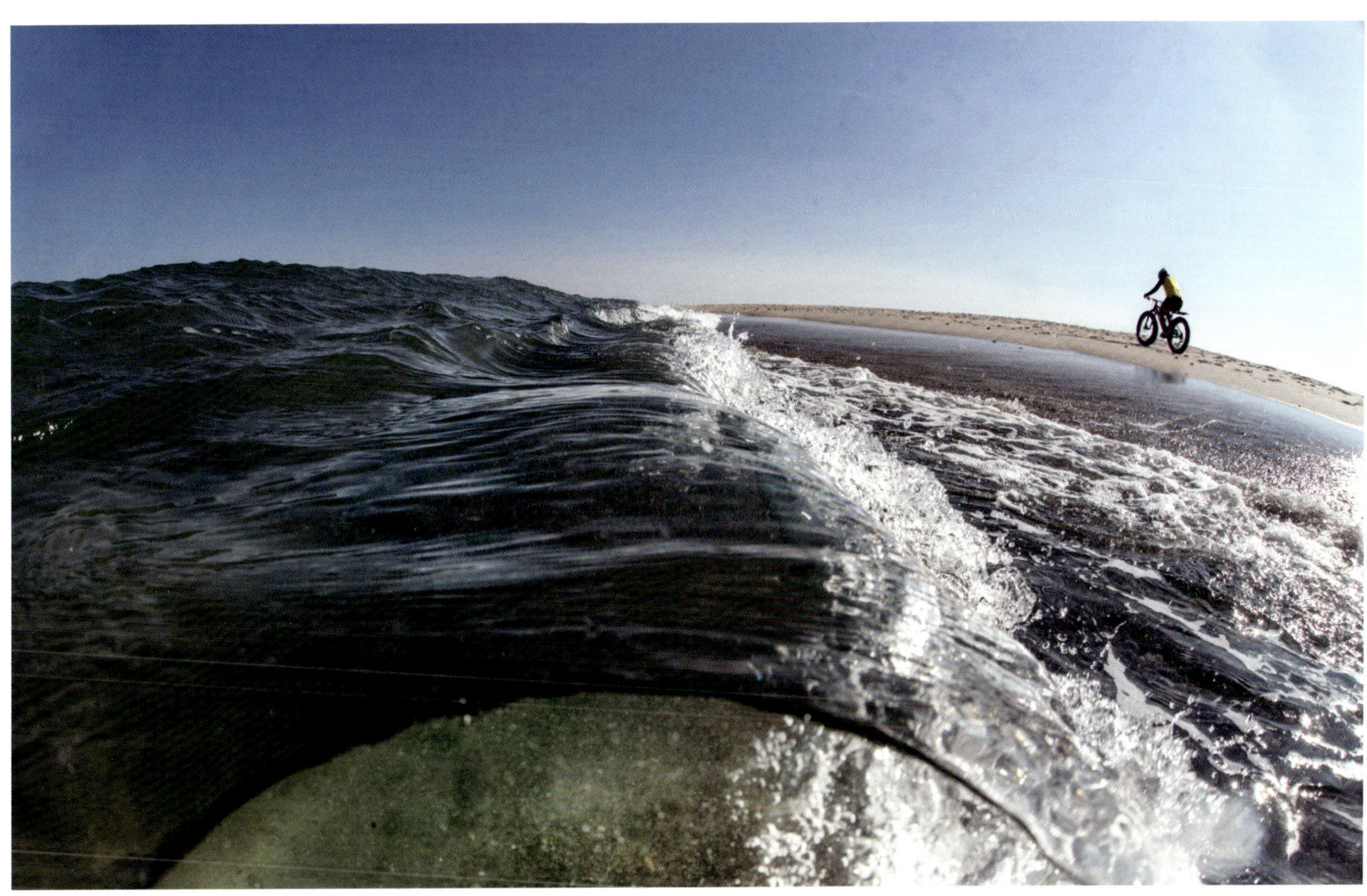

Modern Family

All of these family members seem to be doing their own thing, but doing it together.

Wet Wheels

This cross section of a wave offers a sneak peak at what lies beneath.

Best Friend

Whoever decided that diamonds are a girl's best friend was mistaken.

Stone Setting

A covey of rocks resemble sunning seals on a Nova Scotia beach.

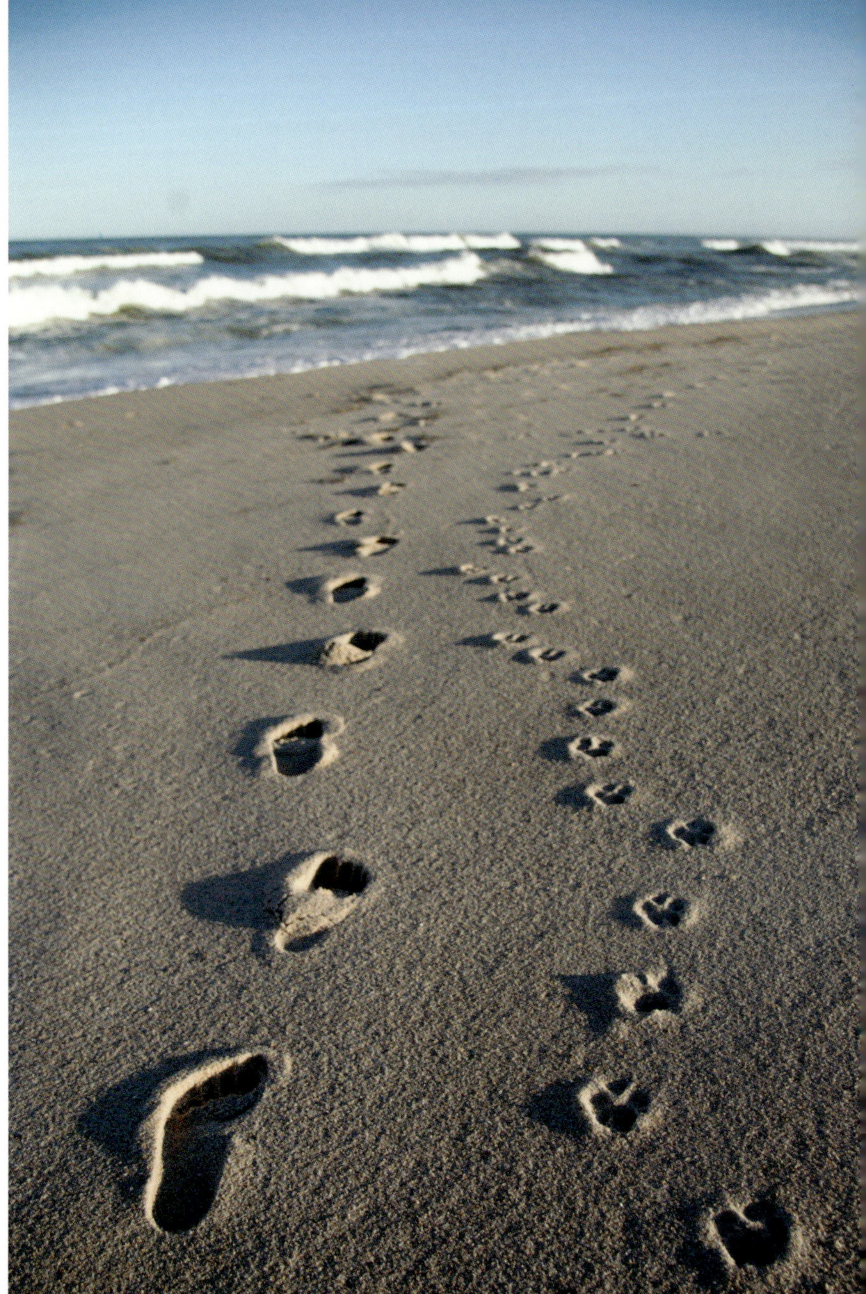

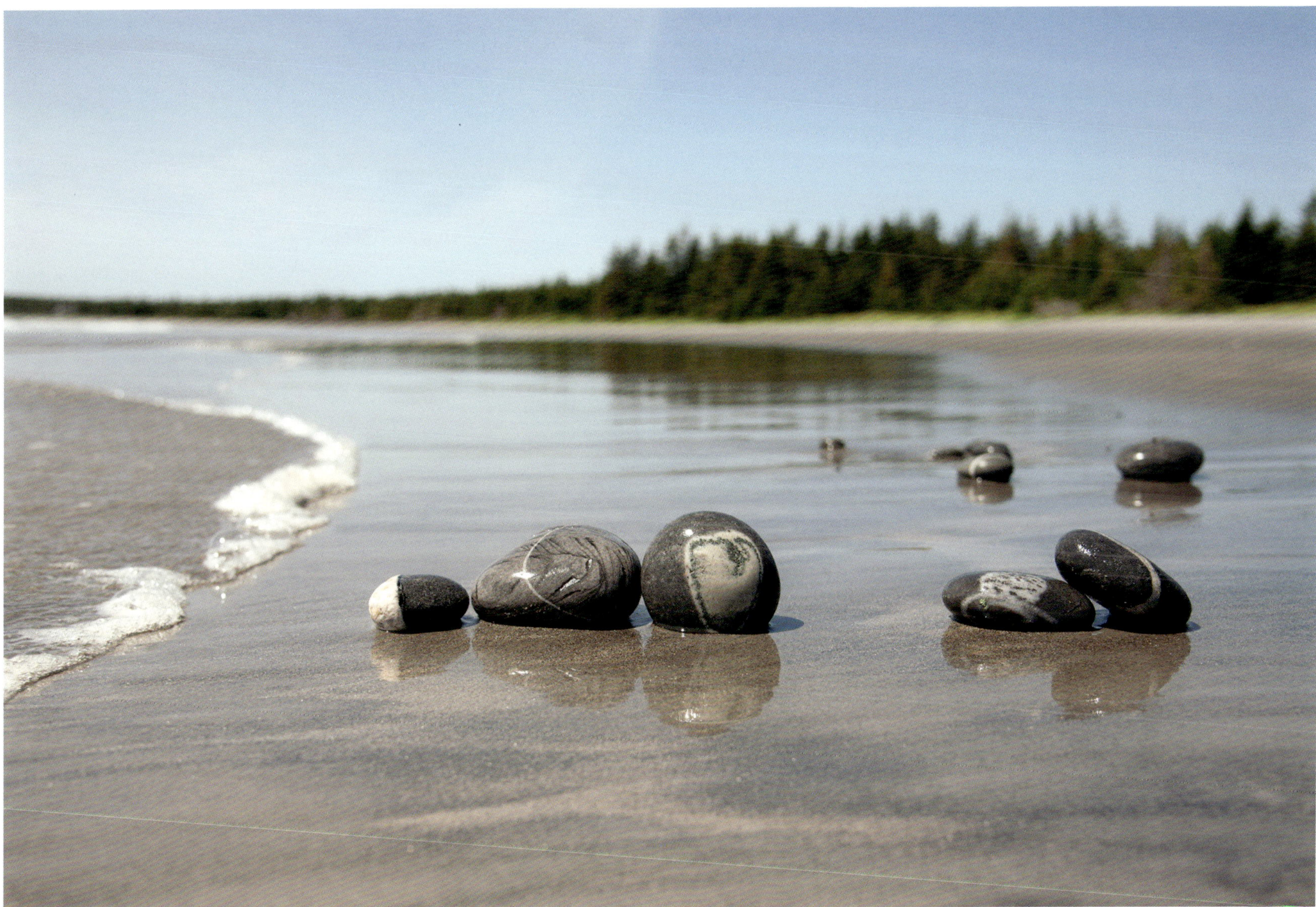

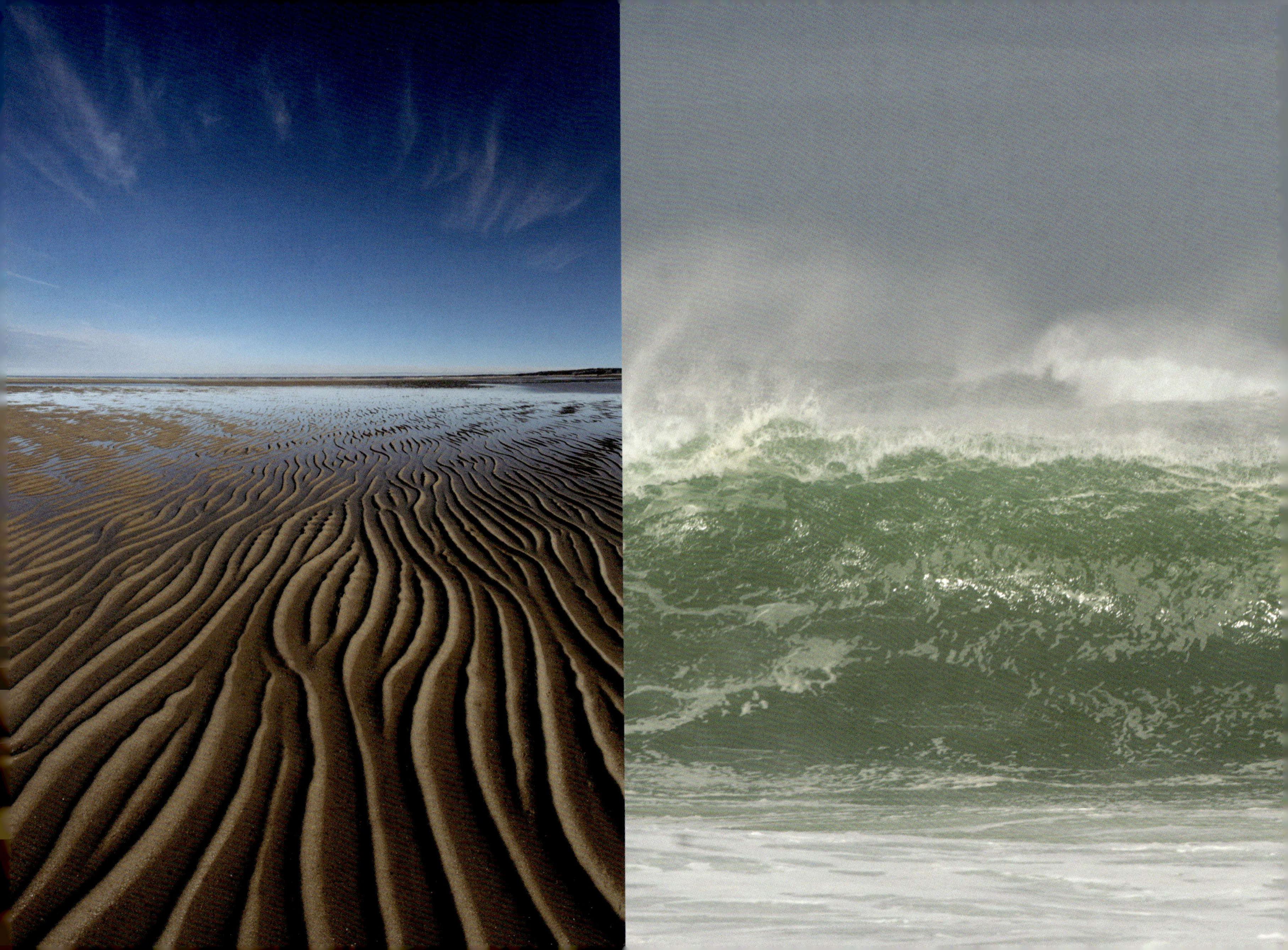

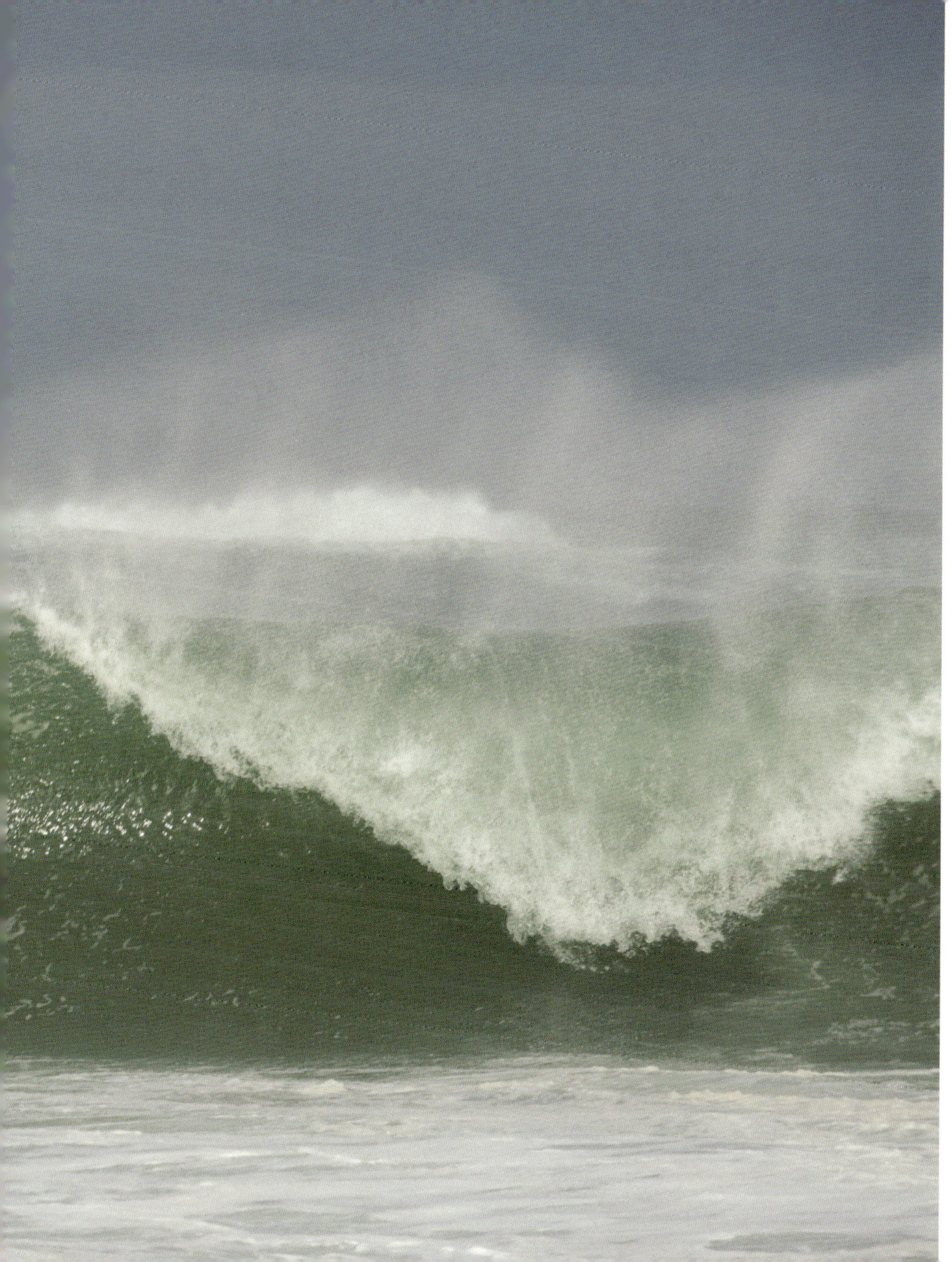

Sand and Sky

It is always a delight when the sky mimics the earth, or is it the opposite?

The Deep Green Sea

I have asked my kids a million times, "What color is the ocean?"

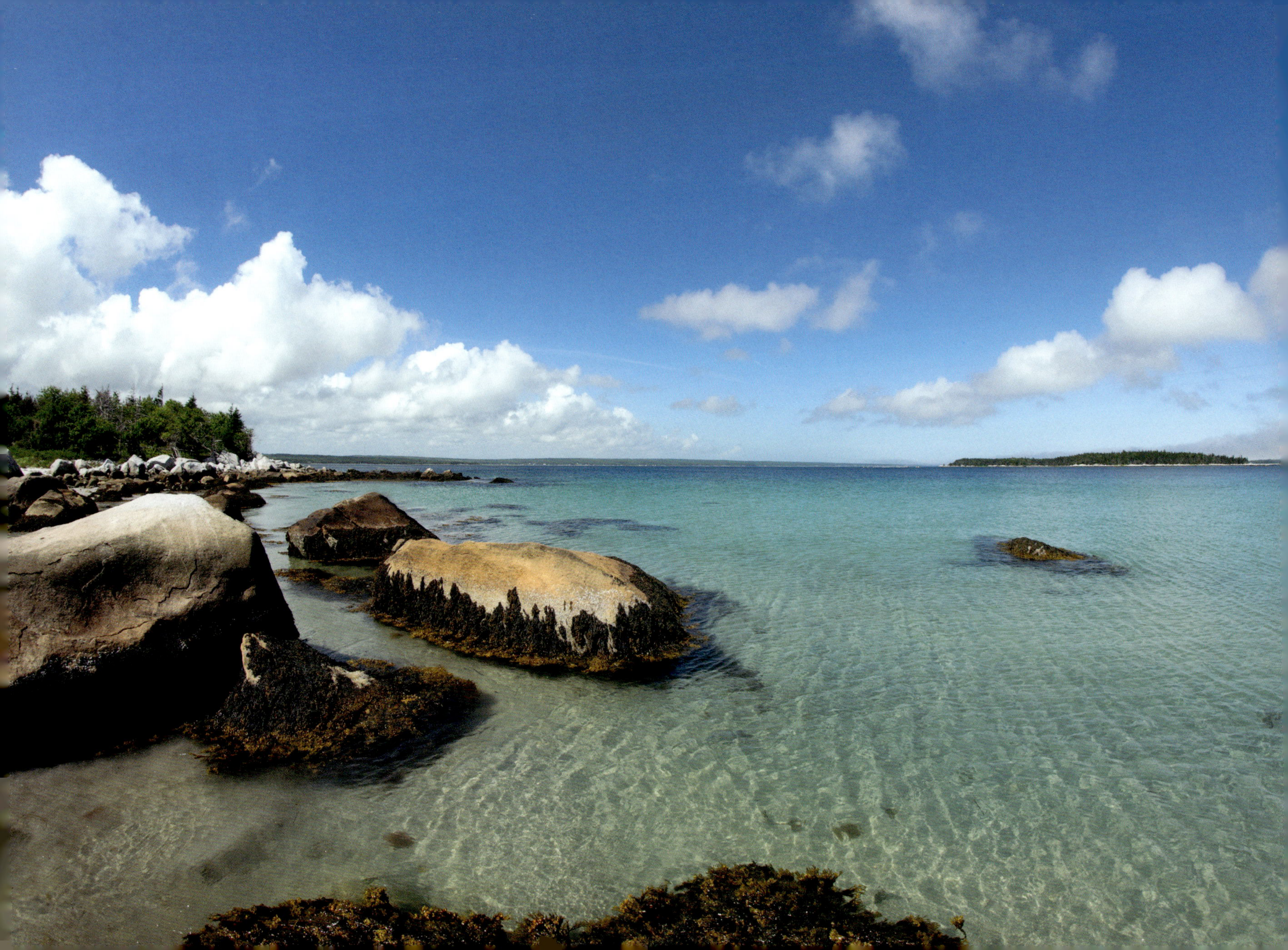

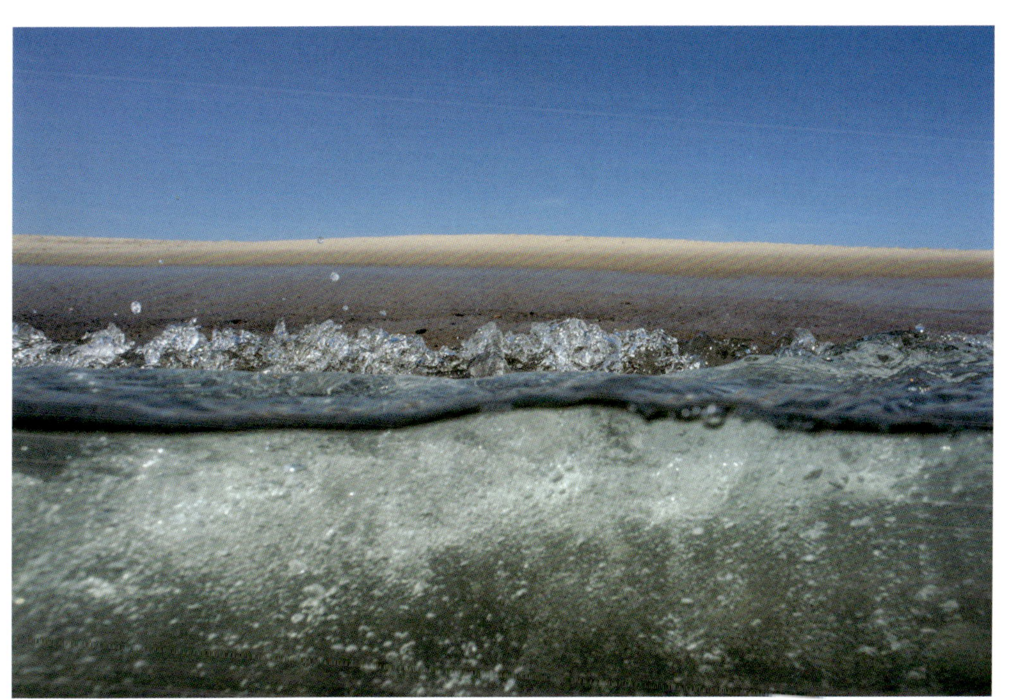

Canadian Tropics

This Nova Scotia beach has the clearest water I have ever seen, and the coldest I have ever felt.

Breaking Waves

As this wave charged the shore, its barrel was captured half below and half above the water, exposing the underwater turbulence. The wave below the surface is similar to what we see on top.

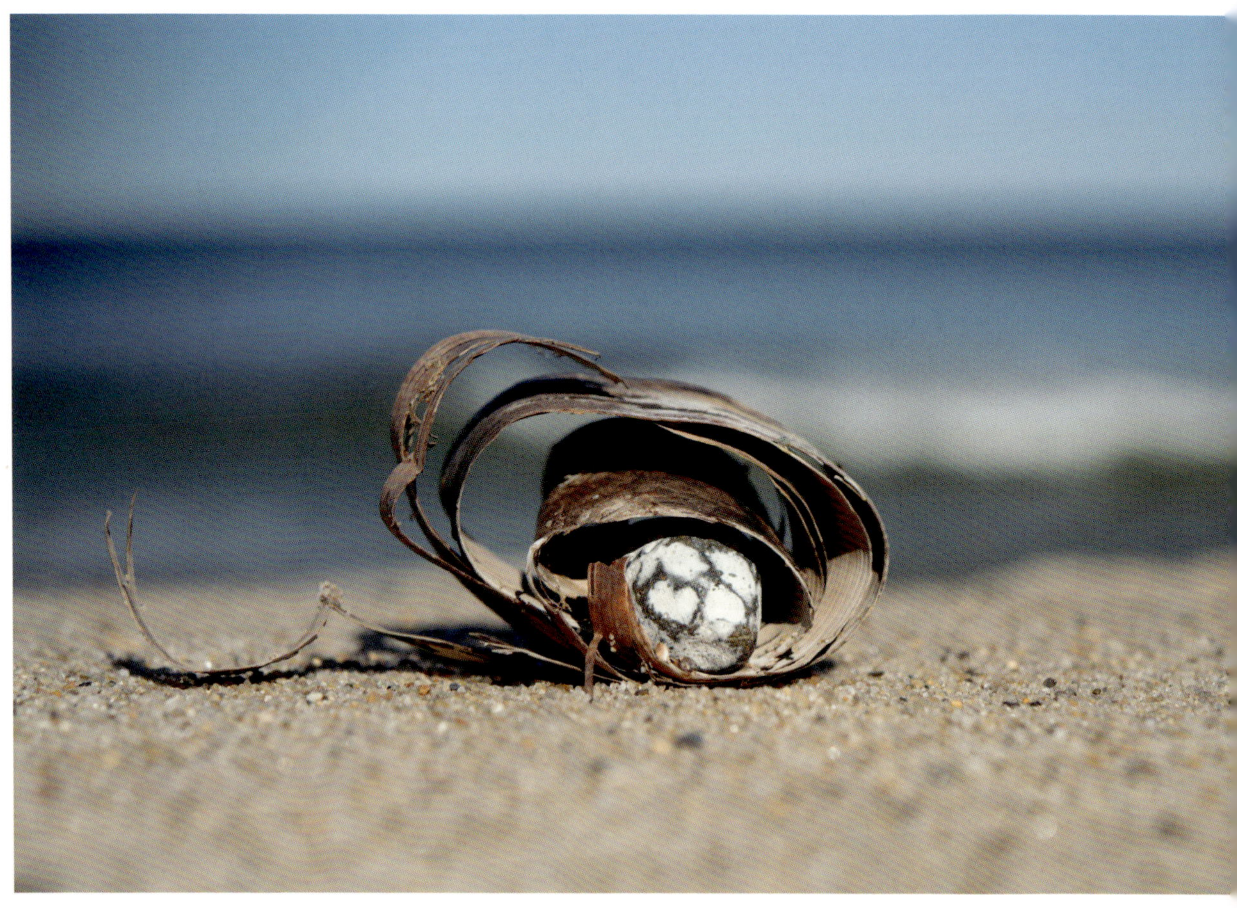

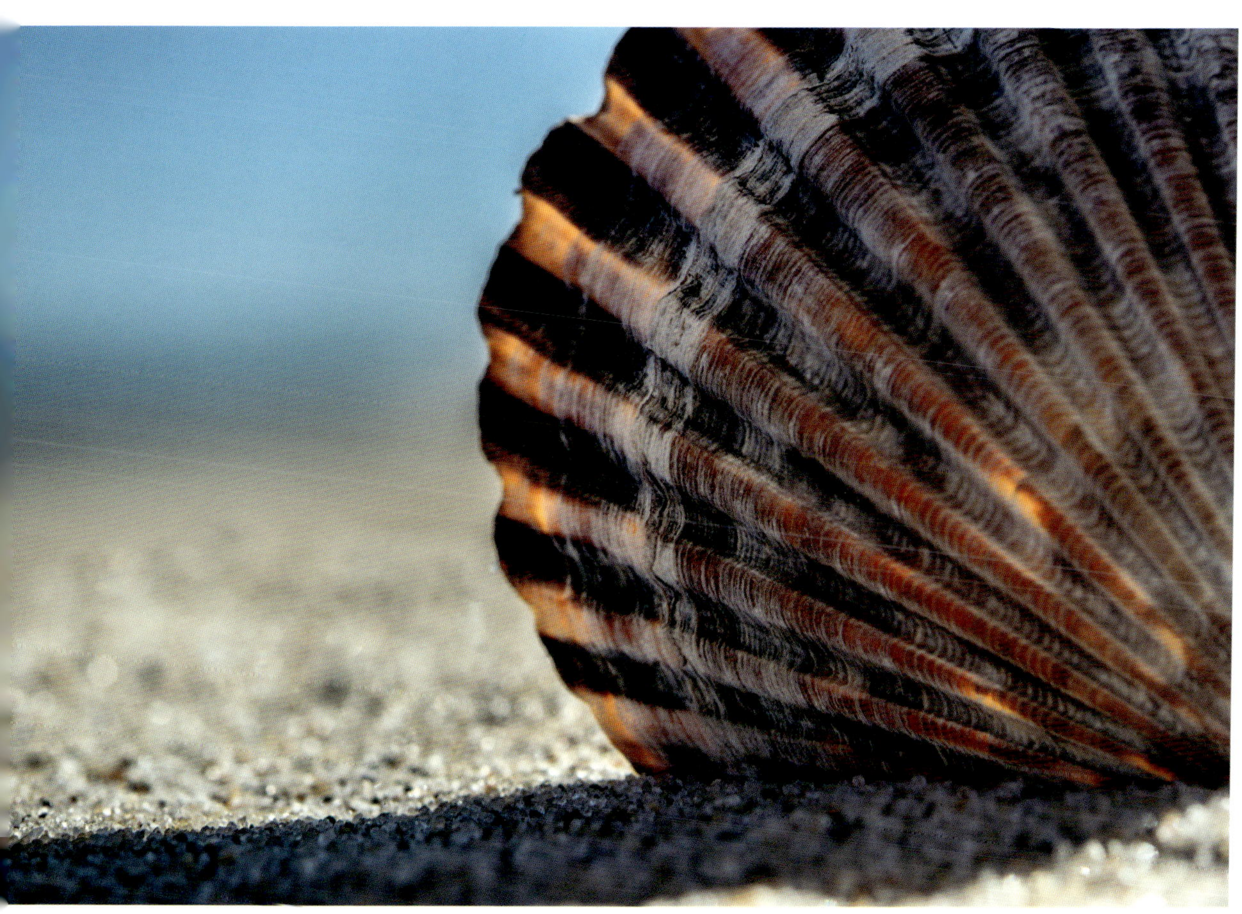

Treasures

This scallop shell looked monochromatic until I held it up to the sunlight.

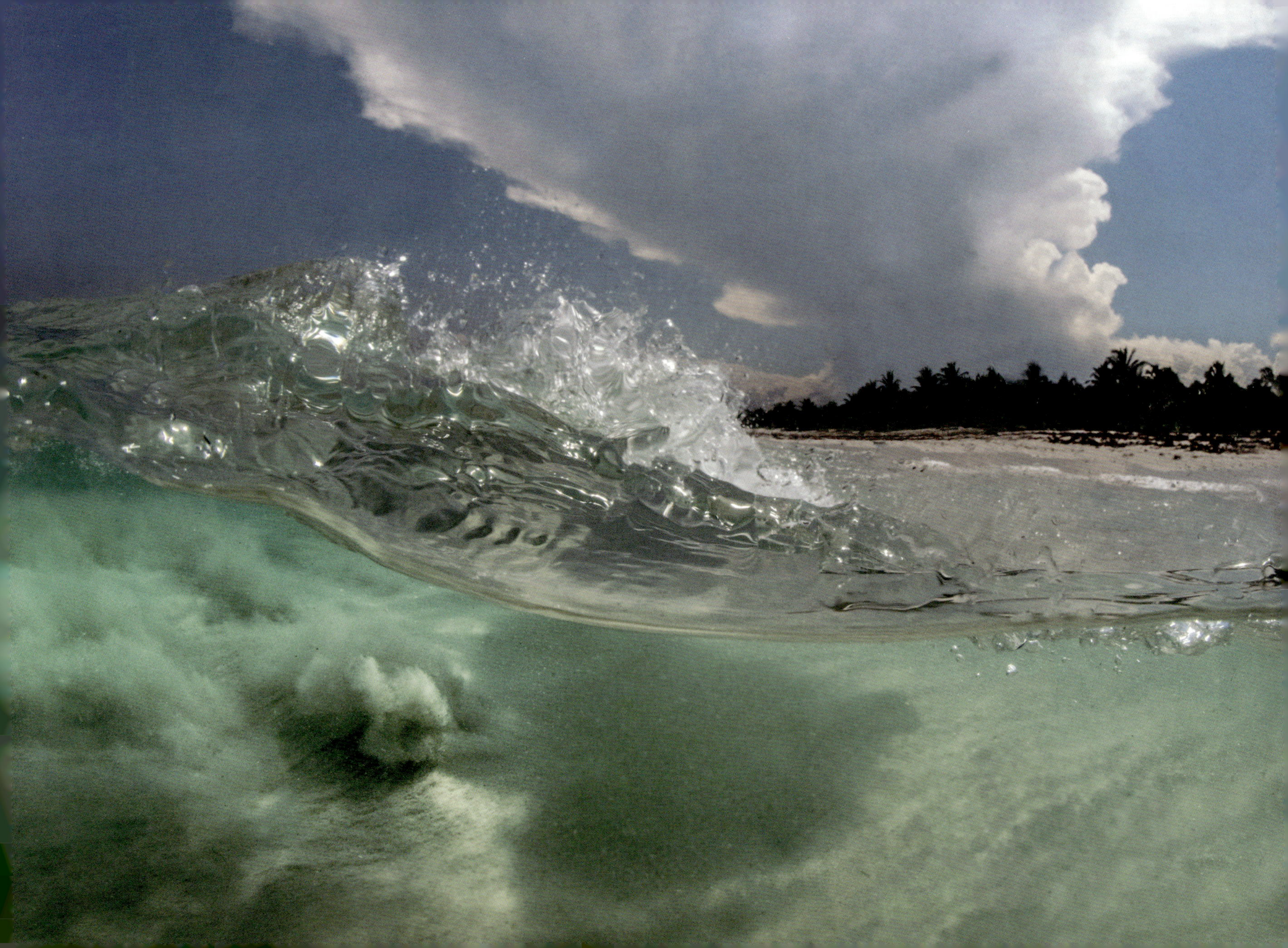

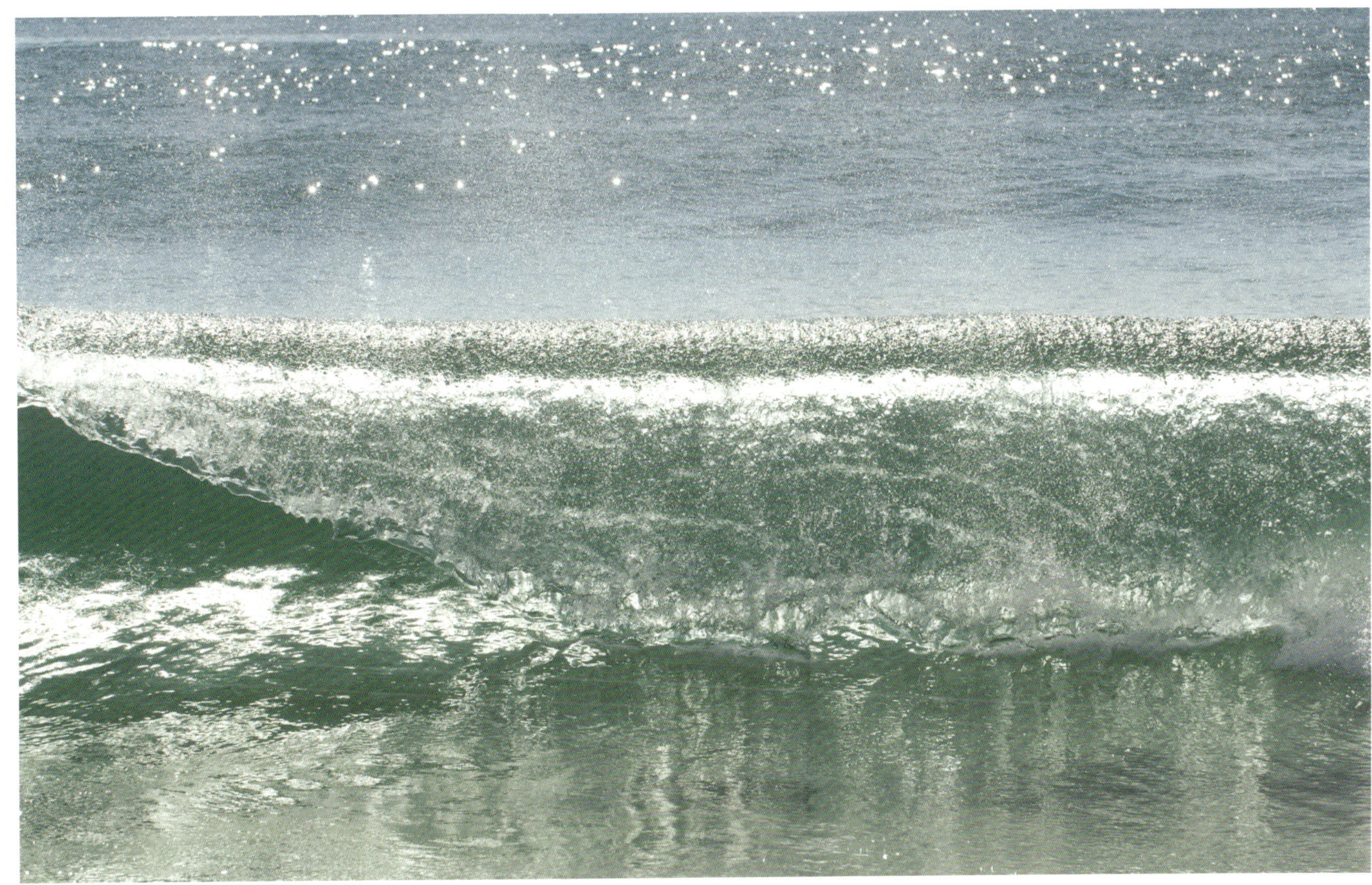

Storm on the Way

This storm came fast—under, on, and over the water.

Frosted-Glass Wave

Shooting straight into the morning light creates a shimmering effect.

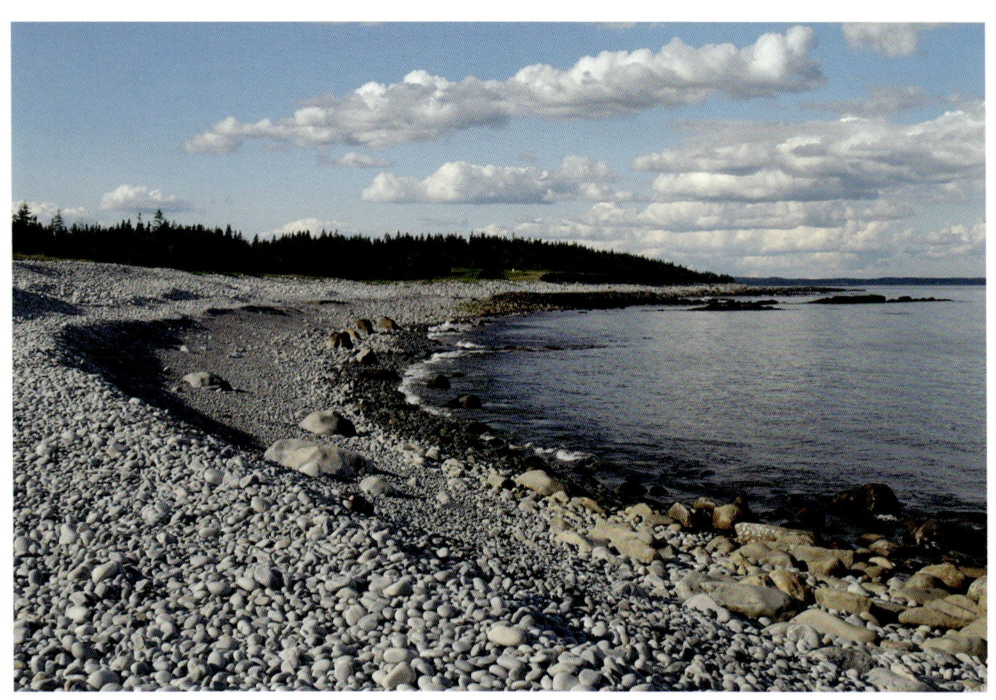

Rockhounds' Delight

This Canadian beach is one of my favorite places to find and photograph rocks. We build forts out of driftwood and anything else that washed ashore. Then we used driftwood for furniture and buoys for decorations, fully aware of their impermanence.

Sunrise

An ebbing wave catches the day's first light just right.

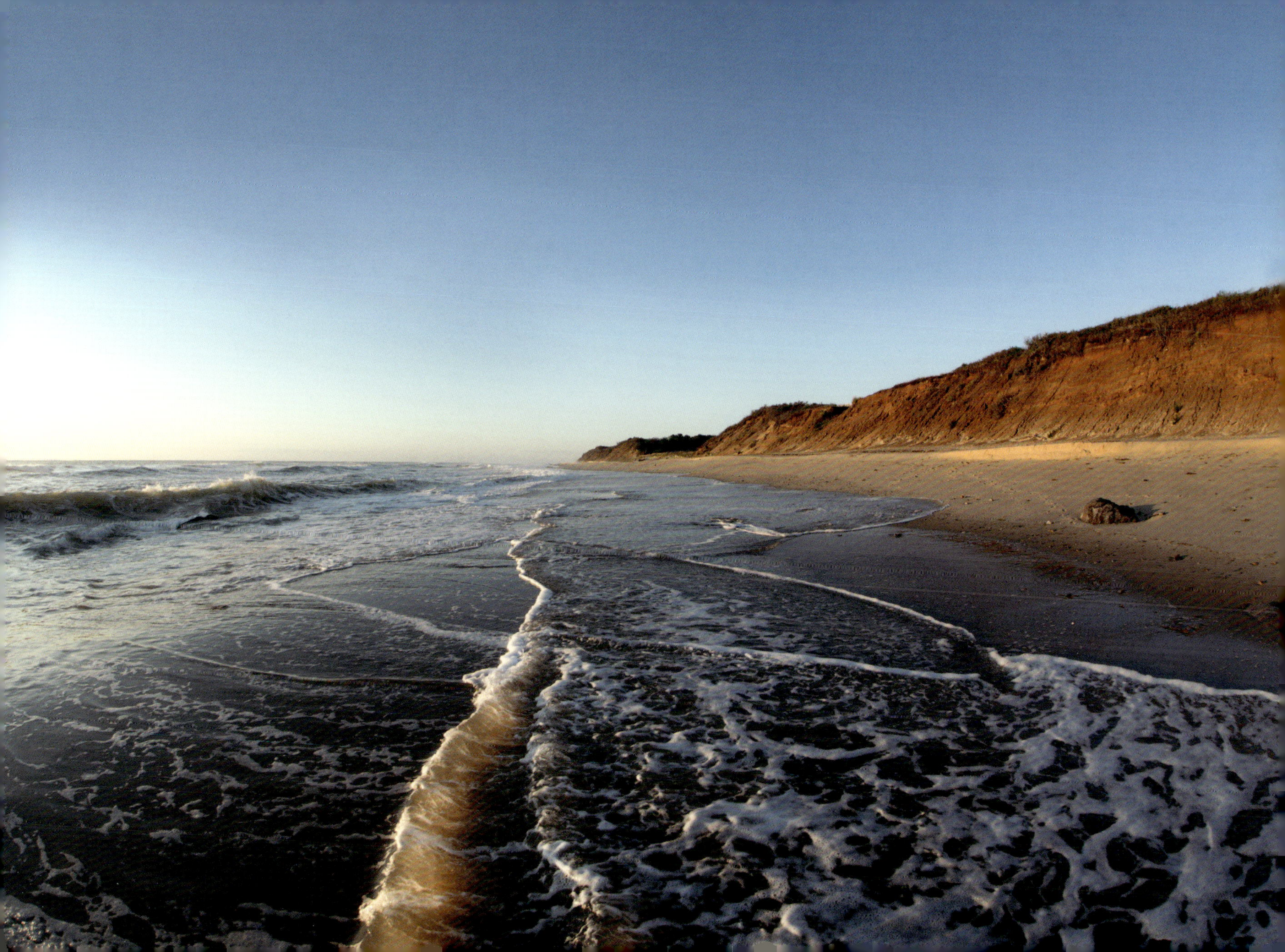

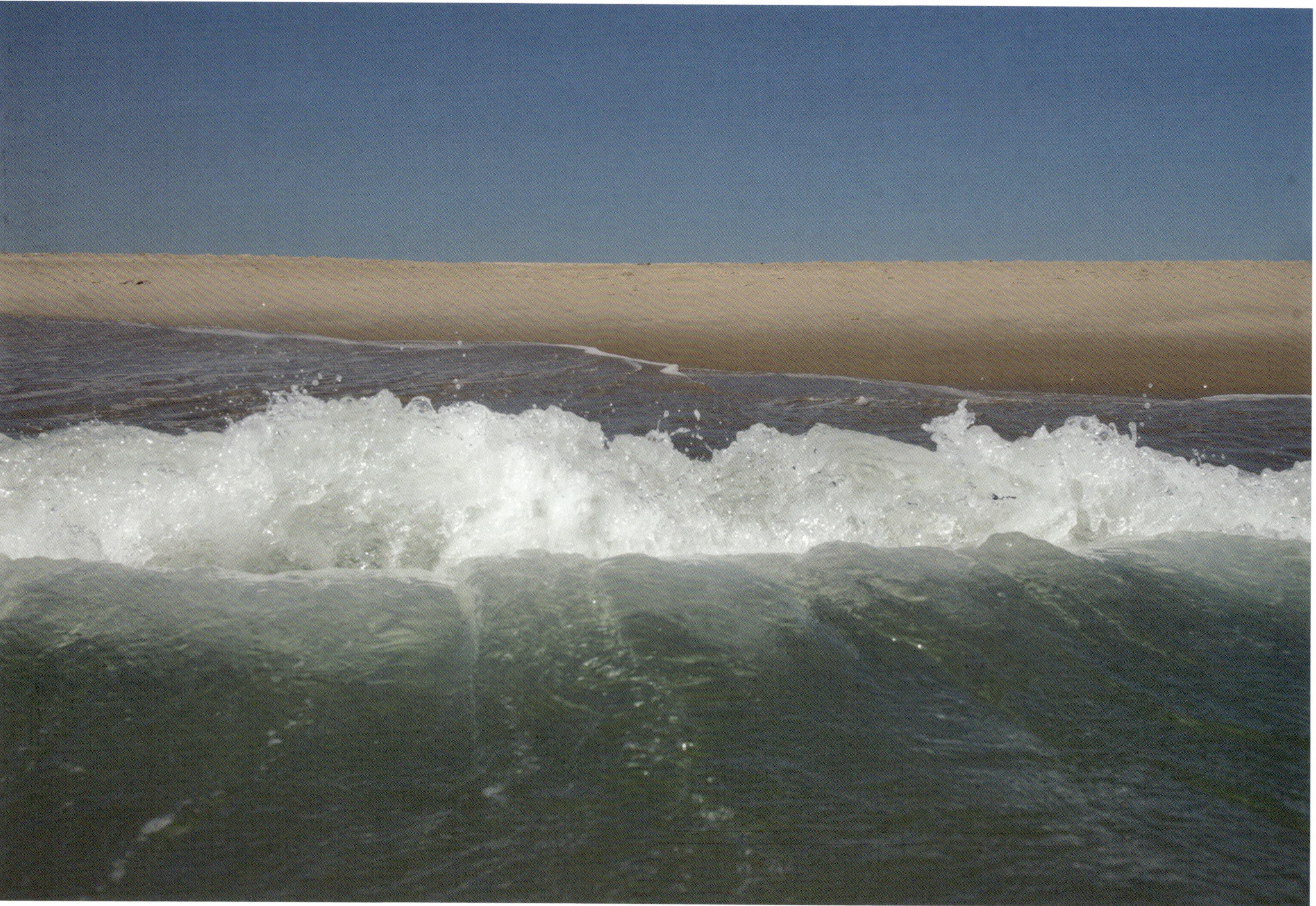

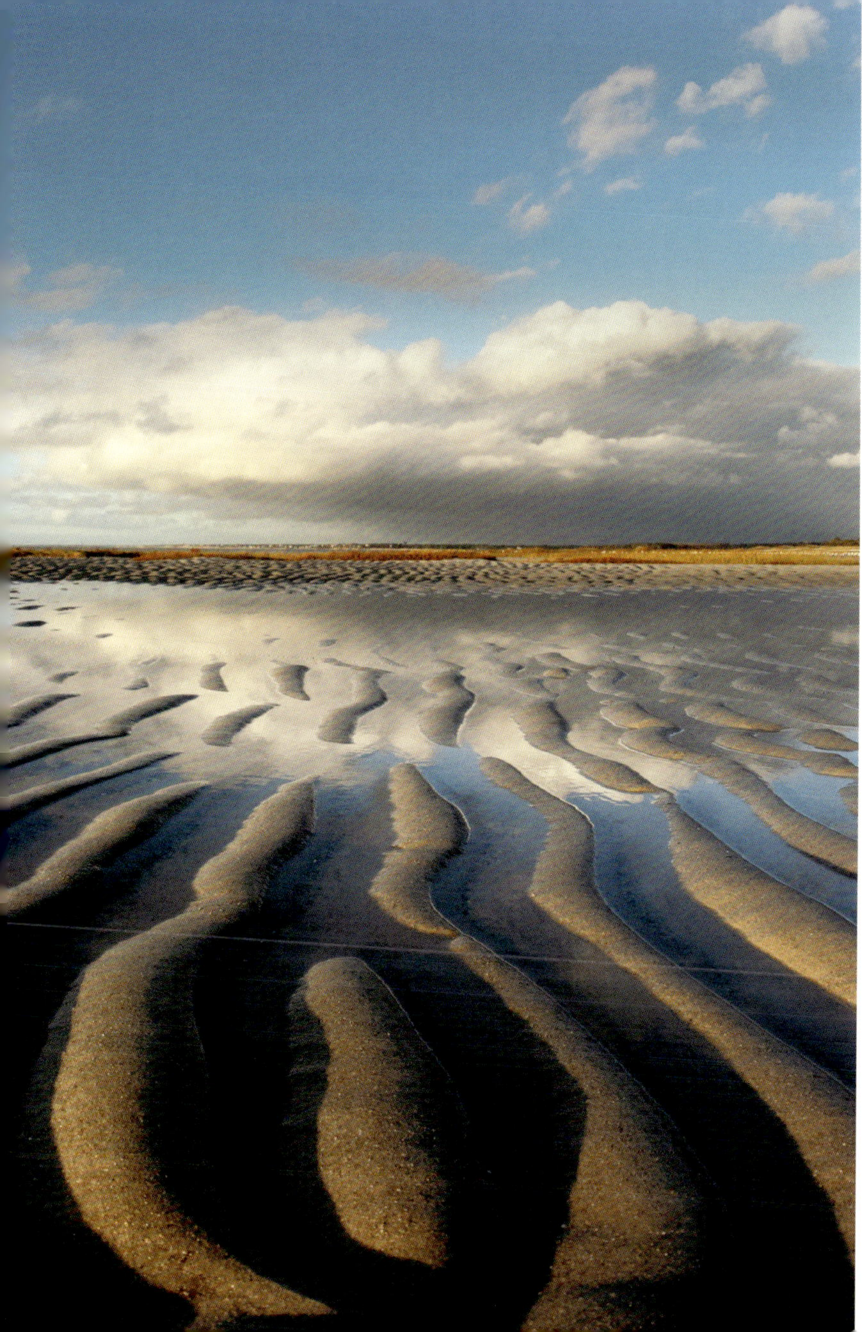

Final Destination

A wave's-eye view as it rolls to shore

Sandy Fingers

Undulating strips of sand and water create an abstract collage.

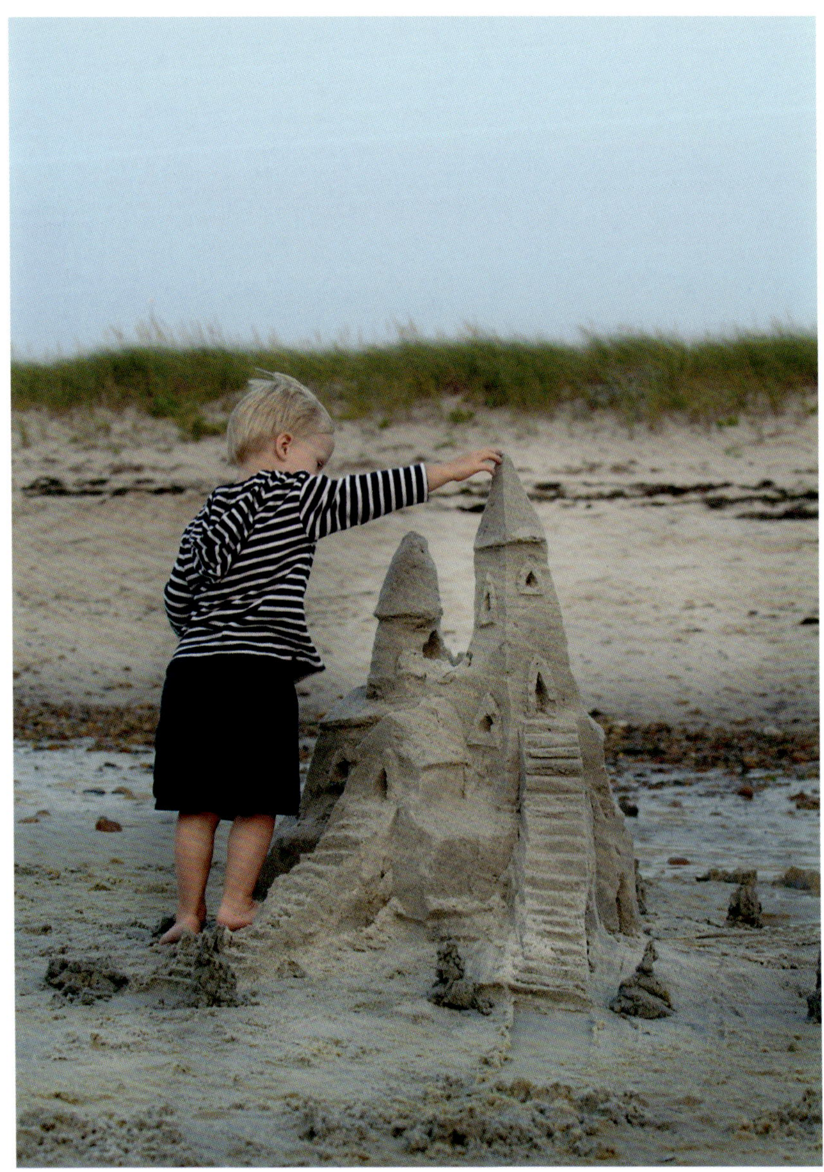

Magical Castle

A child's discovery at the end of the day

Ready to Go

A gorgeous evening for surfing on Cape Cod

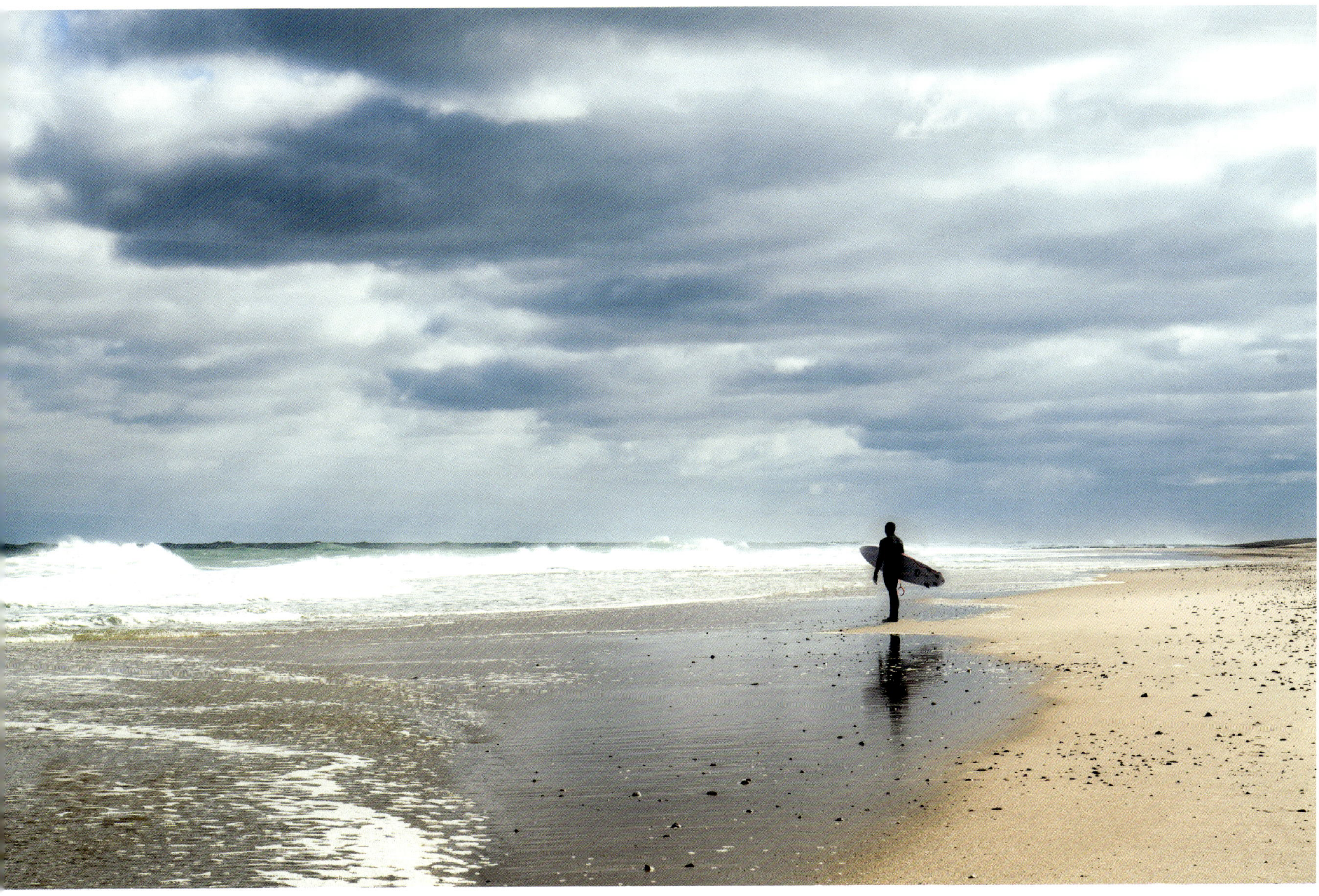

Take a Seat

Beach, bench, and boardwalk under the summer sun

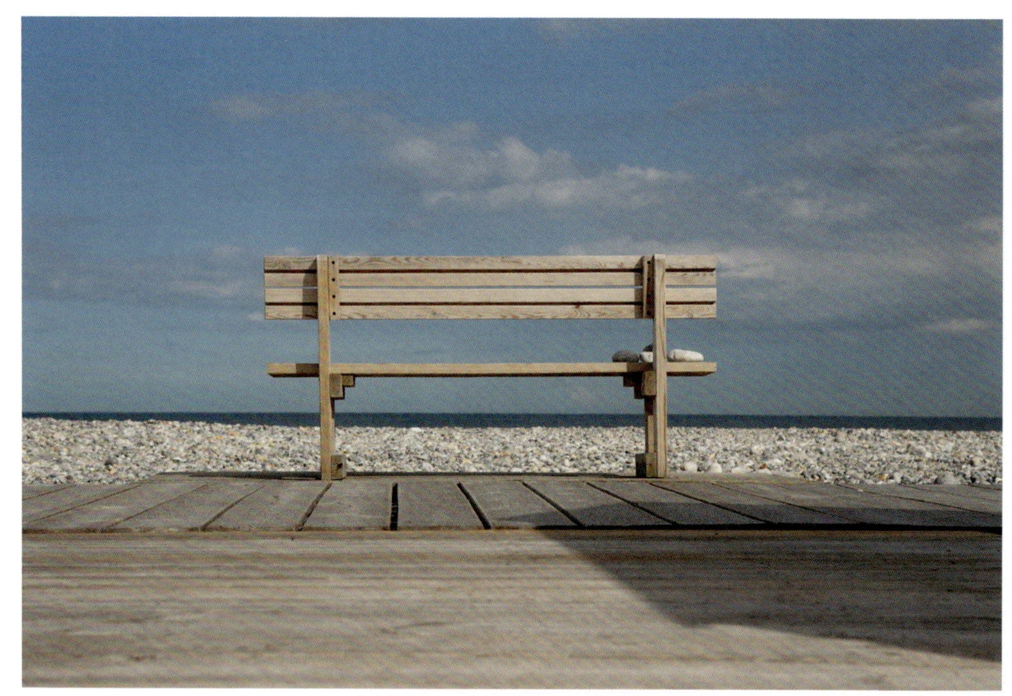

French Poppies

We visited France in June, when the poppies were in full bloom. Many of the poppy fields had paths into the center where you could stand in the middle of acres of vibrant blossoms. Just as phenomenal was the sight of bright-red poppies against the blue sea.

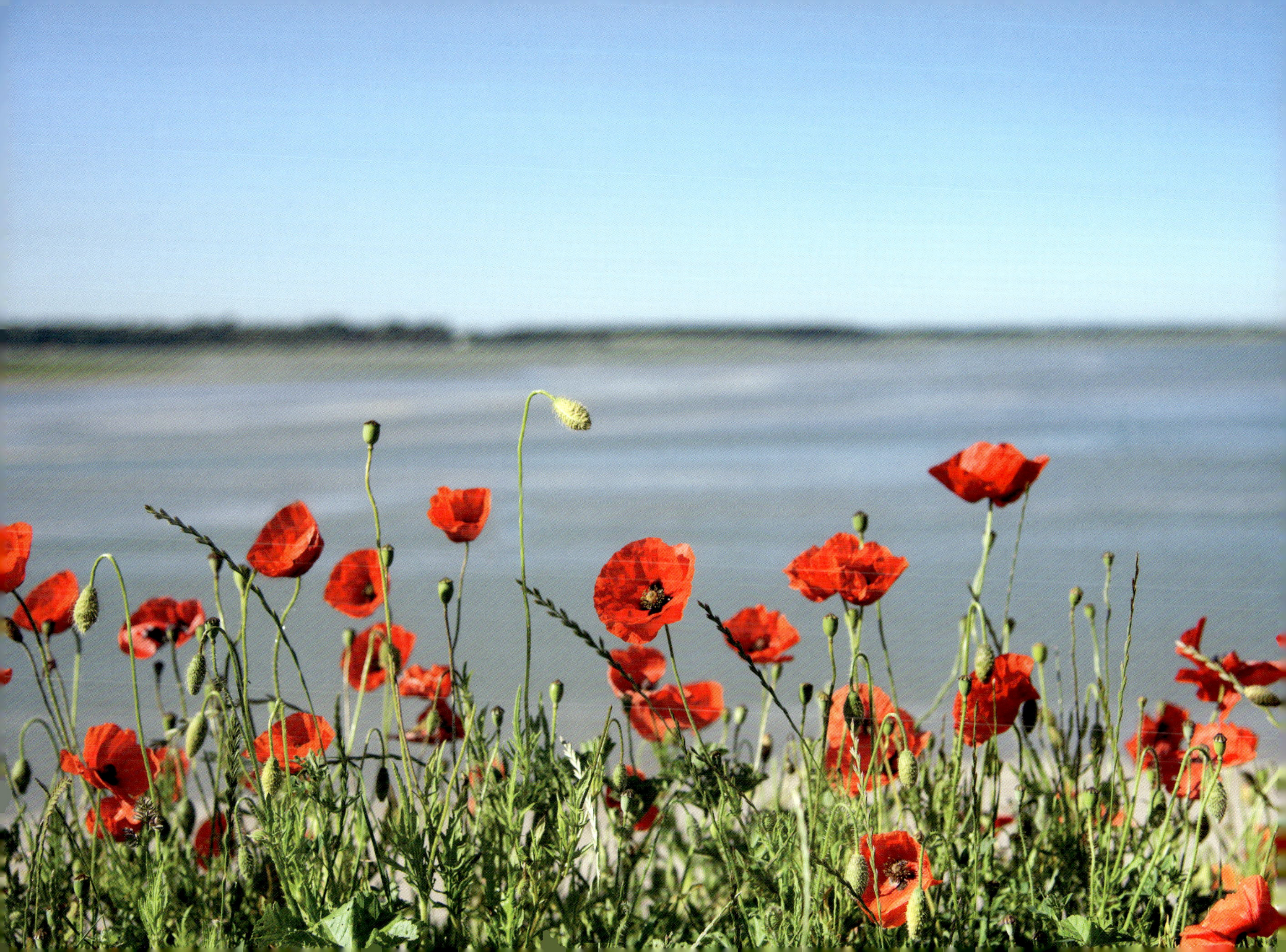

Morning Glory

Morning light gives frothy waves a chartreuse glow.

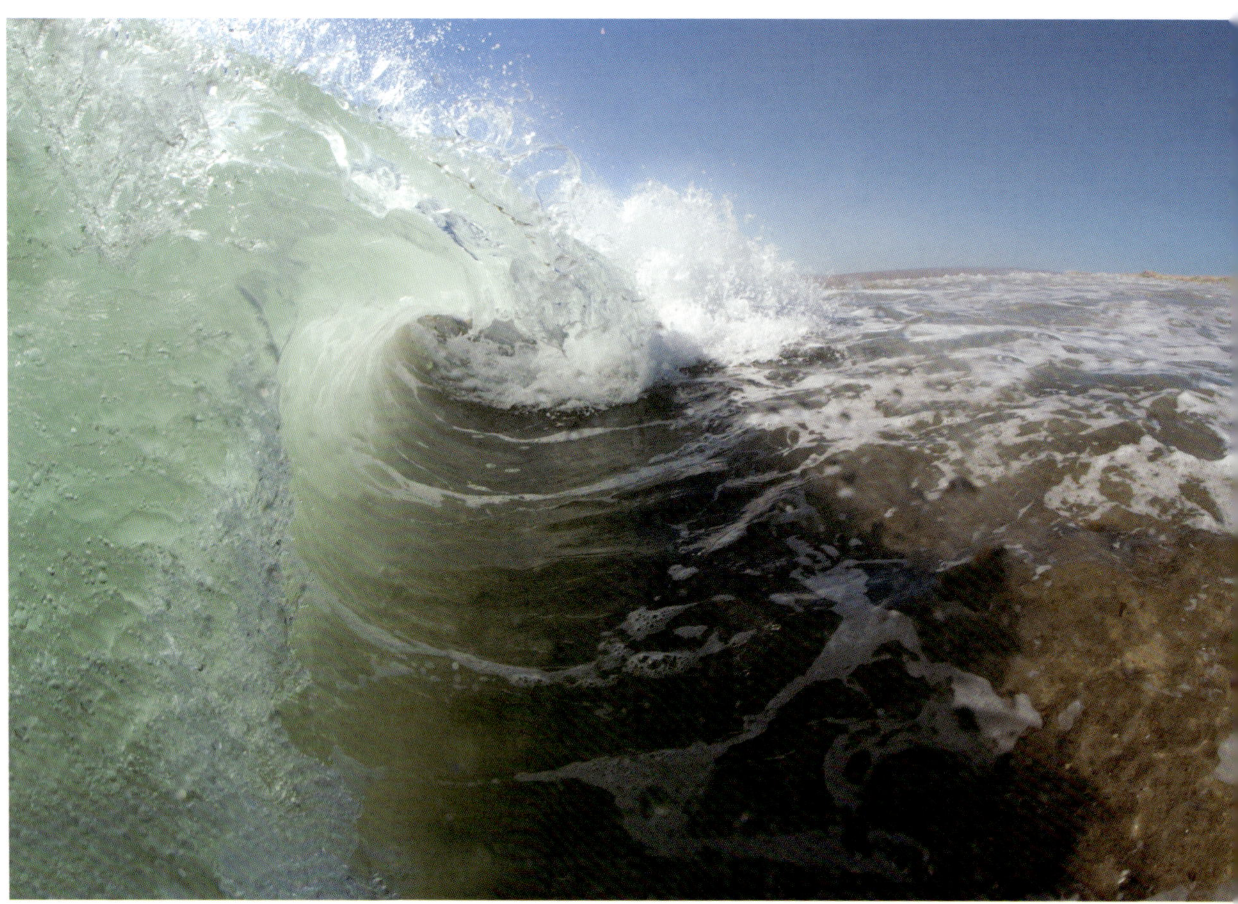

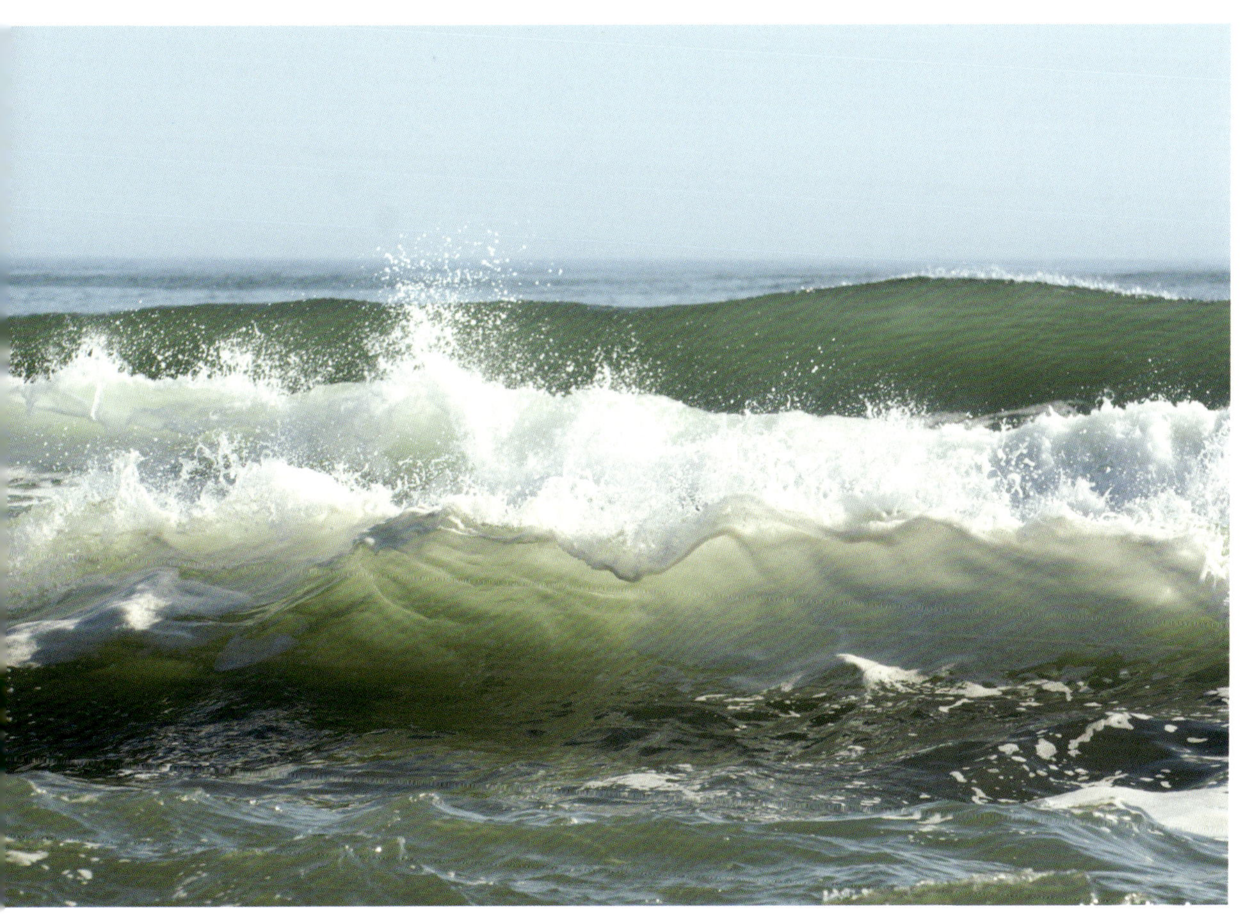

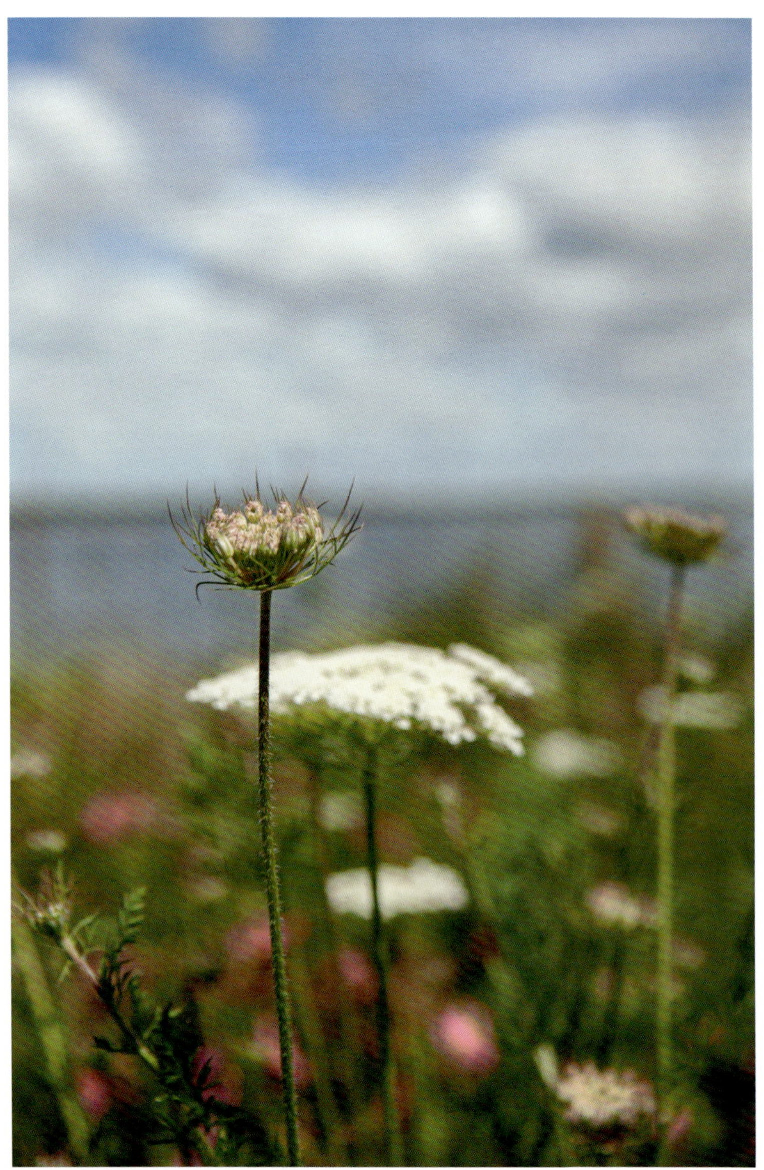

Canadian Queen

Queen Anne's lace unfolds along the shoreline.

Reflective

A stunning moment to pause and reflect

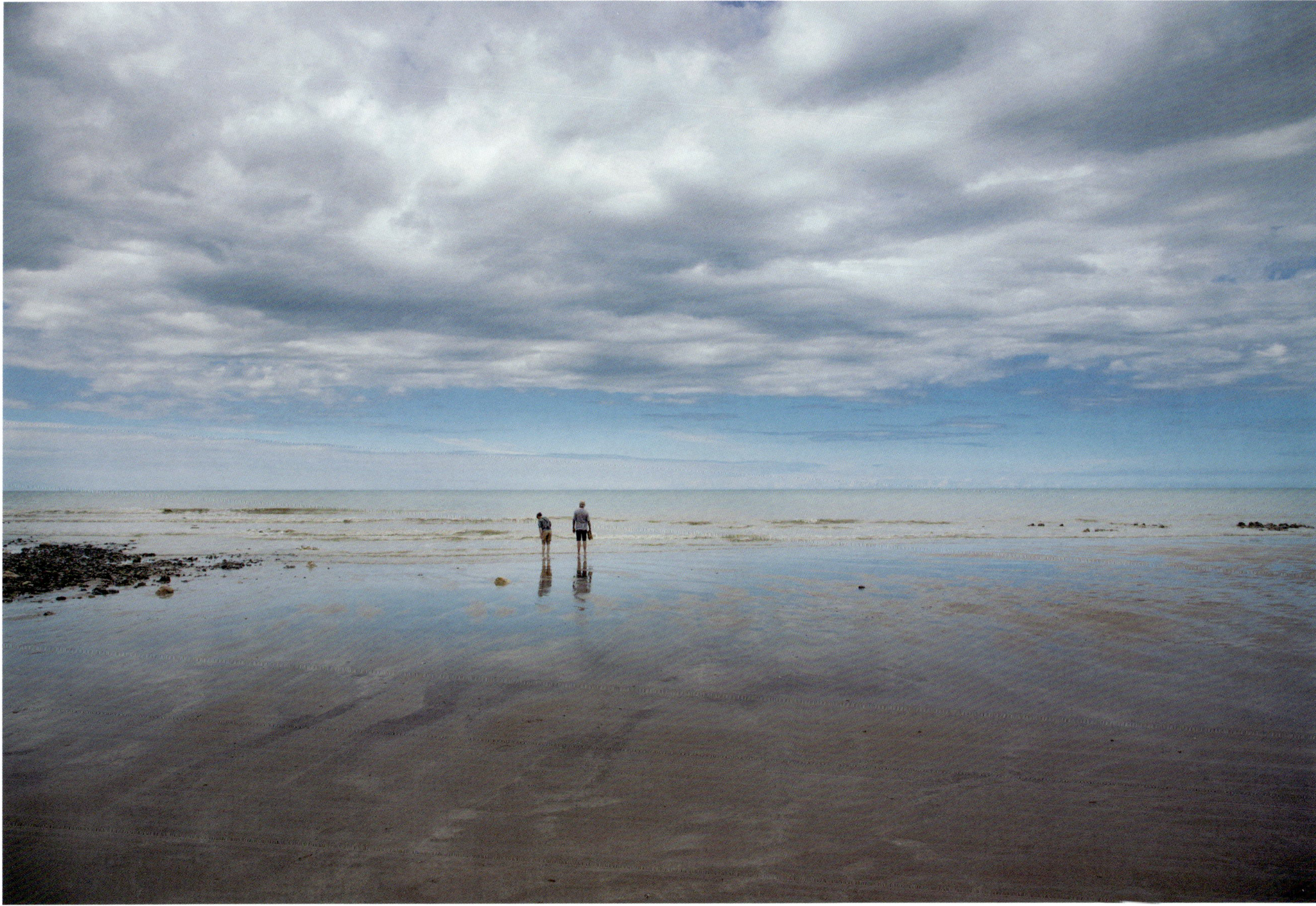

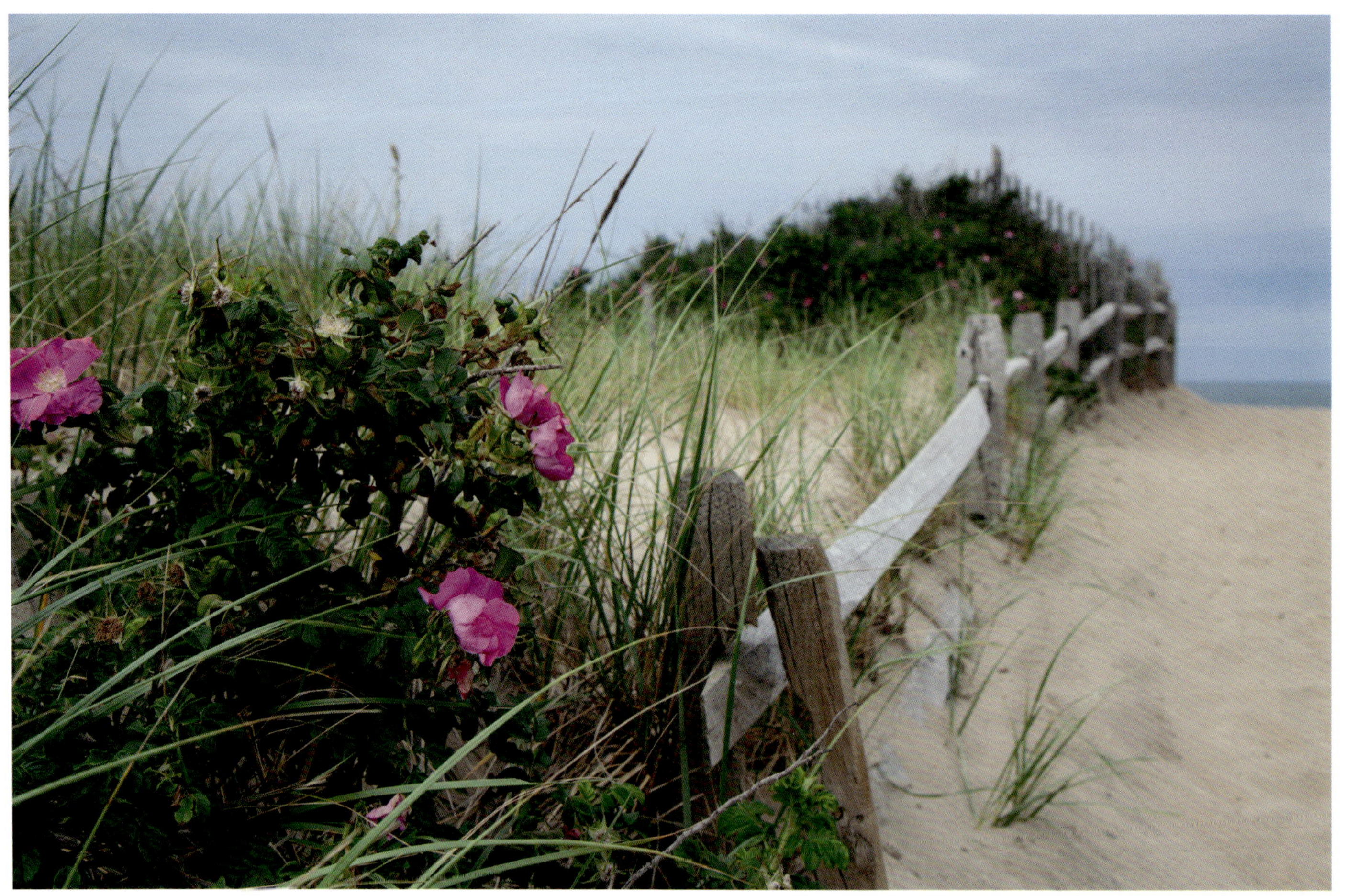

Beach Roses

Beach roses in bloom will soon yield rose hips for jam.

The Beaten Path

A concentration of footprints form a path. It's not the most direct path to the sea, but it's the most inviting.

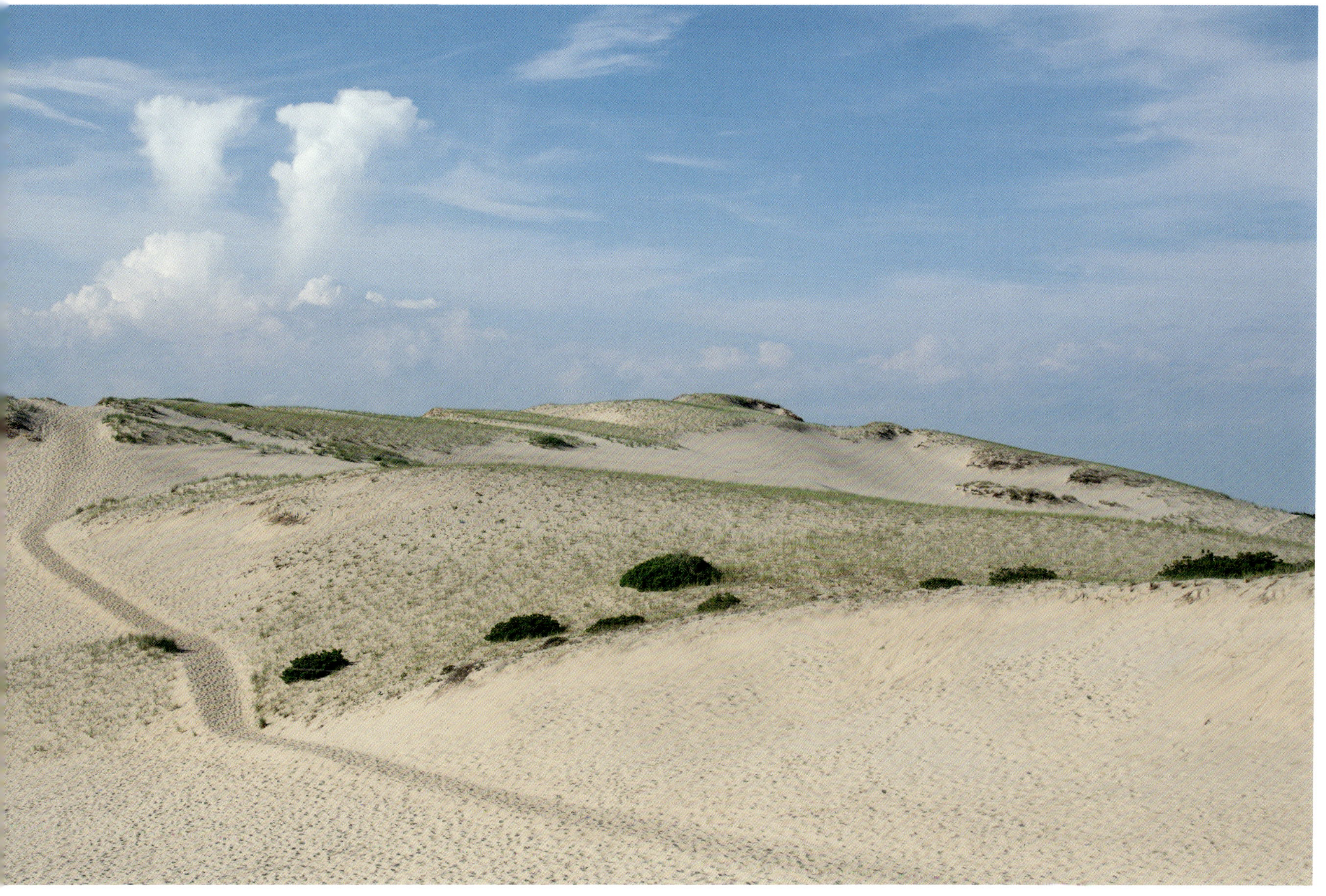

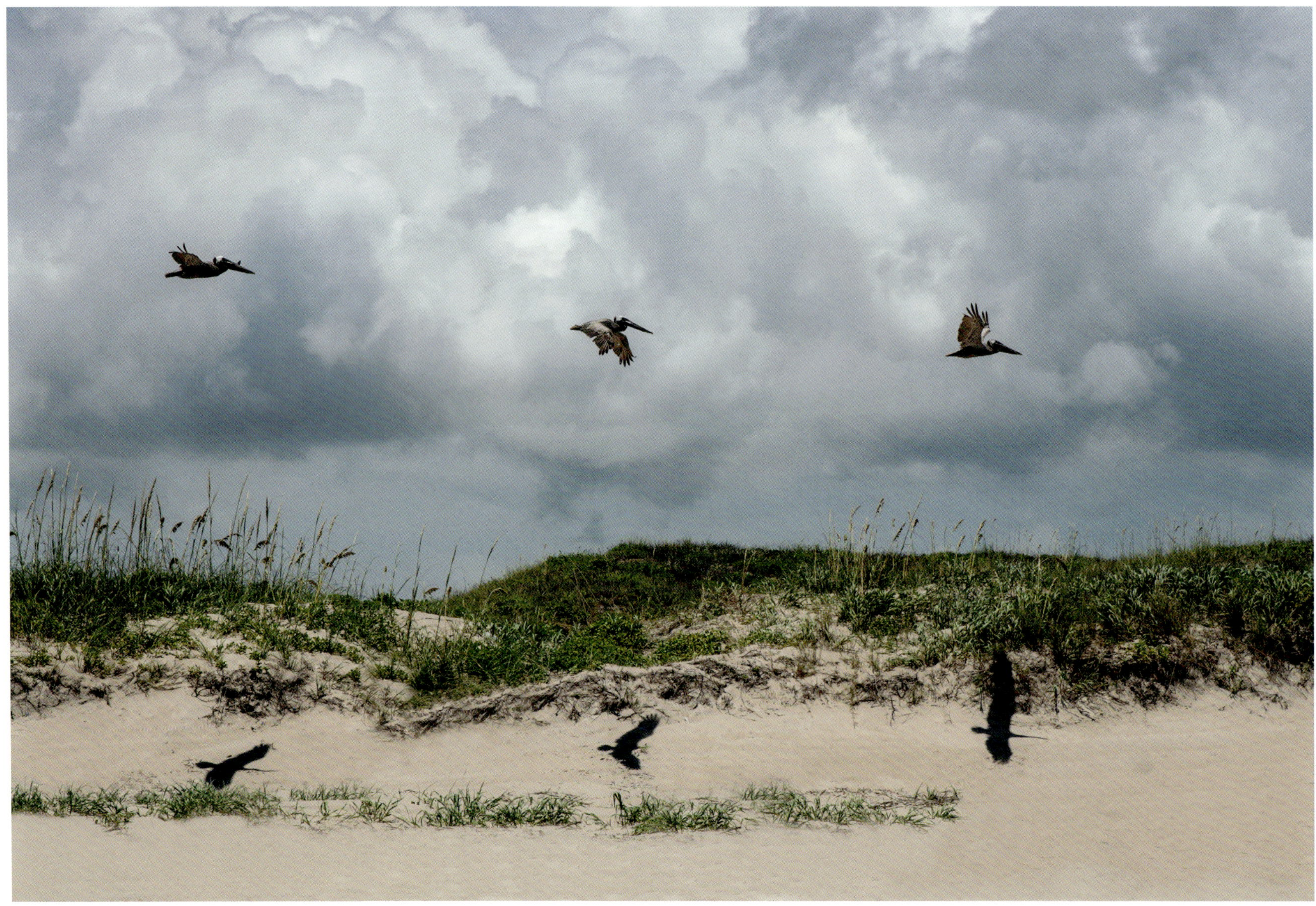

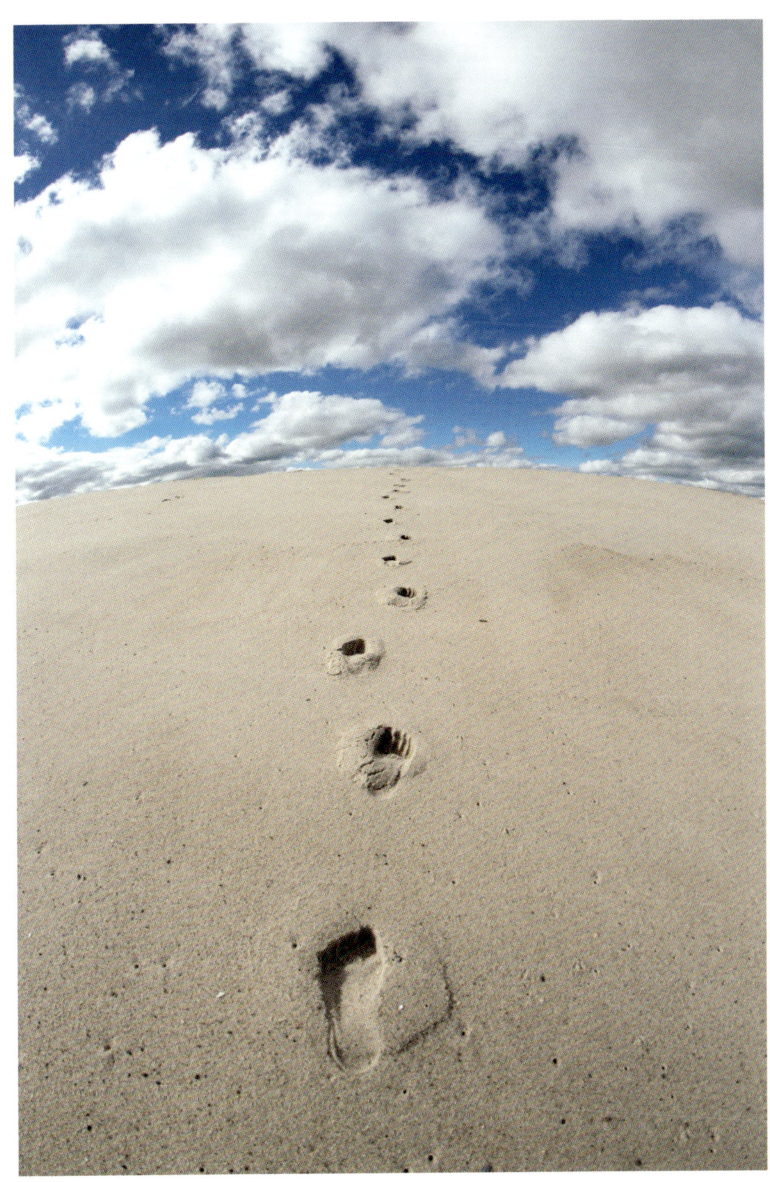

Flight Shadows

Shadows flit by as quickly as the birds.

Footprints

Robinson Crusoe and Friday come to mind.

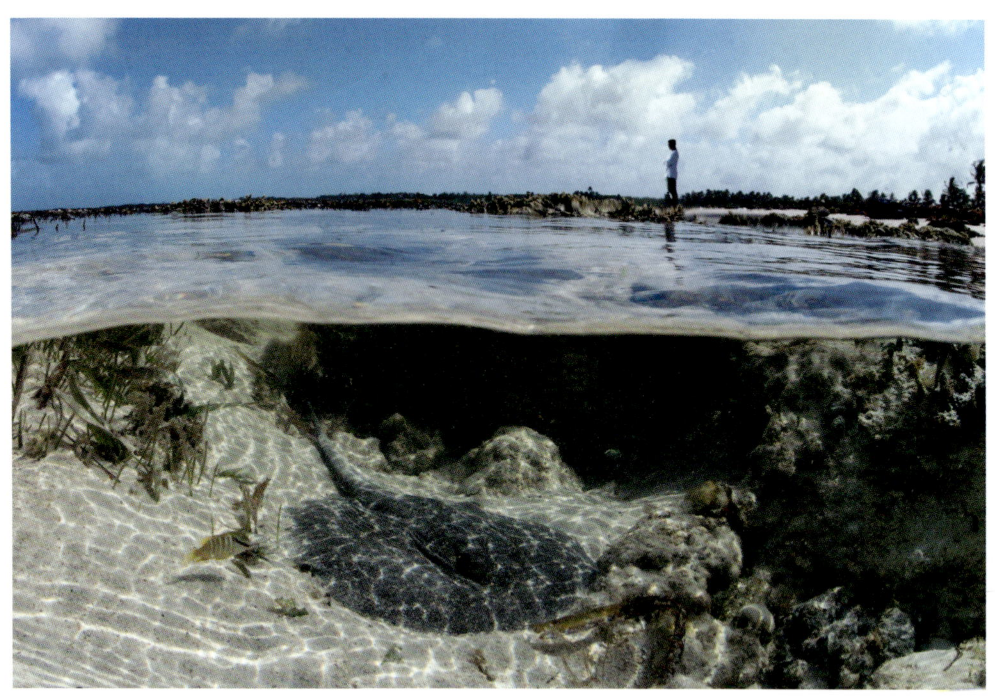

Face-Off

A sea ray came out of nowhere, almost camouflaged in the dappled sunlight.

Juneteenth

So much to ponder on this day. The evening sunset brought solace.

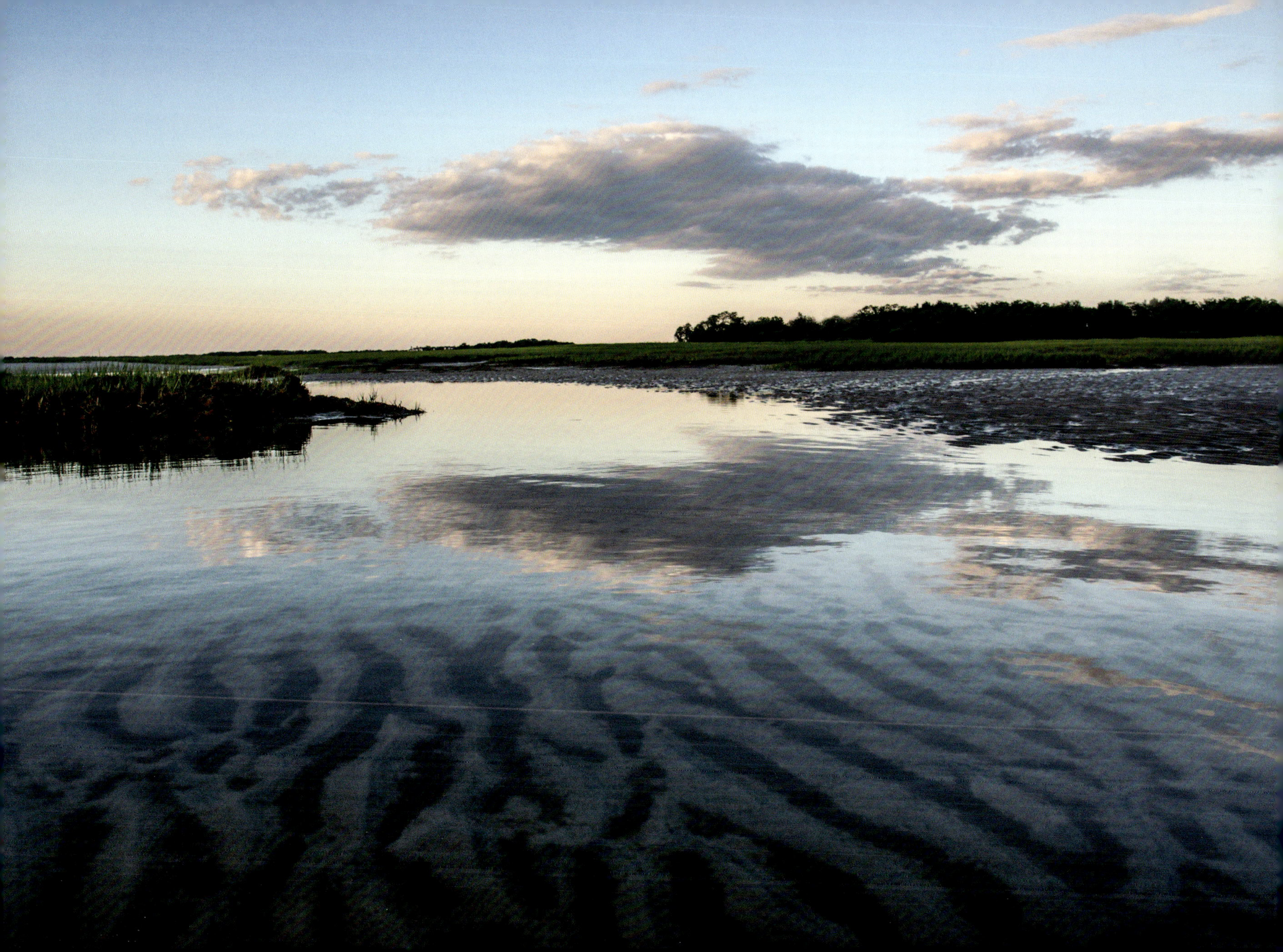

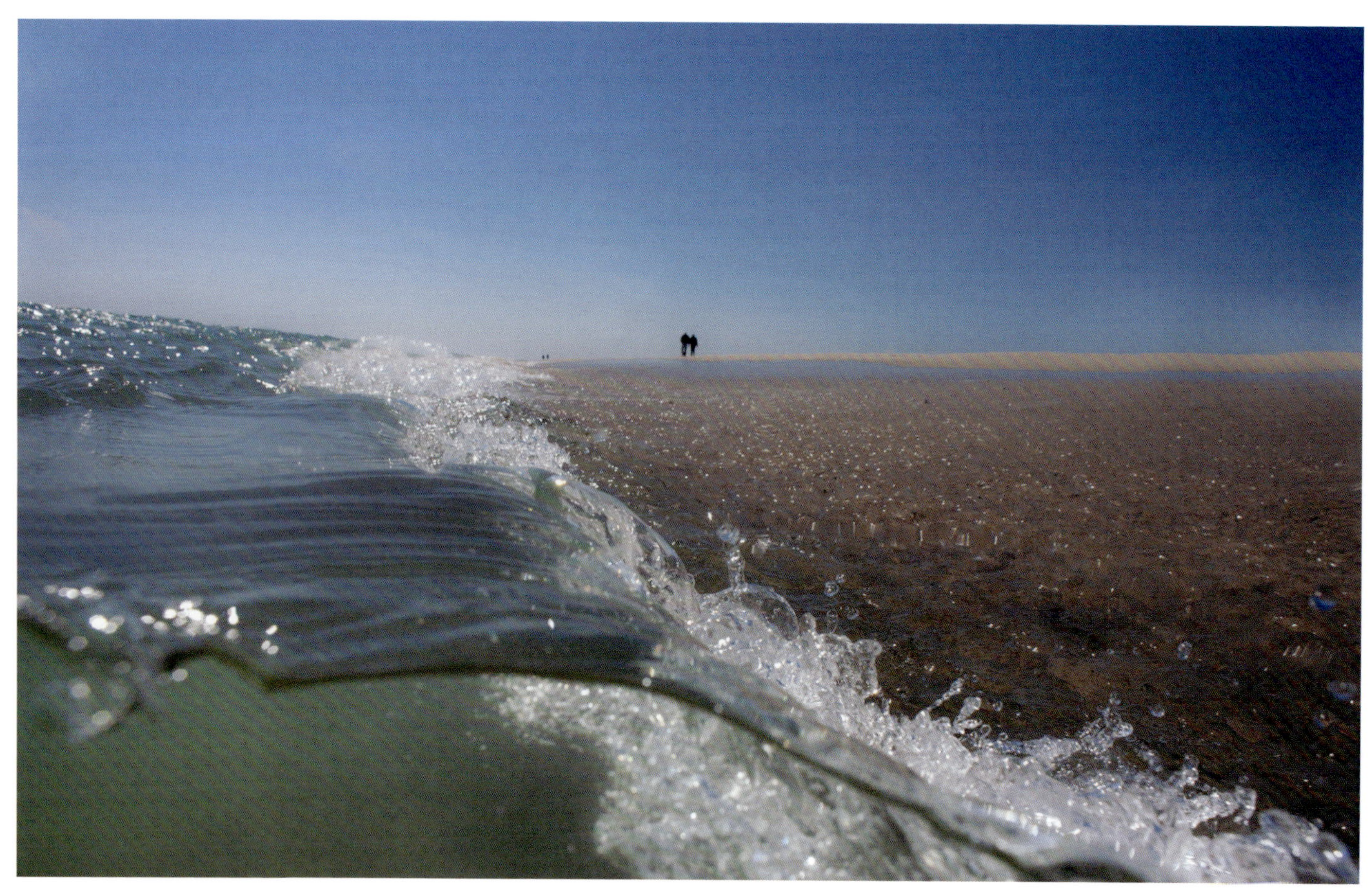

Solitude

Sometimes a walk on the beach fixes everything.

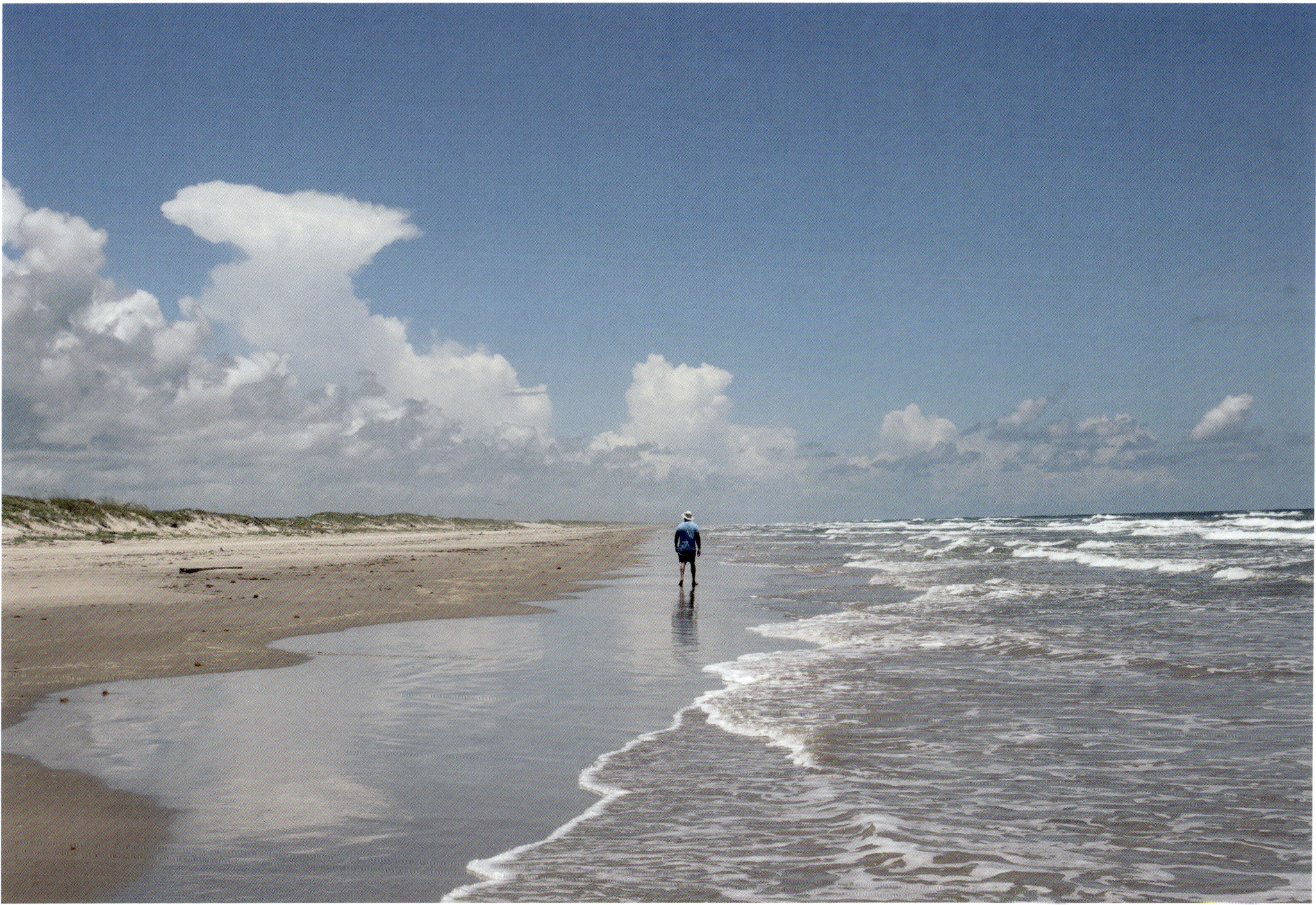

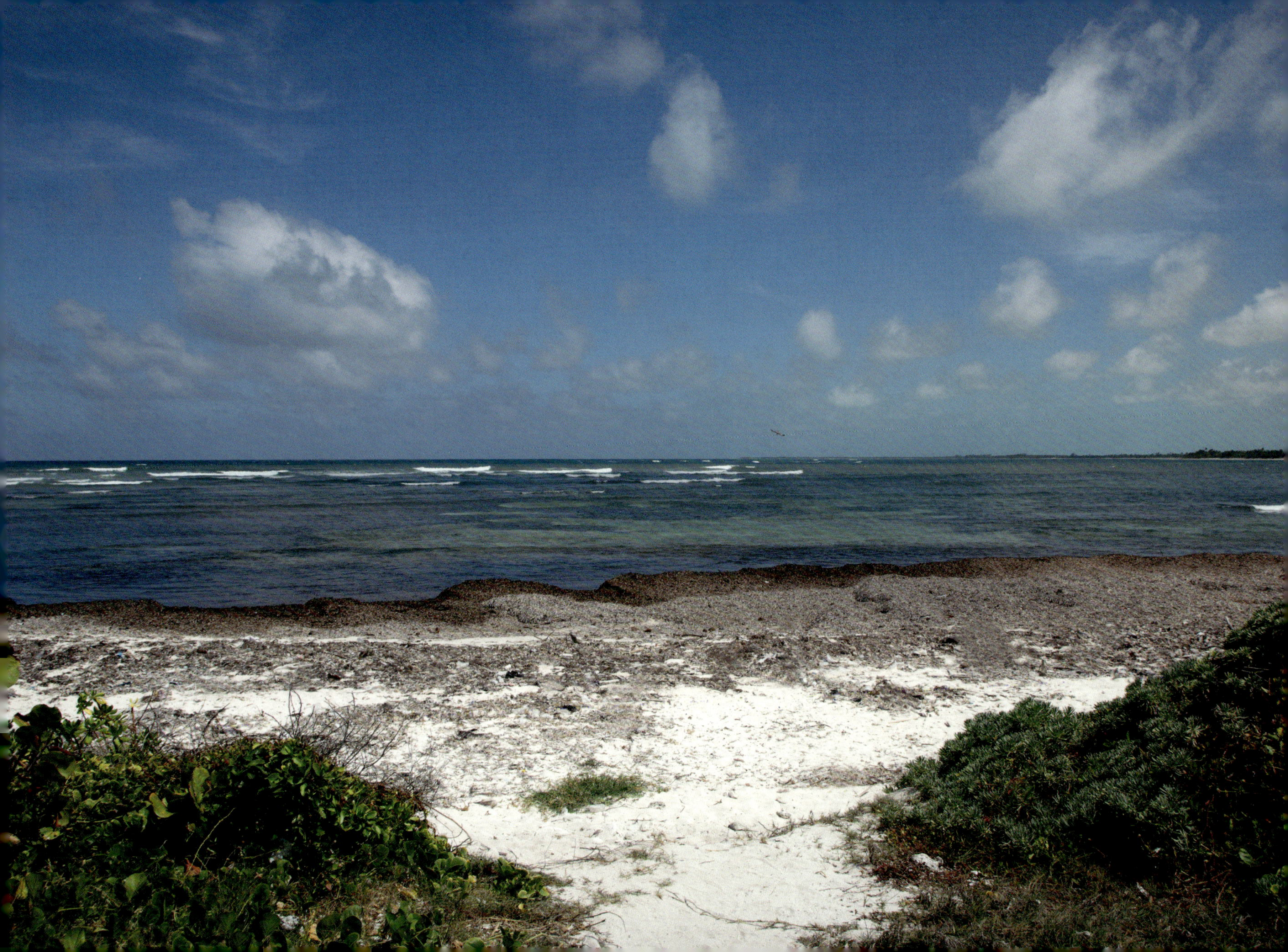

Welcome to the Beach

The path to this extremely remote tropical beach looks so welcoming. What you don't realize at first is that the seaweed is overflowing with plastic debris. It comes as a shock at first, followed by horror. The amount of plastic that had washed ashore in this one area was staggering. Then the sobering realization hits that this plastic is everywhere.

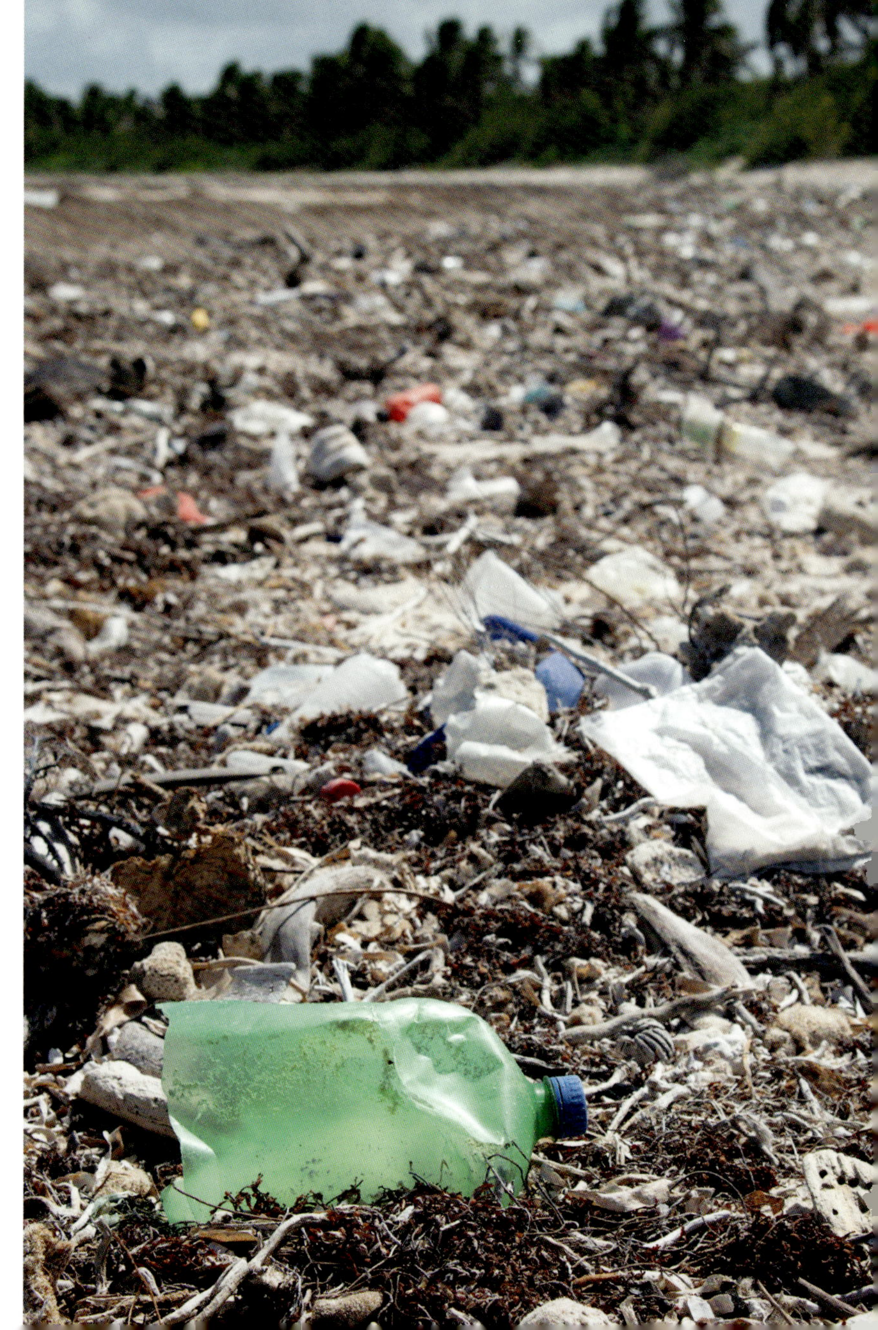

PLASTIC PLOVER

A Year of Plastic

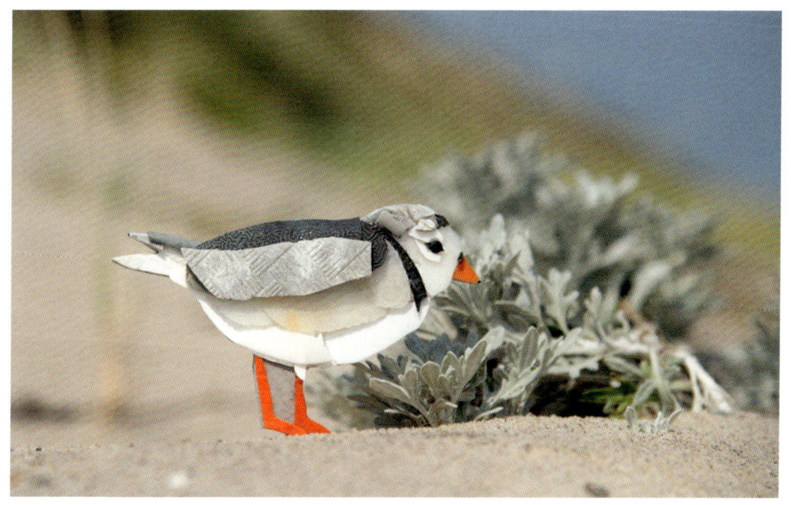

Sarah Thornington-Cericola has launched an environmental conservation organization called A Year of Plastic. She recently finished a yearlong project doing a beach cleanup every day for a year, documenting the found plastics to bring awareness and conversation about our overuse of single-use plastics. When she's not running her photography business or organizing a beach cleanup, she creates art from found plastic, which she exhibits throughout Cape Cod to stress the importance of taking care of our planet. Sarah starts planting conservation seeds early by educating kids at workshops, where they clean beaches together and create art with the found plastic.

facebook: ayearofplastic
instagram: ayearofplastic

AFTERWORD

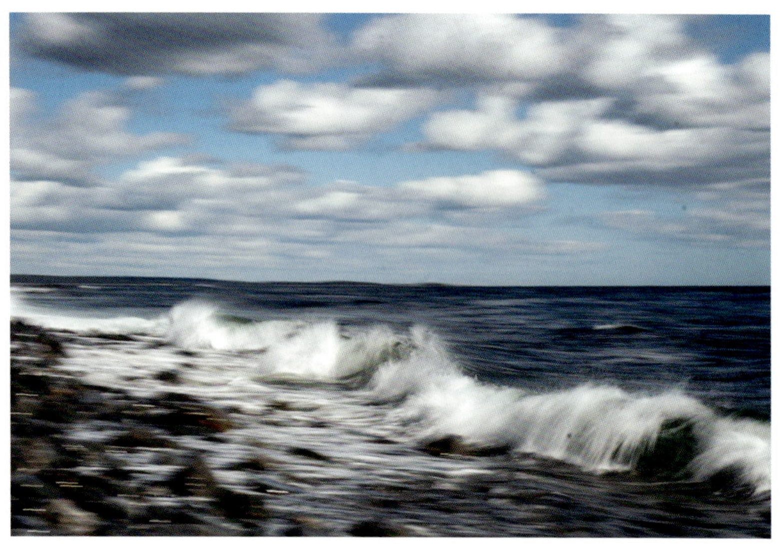

The Beach

Listen to the surf, really lend it your ears, and you will hear in it a world of sounds: hollow boomings and heavy roarings, great watery tumblings and tramplings, long hissing seethes, sharp, rifle-shot reports, splashes, whispers, the grinding undertone of stones, and sometimes vocal sounds that might be the half-heard talk of people in the sea.

—Henry Beston, *The Outermost House*

No two words in the English language better describe a place that evokes onomatopoeia, words that imitate sounds, more than "the beach."

Henry Beston, in his literary classic of the early 1900s, *The Outermost House: A Year of Life on the Great Outer Beach*, captured these majestic sounds in stunning word pictures. Spending a solitary year on an isolated stretch of Coast Guard Beach on Outer Cape Cod, 2 miles south of the historic Eastham Life Saving Station, Beston wrote of this haunting beauty from a snug, windblown, 21-by-16-foot, two-room beach shack with a frugal wooden writing desk overlooking the surf.

A Harvard-educated writer and naturalist, Beston built the cottage in 1926 mostly from scrap driftwood, dubbing it the "Fo'castle," given its ten windows and commanding presence atop a high dune overlooking the open Atlantic that offered the sense of being aboard a ship.

It was here that he planned to spend two weeks writing at summer's end. "The fortnight ending, I lingered on, and as the year lengthened into autumn, the beauty and mystery of this earth and outer sea so possessed and held me that I could not go," wrote Beston.

Amy Dykens, in her elegant book *Beaches: Celebrating Stones, Sand, and Surf*, captures in exquisite photography the word pictures of Beston on Cape Cod, and expanding her journey to Nova Scotia, France, Mexico, Costa Rica, and other enchanted places. Her book offers something for all, conjuring up our own memories and imaginations of the sea.

Wrote Beston, "Nature is a part of our humanity, and without some awareness and experience of that divine mystery" we cease to be ourselves.

Amy's book brought back personal memories for me. As a young man, I often walked south along Coast Guard Beach, pondering nature and next steps in my life. I used to sit on the front steps of Beston's beach shack, drinking in the beauty that surrounded me.

I found God here. I felt at peace, a calm later shattered by the Great Storm of February 1978, with sustained winds of close to 100 miles an hour and an overwash of nearly 15 feet that swept the Fo'castle out to sea. Memories of the beach shack survive for me and are preserved in the pounding surf and in the stillness that surrounds me.

—Greg O'Brien, a career journalist and author, lives with his family in Brewster on the Outer Cape.

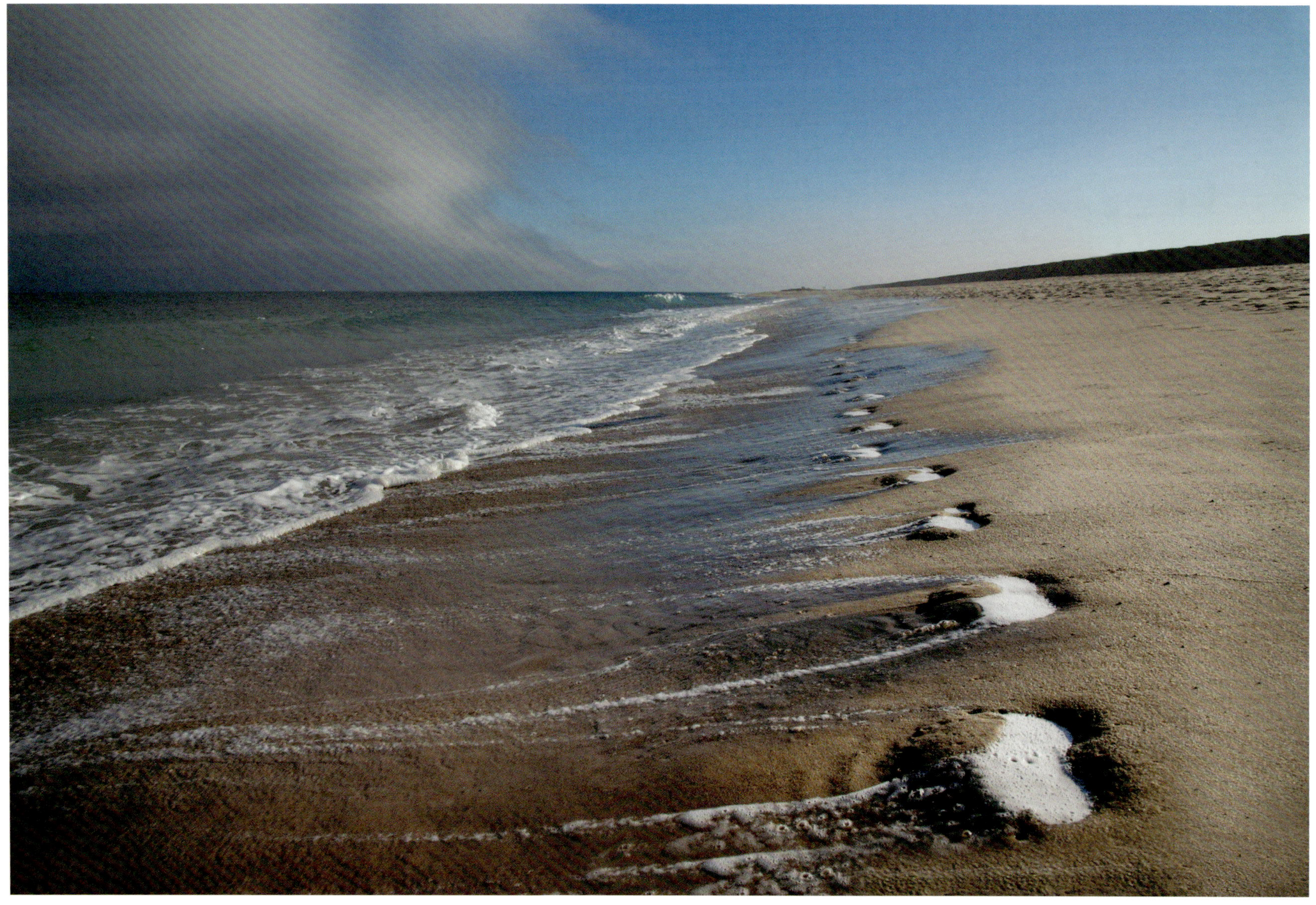

ACKNOWLEDGMENTS

Heartfelt thanks to Pete Schiffer for appreciating the generosity implicit in my work, and to editor Cheryl Weber and book designer Molly Shields.

Thanks also to my sons, Charlie and James Kiernan, for being the best part of my life, and for understanding when the beach is calling me. Very special thanks to my son James, brother Jim, sister Elisabeth, and brother-in-law Robert Hodapp for excellent editing and guidance; I cannot thank you all enough.

I could never adequately thank my sisters: Elisabeth Dykens, for her lifelong support, for believing in my projects from day one, and for being my kindred spirit and beachcombing soulmate; and Nancy O'Neil, for her lifelong love, interest, and support. Many heartfelt thanks to Tom Webber for supporting my ideas, exploring with me, and being patient when I wander off to shoot. Special thanks to my goddess friends Katie McConnell, for her friendship, positivity, artistic advice, and support; Tara Owen, for her heartfelt, creative enthusiasm; and Anisa Raoof, for patiently teaching me how to use a computer all those years ago. I am forever grateful to my sister-in-law, Julie Dykens, for sharing her sea glass collection and for generously selling my work in her gallery, Local Color, in Chatham. Many thanks to all who have walked beaches with me, especially Sissy and Bob, Tom, Bella Penkwitz, Lisa Bacon, John Proudfoot, Julie and Abby Dykens, and my kids.

Thank you to Greg O'Brien, Lisa Genova, Sarah Thornington-Cericola, Courtney Milley, and Joanne Doggart for giving me their time and advice. Thanks to my loving friends and family who have encouraged me (then and now) and provided much inspiration: Bob Lassiter, Joanne Bergquist, Sean O'Neil, Mike Kiernan, Virginia Osborn, Charles Bell, Jeff Dykens, Jennie and Jay Dykens, Page Malinowski, Wanda Pells, Aline Lindemann, Paul Critikos, and Martha Longley.

Special thanks to the many friends who have supported and encouraged me with my photography over the years, I am grateful for all of you—especially Patricia Parker, Kalson Pang, Amy Farrell, Rene Votteler, Megan Seamans, Shelly Hippler-Conway, Karen Rood, Danny Walsh, Patrice Milley, Michele and Steve Rowan, Steve Sedman, Diane Marshall, and Susan Crowley.

An enormous heartfelt thanks to my parents: James Dykens, who instilled in his six children the wonder of art as well as the joy of the beach at an early age, and Thelma Dykens, who has supported my art since I was a child painting violets in the garden, and supports it still at age ninety-seven with her encouragement and enthusiasm.

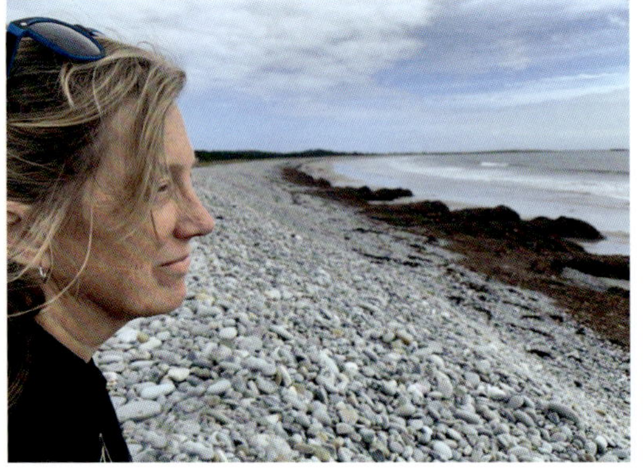

Photographer Amy M. Dykens captures the world in ways that surprise and delight. With a bachelor's in art and a master's in health coaching, her photos reveal to each of us nature's life-affirming wonder. A beach, wedding, and portrait photographer, Amy is a lifelong resident of Cape Cod. Her previous book, also published by Schiffer, was *My Heart Rocks*.